vision on

Nonfictions is dedicated to expanding and deepening
the range of contemporary documentary studies.
It aims to engage in the theoretical conversation
about documentaries, open new areas of scholarship,
and recover lost or marginalised histories.

General Editor, Professor Brian Winston

vision on

FILM, TELEVISION AND THE ARTS IN BRITAIN

John Wyver

 WALLFLOWER PRESS LONDON & NEW YORK

for Clare

First published in Great Britain in 2007 by
Wallflower Press
6 Market Place, London W1W 8AF
www.wallflowerpress.co.uk

A catalogue record for this book is available from the British Library.

ISBN 978-1-905674-39-8 (pbk)
ISBN 978-1-905674-40-4 (hbk)

Book design by Elsa Mathern

Printed and bound in Poland; produced by Polskabook

The Arts on Film Archive is supported by the AHRC
www.artsonfilm.org.uk

Arts & Humanities
Research Council

CONTENTS

ACKNOWLEDGEMENTS

I am grateful to Joram ten Brink for inviting me to write *Vision On* and also to David Curtis for suggesting to him that the idea of such a book might interest me. Joram has been an immaculate collaborator, prodding me towards the completion of the manuscript, plying me with film copies and offering valuable and encouraging responses to my first drafts. My sincere thanks are also due to Elaine Burrows, who has been cataloguing the Arts Council films collection, who also provided support and cassettes, as well as essential information and fact-checking. Steve Foxon, another key member of the digitisation project, assisted with the illustrations.

The cataloguing and digitisation of the Arts Council-funded films is an initiative of the School of Media, Arts and Design at the University of Westminster, undertaken with funding from the Arts and Humanities Research Council, and I am delighted to be working at Westminster now with Professor Annette Hill, Rosie Thomas and their colleagues.

Rodney Wilson, who between 1970 and 1999 ran the Arts Films initiative at the Arts Council and then the Film, Video and Broadcasting department there, generously submitted to detailed interviews as well as loaning me essential documents and providing valuable comments on a draft of Chapter 3. At Arts Council England Richard Gooderick facilitated access to films and Kim Evans, Gill Johnson and others contributed information and insights.

The papers of the Arts Council of Great Britain up until 1997 are kept in the Victoria and Albert Museum Archives in west London. This is a treasure trove of documents overseen by unfailingly helpful and knowledgeable staff. I am also immensely grateful to the London Library, which provided many essential volumes as well as a delightful environment in which to work.

A number of filmmakers and others helped with specific information about films including Sophie Bowness, Louisa Buck, David Hinton, Julian Leigh, Laura Mulvey, James Scott and James van der Pool. And among those, in addition to some of the above, who read parts of the manuscript and saved me from stupid mistakes are Keith Griffiths and Michael Jackson; needless to say, the errors that remain are mine.

Many other colleagues, long ago at *Time Out*, and for the past 25 years at Illuminations, have contributed in so many ways to shaping my ideas about arts programmes and about independent production; among these are Andrew Chitty, Mike Dibb, Geoff Dunlop, Carl Gardner, Seb Grant, Michael Kustow, Robert McNab, Louise Machin, Sandy Nairne, John Read and Rod Stoneman as well as my partner at Illuminations Linda Zuck and, a guiding spirit for me in so many ways, the late Marc Karlin.

Professor Brian Winston, the general editor of the *Nonfictions* series in which *Vision On* appears, offered generous and rigorous comments on the manuscript. I have known and admired Brian since I witnessed a typically explosive contribution by him to a debate at the 1978 Edinburgh International Television Festival and it is a particular pleasure for me that *Vision On* appears with this association. I am also very pleased to have worked closely and productively with Wallflower Press, with their editorial manager Jacqueline Downs and especially with the company's editorial director Yoram Allon.

My final thanks are reserved for my children Kate, Ben and Nicholas, and also Beryl, who have all helped in far more ways than they can imagine. And of course, I am grateful in so many, many ways to my wife Clare. This is a book for her.

John Wyver
London
October 2007

LIST OF ILLUSTRATIONS

PREFACE

Like many other projects, it all started from a personal event – the death of the director, producer and cameraman David Rowan in 2001. In the last stages of his career David taught film with me at the University of Westminster in London. A quiet, modest and dedicated lecturer, he never spoke in great length about his own career in film. Following his death, the university organised a memorial screening of his films, mainly of those made with the Arts Council Film department in the 1970s and 1980s.

As a result of that memorial screening, and not very long afterwards, the Arts on Film Archive was born with the help of the Arts and Humanities Research Council (AHRC), University of Westminster, the Arts Council and the British Film Institute (BFI). The archive comprises a complete database of the Arts Council film collection, and a digital copy of every film which is available online for viewing by all researchers both in the UK and internationally. The Arts on Film Archive provides a key resource for the study of both British and international post-war art, and British documentary filmmaking.

And the archive begat this book. The Arts Council film department production of nearly five hundred films from 1953–99 can only be seen as part of a much larger picture – film, television and the arts in the UK during the second half of the twentieth century. With very little to rely on in terms of tradition, broadcasters, filmmakers and public institutions developed – and often struggled with – the complex world of presentation of the arts to the public via broadcasting, art galleries, film festivals or even screenings in village halls. In a period which saw both the expansion, the proliferation of exhibition of the arts in Britain and the rise and rise of broadcasting and public support to the arts, this book charts, for the first time, the complete story of film, television and the arts across the whole spectrum of broadcasting and film production in the UK since World War Two. The book embarks on a journey of highly significant analysis through the political, cultural and aesthetic landscape of the arts and film in Great Britain since the early 1950s to the beginning of the twenty-first century. Moreover, the book sets out to open the discussion about the arts and the moving image in the twenty-first century as it is just beginning to unfold. Alongside its critique of the work of the last century, the book offers a coherent argument for the way forward.

Coming out of an archive project, it is often tempting to look at the past as a 'golden age' with a strong sense of nostalgia. Far from it. Alongside stories of success there were missed opportunities and failures. One can only hope that the experience of the past sixty years will contribute to a robust future for the representation of the arts through the moving image in a landscape which is now much wider than the traditional world of television broadcasting or publicly-funded film productions.

Joram ten Brink
Director, AHRC Arts on Film Archive
School of Media Arts and Design
University of Westminster
www.artsonfilm.org.uk

'The values which we hold to be supreme must be shared and no better instrument for sharing them has been invented than television.'
                                        – Stephen Hearst, BBC producer, 1968

'The golden age has not passed; it lies in the future.'
                                        – Paul Signac, artist, 1895

INTRODUCTION

Exterior; day. Long-shot of Cathédrale Notre-Dame de Paris. The title-card 'The Skin of Our Teeth' has disappeared and a stirring organ voluntary falls away. A bright sun pours soft light across the medieval stonework. We are on a bank of the Seine as it streams around the Île de la Cité. Into the left of frame steps Lord Clark, in his mid-sixties, tanned and smartly attired. With a white handkerchief peeking from his breast pocket and a tie just slightly askew, he returns us to a turbulent time after the Romans when Western civilisation almost disappeared. His conclusion, however, is reassuring: 'We got through by the skin of our teeth.' Clark speaks of the survival of fundamental values across centuries with a quiet self-possession. Yet he confides that he is uncertain about his subject. 'What is civilisation?' he asks us. 'I don't know. I can't define it in abstract terms. Yet. But I think I can recognise it…' – here he turns to look back at the shining cathedral – '…when I see it…' – the image cuts to the west front – '…and I'm looking at it now.'

Lord Clark and me

As a painfully unself-confident 13-year-old, I marvelled at Clark's effortless communication of his lifetime's learning. Nearly forty years on, I can recall the dissolve that follows moments later as the camera tilts down into the waters. 'Some time in the ninth century' – it is as if Clark is reminiscing – 'one could have looked down the River Seine…'. Emerging from the waves is a striking shot of a carved Viking prow around which the camera moves with an ease that parallels Clark's delivery. And today I can reassure my memory about the transition by accessing on DVD, with sound and image lovingly restored, this first episode of the BBC series *Civilisation* (1969). The 13 films, written and presented by Kenneth Clark and directed by Michael Gill and Peter Montagnon, remain in many ways the touchstone of documentaries about the arts. In 2006, it was inevitable that both professional critics and critical bloggers would compare Simon Schama's ambitious series of artist profiles, *Power of Art* (it is not not entirely clear if the author's appellation is part of the title), to Clark's films. 'From Kenneth Clark's *Civilisation* in 1969 to Simon Schama's *Power of Art* in 2006. Can anyone possibly call that a cultural progression? No, I don't think any sane person would say so', offered the online contributor 'cyboman' in response to some self-justificatory musings by Schama on *Guardian Unlimited*.

Vision On: Film, Television and the Arts in Britain tackles the questions prompted by that notion of 'a cultural progression'. After a brief look at the prehistory of the arts on film, it chronicles the intersections between the moving image and the arts from the first film documentary on BBC Television in 1951 to the present. There is in addition an outline exploration of a typology of the arts on-screen, a discussion of mainstream and alternative approaches to engaging with the arts on-screen and, as a conclusion, some speculations about the near future. The book's catalyst and focus is a specific and substantial group of films. These are the documentaries and screen performances funded or part-funded by the Arts Council of Great Britain, which in 2007 have been restored, catalogued and digitised. My aim, however, has been to set these films in a wider context and to outline other histories, most notably that of broadcast television's engagement with the arts.

More specifically, this is a book about documentaries made with Clark and with Schama (both of whom contributed to Arts Council-funded films), and about numerous documentaries created by producers and directors like John Read and James Scott, Leslie Megahey and David Hinton, Marc Karlin and many, many others. It is also a book about dramatised biographies of artists and about framed performance, about how paintings can be filmed, about the creative use of images and sounds, about screen poetry and ambiguity, and about how television and film can ask questions of art and of ourselves. My hope is that *Vision On* has an objective value for filmmakers and those studying film and television histories, as well as those simply interested in how media has contributed to shaping our ideas about the arts. But as the opening above suggests, the book also has a personal dimension that I have not been able entirely to suppress.

I am, perhaps understandably, cautious about claiming that Lord Clark changed my life, but there is no doubt that at times his screen presence has been immensely important. *Civilisation*, watched avidly in an uneasy family environment, was a central part of my teenage education. I learned about the topics that it covered and, as I recognised later, about its filmmaking strategies. Clark's series, however, also shaped who I was and the person that I would become. In my early fifties I believe that I am, simply and straightforwardly, a better person for the series having been part of my life, and I am happy to acknowledge the same about a host of other documentaries and performance films. Nor was it just the first broadcast screening of *Civilisation* that made an impact. I clipped and saved for years the transcripts of the episodes published each week in *The Listener*, and the illustrated paperback drawn from these served as a guide to the Renaissance when three friends and I drove through Italy after a first year at university. I caught repeats of the series from time to time and when I began to work as a journalist I wrote occasional articles that considered it. I have critiqued its analytical framework and despaired of its conservatism yet I continue to admire and celebrate its achievement. In part to acknowledge how important *Civilisation* had been for me, I wrote and directed the documentary *K: Kenneth Clark 1903–83* (1993) for BBC2 to mark the tenth anniversary of Clark's death. For this production I interviewed each of his three children, placing the politician and diarist Alan in the library at the family home of Saltwood Castle exactly where the final scene of the closing episode of *Civilisation* was shot. My response to the series now is impossible to disentangle from these experiences. And although I intend to confine (most of) my personal memories to this Introduction, I need here to acknowledge that I have had a minor, marginal part in the stories that *Vision On* explores.

Kenneth Clark and Notre-Dame de Paris
in the opening sequence of *Civilisation*

Take three histories

The shot in *Civilisation* of the sculpted Viking prow that issues from the Seine makes another appearance in the half-hour film *Carved in Ivory* (1975). This too was directed by Michael Gill and written and narrated by Kenneth Clark, and it looks with a careful, educated eye at English medieval ivories sculpted between 700 and 1200. Many of these exquisite works were brought together in 1974 for a once-in-a-lifetime exhibition at London's Victoria and Albert Museum organised with the Arts Council of Great Britain. The Arts Council published a catalogue for the show, written by the curator John Beckwith, and it also funded the film, which was one of the last with which Clark had an active involvement. *Carved in Ivory* is a simple but exceptional documentary, with the camera taking you close to the artworks, guiding and instructing your eye, as Clark's authoritative but never alienating voice sketches the historical context and explores his sense of these artworks' 'Englishness'. He describes, for example, an Adoration of the Magi as 'a great piece of ornamental abstract art … of course it's a masterpiece but there is a coldness about the head of the Virgin that seems to me un-English.'

Carved in Ivory is one of the 480 films funded or part-funded by the Arts Council between 1953 and 1999. Much like the acquisitions of paintings, sculptures and more made by the Arts Council from 1946 onwards, these films form a collection of surpassing richness. In them the camera encounters many key British artists of the twentieth century's second half, from Graham Sutherland and John Piper to Sarah Lucas and the Chapman brothers. But there are also numerous profiles and biographies of visual artists whose earlier deaths cheated the camera's access: William Hogarth and Alfred Wallis, Käthe Kollwitz and Edward Hopper. There are films about architects, including Frank Lloyd Wright and James Stirling, and documentaries focused on individual buildings, such as Beaubourg in Paris and Kensal House in north London. And from 1976 onwards, films consider composers like Alan Bush and Elizabeth Maconchy, poets such as Basil Bunting, and avant-garde filmmakers including Jeff Keen and Malcolm Le Grice. Quirky encounters with folk art feature too, such as *Our Business is Fun* (1975), about two fairground sign decorators, and a brief, entirely delightful meeting with music hall novelty act Sam Sherry.

Major exhibitions are documented in the collection, as in *Carved in Ivory*, and there are polemics about the destruction of the built environment and, *plus ça change*, the media's hostility to contemporary art. Shifts in commissioning decisions over the years reflect the changing concerns of the arts and arts funding in Britain. Early on there is a focus on community arts and then the impact of feminism is felt as well as a much deeper engagement with black arts and issues. Performance becomes more and more central, especially once the Arts Council starts to work closely with broadcasters. Celebrated initiatives like *Dance for the Camera* (1993–2003) and *Sound on Film* (1995–98) bring together choreographers and musicians with creative directors. There are dull films in the collection, and a few that it seems inconceivable now were either funded or produced. But overall the quality level is high, and the roster of filmmakers is almost as distinguished as the subjects, even if the names are less familiar: Basil Wright, Bruce Beresford, Lutz Becker, Tristram Powell, Jana Bokova, Phil Mulloy, Keith Griffiths and the Quay Brothers. Perhaps the most interesting of all the aspects of the Arts Council film collection, at least as it will be argued through *Vision On*, is its holding of films that strive to find alternatives to the dominant ways in which the arts have been presented on-screen. Part of my argument is that continuity in approaches to arts documentaries, especially within broadcast television, is far stronger across fifty years and more, than is any sense of significant change. Films that offer new challenges for filmmakers and subjects, and especially for audiences, are to be cherished and celebrated, and these visions, whether made for television or for the Arts Council, are central to the focus of this book.

The history traced by the works created with funding support from the Arts Council is one of three intimately overlapping histories of production that are entwined throughout *Vision On*. The second history is that of what, for all of the complexities associated with the term, can be called independent production, and the third is the creation of programmes with and about the arts for broadcast television. None of these strands or traditions is in any sense homogenous and drawing out the differences and contradictions within them is a key element in what follows. 'Independent' in particular is a tricky term, bringing together questions of ownership, financing and control with ideas of aesthetic strategy.

Post-war independent production embraced an extraordinarily diverse range of alternatives to the mainstream film and broadcasting structures: Free Cinema at the end of the 1950s which developed an influential idea of filmmaking as personal expression; 'amateur' projects like Kevin Brownlow and Andrew Mollo's vision of a Nazi invasion of Britain, *It Happened Here* (1966); from 1966 the London Film-makers' Co-operative (LFMC), a production, distribution and exhibition centre for experimental filmmakers; and through the influential leftist collectives of the 1970s given a focus by the Independent Filmmakers' Association (IFA). Around 1980 a new notion of independent production emerged in parallel with the debate about the form of the proposed fourth channel. Independent producers in this context were those not wholly or largely owned or controlled by a broadcaster, and while many of these first independents cherished the earlier ideas of an oppositional film practice, these concerns became increasingly submerged by, in hindsight, the relentless development of a solely commercial drive to the idea of independence.

Independent production frequently intersected from the early 1980s on with broadcast television, which was and remains by far the dominant context for the creation of programmes and other media about the arts. Faint traces remain today of studio features related to the arts from the 1930s and from after the resumption of BBC transmissions in 1946. Individual film documentaries were made for the BBC from 1951 onwards and occasional programmes were shown after 1956 by ITV, including several series of engaging lectures by Kenneth Clark. The immensely influential *Monitor* (1958–65) was the first regular strand of arts programming, and it was joined by ABC Television's *Tempo* from 1961 to 1968. Subsequent series working with a variant of the *Monitor* model include *Omnibus* (1967–2002), *Arena* (1975–), *The South Bank Show* (1978–) and *Imagine* (2003–). More topical, faster turnaround coverage was provided in the 1960s by *Late Night Line-Up* (1964–72), in the 1990s by *The Late Show* (1989–95) and now by *The Culture Show* (2004–). Complementing these regular series was a host of additional performances, events and documentary series. In arts programming, as in so many other areas, Channel 4 changed the rules, bringing a far greater diversity of subjects covered and approaches taken. Independent producers drove much of this opening up of arts programming and, as *Vision On* details, a significant number of their projects were part-funded by the Arts Council. From the late 1980s, independents began to make arts programming for the BBC and other broadcasters, and again these collaborations feature prominently in the Arts Council films.

The films funded by the Arts Council have an important place in the histories of both arts broadcasting and independent production. Films made for the Council in the 1950s and 1960s were produced by independent companies and also by the British Film Institute. From 1970 the Art (later Arts) Films committee oversaw this initiative as part of the Art department, and then from 1986 the funding became part of the responsibility of the Film, Video and Broadcasting department. Independent producers developed and made all of this work, and from the early 1980s many of the projects were co-produced with television companies, first with Channel 4 and later with the BBC and others. Initiatives like *Dance for the Camera* and *Sound on Film* were developed as direct collaborations, and for a decade and a half the relationship, whilst at times bumpy in its details, was a mutually productive one. But there is an argument that the smaller partner became too dependent on the larger, and as terrestrial broadcasting began to move away from a commitment to the arts, the rationale for a funding structure for arts media through the Arts Council separate from broadcasting had been weakened, and this contributed to the ending of the Council's initiative.

The Arts Council's Film, Video and Broadcasting department was closed in 1999, although the funding and production of some dance works continued into 2003. Recognising the importance of the collection and also the lack of documentation and difficulty of access (although films and excerpts continued, as they still do, to be licensed to broadcasters and digital channels) Joram ten Brink from the School of Media, Arts and Design at the University of Westminster assembled a successful bid to the Arts and Humanities Research Council for research funding focused on the collection. The aims of the research project were to catalogue the films produced with Arts Council funding, to locate and restore the complete collection for digitisation and to produce an archive for online access by academics and researchers. *Vision On* is an additional element in this project and its publication in 2007 complements the completion of the research initiative and the launch of the online archive.

Things to come

The detailed history of the Arts Council's support of film production and the context of this within the Council's development as a whole is the focus of Chapter 3. Before this, Chapter 1 outlines the history of the arts on British television until the arrival of Channel 4 in 1982. Neither this nor the next chapter, which chronicles arts programming from 1982 onwards at the BBC and ITV as well as the ways in which Channel 4 and subsequent broadcast and digital channels have engaged with the arts, is intended to suggest that the 1960s or the 1980s, or indeed any other period, was a 'golden age' for the arts on television. Nor is the theme of the book as a whole a lament for the lost shows of yesteryear. That this point needs to be stressed so early in the discussion is a pre-emptive response to a familiar refrain of broadcasters when contemporary arts programming is critiqued. Caricaturing historical explorations as simple-minded celebrations of a 'golden age', executives are more easily able to dismiss the lessons that can be drawn from the past.

One strand of my argument is that the arts were taken more seriously by terrestrial broadcasters in the past than they are now and that there are unquestionably deficiencies about broadcasting's provision of cultural programming in the early twenty-first century. This is less to do with a quantitative assessment, for many arts programmes are still presented today, but depends rather on a more nuanced discussion about the type of programmes, their aims and aspirations, their commitment (or lack of such) to cultural ideas and values. But I want also to celebrate recent successes and to look forward to the emerging possibilities of new forms of cultural media. The arts on-screen, as so much else, have entered a world where the production and distribution, the exhibition and uses of media are – and will be even more so – fundamentally different to the structures of 1951.

Given that much of the work for broadcast was funded by public monies through the BBC licence fee, it is perhaps a paradox that the history of television programmes in any genre remains so difficult to study in detail. Although this may change with new online archives, and although DVD releases are making available once again a very limited number of programmes (like *Civilisation*), access to many, many programmes has for decades been difficult and, for academic researchers, often prohibitively expensive. In part as a consequence of these problems, television studies have focused on policy development and the history of institutions, or on a theoretical analysis of the medium, and there is still a significant lack of documentation and study of individual programmes and genres. *Vision On* is a modest contribution aimed at correcting this for broadcast programmes about the arts.

Chapter 4 of *Vision On* attempts a typology of arts programming, highlighting the three forms of the lecture, the encounter and the drama and discussing the dominant approaches within each. In response, the second part of this chapter considers strategies that offer alternatives to television's dominant forms of exploring the arts. Throughout this book, 25 of the Arts Council-funded films (or groups of them) are considered in detail in sidebar sections. My intention here is to highlight and discuss distinctive and distinguished productions, and to suggest implicitly that these films in particular offer alternative strategies which media producers might develop in the future. This '25' also allows me to celebrate those films that during an exhaustive viewing of all of the 480 Arts Council productions have emerged as my favourites, such as *Richard Hamilton* (1969), a collaboration between James Scott and Hamilton, and *The Impersonation* (1984), made by Noël Burch and Christopher Mason.

Inevitably there are topics that *Vision On* might have covered but does not. These include, beyond an occasional reference, the history of music and dance on television and also the presentation of theatre and classic drama. Although they are comparatively few in number, British feature films focused on artists, such as Tony Hancock's *The Rebel* (1960), Ken Russell's *The Music Lovers* (1970) and Peter Greenaway's *The Draughtsman's Contract* (1982), are not treated in any depth in the pages to come. And films and videos made by artists as artworks are, with a few exceptions, also left for consideration elsewhere. The focus too is almost exclusively on work made in Britain, although significant alternatives from continental Europe and elsewhere are brought into the argument where, as contrasts, they can be illuminating. I recognise, too, that there is a bias throughout towards films about the visual arts. Painting and sculpture have, for me, been the subjects of many of the most stimulating arts documentaries, and perhaps as a consequence the visual arts is also the context in which I have most often worked as a producer.

The final chapter of *Vision On* looks forward, asking what we can learn from the history of arts films in Britain, and specifically from the productions of the Arts Council, as we face an undetermined but exciting digital future. With terrestrial television having largely marginalised the arts, what new strategies can be developed for the financing and production of arts media, and for distribution and the development of new audiences? The Arts Council films, crucially, were created with public funding, and the collection is the single extensive group of such films about the arts produced largely outside the structures of broadcasting. As the debates continue about the BBC's licence fee and about the regulation of television and the Internet, are there lessons to be drawn from these films and indeed from the history of arts programming as a whole which can inform how public monies might be committed to new kinds of arts media in the future?

Two other themes run through much of this history. One is the perennial perception on the part of broadcasters of the *difficulties* of art, and especially modern art, along with the expectation that television ought to be able to resolve these difficulties for audiences, whatever their levels of prior knowledge and refinement. The second idea to which producers and commentators persistently return is an agonising about arts programmes, about whether they are essential when it is recognised that they can never be justified simply in market terms. From the beginning there is the problem, for the broadcasters at least, of reconciling the presence of the arts on television with the medium's mass-market imperatives and expectations, which even from the beginning are commercial and which become ever more so. If television embraces the expectations of the mass audience, can the ideas and values of art survive?

'Can Art be box office and remain Art?' asked Peter Lewis in the spring 1962 edition of the BFI-funded television journal *Contrast* – and it is still the question that preoccupies television today. 'Of course the answer ought to be a resounding Yes. But it is a damned hard thing to prove. Picasso is box office. Beethoven … Shakespeare … But lump them together and call them Art and the queue dwindles' (1962: 202).

The dilemma of whether to 'dumb-down' or 'brain-up' is always with us. Discussions about whether arts programming, especially on the BBC, is 'elitist' is another strand of this knotty nexus of concerns. How can the BBC justify producing arts programming for small (and predominantly metropolitan and southern) minorities when everyone pays the licence fee? Why should broadcasters 'super-serve' the arts audience and as a consequence, they suggest, short-change everyone else? Again, if the values of the market take precedence, the argument is hard to refute. But broadcasting in Britain has constantly negotiated between numbers and other constructions of value, whether social, political or cultural. The story of the arts on-screen is a strand, albeit a particularly pointed one, of this negotiation.

Back, briefly, to autobiography. The first film on which I worked as a producer, *Just What Is It…?* (1984), was co-funded by the Arts Council and Channel 4. I made other films with similar funding arrangements and I also served on Arts Council funding committees. I am pleased to have had opportunities to work in this way, and to have produced numerous films for the BBC and Channel 4, but in 2007 my primary interest is in the future forms, in publishing films on DVD and online, in working directly with arts institutions to produce their own media, and in developing original media configurations that take advantage of broadband and other non-linear delivery mechanisms. My regret is that in the absence of the kind of support that the Arts Council once offered, there is currently next-to-no public funding for media development in the context of the arts. I believe that an opportunity was lost in the 2004–6 round of BBC licence fee discussions to put in place a system by which producers and arts organisations, with and without broadcasters, could have had access to partial funding to develop the kinds of work that terrestrial television is so clearly not developing. It is possible that the Public Service Publisher, proposed by Ofcom, the independent regulator for the UK's communications industries, will fulfil at least part of this need, and doubtless other kinds of creative collaborations for funding and production will emerge. Working towards these new forms is important, and *Vision On* aspires to offer in a modest form some lessons from history to inform future develop-ments. I have no interest in seeing *Civilisation* re-created now or in the years to come, but my hope – and expectation – is that there will be new forms of arts media which will excite and shape and inspire and challenge just as Lord Clark's offering did for the 13-year-old me, and as so many other films have done for me and for many others since.

CHAPTER 1
'A MEANS TO RAISE THE PUBLIC TASTE':
BRITISH TELEVISION AND THE ARTS 1951–82

On the evening of 30 April 1951 BBC Television transmitted *Henry Moore*, a half-hour film profile of the artist produced by John Read. The following day, a retrospective exhibition of the artist's works organised by the Arts Council, 'Sculpture and Drawings by Henry Moore', began at the Tate Gallery in London. Two days later, on London's South Bank, King George VI opened the Festival of Britain. Adjacent to 'The Origin of the Land' exhibit, and round the corner from a display devoted to the still comparatively new medium of television, stood Moore's 'Reclining Figure', the creation of which was chronicled in the BBC documentary. Television, exhibition and festival reinforced Moore's status as *the* emblematic visual artist of the moment.

Television had been on air for less than a decade (leaving aside its enforced break during wartime) and the Arts Council had been in existence for only six years. The Festival of Britain marked the end of wartime austerity and suggested the country's dynamic future. This was tomorrow, and as Alan Bennett has the playwright Joe Orton say in the film *Prick Up Your Ears* (1987), this was 'when it all came off the ration … food, sex, life, everything'. Many stories start here, including the one with which this book is concerned: the representation of art and artists on film and television in Britain. A fifty-year cycle of television's engagement with the arts effectively begins with Read's film and enters its endgame around the millennium as the impact of multi-channel television simplifies and marginalises the arts on-screen.

This chapter traces the rising arc of this tale, through to just before the establishment of Channel 4. It sketches a pre-history of the arts on-screen prior to 1951 and explores early programming from both the BBC and the ITV companies. The chapter also introduces the three figures who are central to the history of arts television in Britain. One is the producer of *Henry Moore*, John Read; another is the mandarin intellectual and art historian, populariser and cultural bureaucrat Kenneth Clark; and the third is the imaginative, eccentric director Ken Russell. Clark, Read and Russell established the ground rules for three dominant programme forms – the lecture, the encounter and the drama – that persist more than five decades later (and that are considered further in Chapter 4).

A pre-history for the arts on film

Given how few examples have been identified in archives and how little research has been published, films about art and artists from before World War Two can best be seen as a kind of pre-history of our subject. In Britain, leaving aside glimpses of prominent figures such as Laura Knight, Wyndham Lewis and Jacob Epstein in the newsreels of British Pathé and Movietone, I know of no significant documents from the 1920s and 1930s presenting painters or sculptors, exhibitions or cultural events.[1] There are imaginative works of film art made under the patronage of sponsoring bodies, such as Basil Wright's elegiac *The Song of Ceylon* (1934), sponsored by the Empire Tea Marketing Board, and Len Lye's *A Colour Box* (1935), completed at the GPO Film Unit, but for the most part British documentary makers were more interested in social and political issues than aesthetic ones. In contrast, filmmakers in continental Europe were fired with a greater cultural curiosity.

The most remarkable early traces of artists on film are in documentary footage shot with an amateur camera by Sacha Guitry in 1914–15. Guitry was an actor, a prolific dramatist and, later, a director of elegant movies. Concerned to celebrate his nation's culture in the first years of the war, he filmed short sequences with a number of prominent artists, and assembled these into the 22-minute *Ceux de chez vous* (often translated as *Those of Our Land*, 1915). Alongside shots of the writer Anatole France, actress Sarah Bernhardt and composer Camille Saint-Saëns, Guitry captured Auguste Rodin sculpting in his studio, Edgar Degas walking in the street and Claude Monet in his garden at Giverny. These figures, he said in a filmed preface appended to a later release of the documentary, were incarnations of the French genius and he presented them on-screen 'as an indirect and modest response to the odious proclamations of German intellectuals'.[2] If only the cinema had been invented earlier, he reflected, how moving it would be to observe Michelangelo carving Moses or Leonardo painting the Mona Lisa: 'How beautiful it would be to see the faces, the glances, the gestures of those men.'

A decade later the German filmmaker Hans Curlis began to document contemporary painters and sculptors at work.[3] His extensive series of short films under the collective title of *Schaffende Hände* ('creative hands') includes *Lovis Corinth* (1922) and *George Grosz* (1924), and he subsequently produced compilations, such as *Schaffende Hände: Die Maler* (1929) which includes Kandinsky at work on an abstract design, Max Pechstein painting a lifeboat in high seas, and the novelist Heinrich Mann posing for the artist Max Oppenheimer. In several of these films Curlis positions the camera behind the artist, shooting over the shoulder onto a canvas or sketchbook across which a brush moves; this shot later became a staple of numerous artist profiles. Curlis also made a film with the American sculptor Alexander Calder at work on his wire figures when the artist was in Germany in 1928–29, and he continued to work as a documentary producer through to *Rembrandt* in 1973.

In the years around World War Two a true tradition of documentary films about the arts began to develop across Europe. In Belgium, for example, André Cauvin used close-ups and travelling shots across photographic images of paintings in his *L'Agneau Mystique de Van Eyck* (1938) and *Memling* (1939). But for filmmakers and critics a decade later, Henri Storck was by far the most influential Belgian arts filmmaker. His *Le Monde de Paul Delvaux* (1946) was a collaboration with the Surrealist painter which also involved the poet Paul Eluard. Delvaux's paintings are employed here in the service of an imaginative poetic fantasy, but Storck's *Rubens* (1948), made with art historian Paul Haesaerts, is a far more rigorous and analytical film. Storck's camera interrogates the canvases, often superimposing lines across them to demonstrate their formal structure.

Critic Paul Davay wrote:

> New prospects open before us. We are no longer passive. We participate in the work. We accept or reject ... Storck and Haesaerts oblige us to remain in front of the picture, to see it with their eyes, but they give us the right to protest, to disagree, and to join in a discussion which is always open to our intelligence. (UNESCO 1949: 18)

In Italy in 1941 the filmmakers Luciano Emmer and Enrico Gras started on a series of films from photographs of Renaissance masterpieces. They began with *Earthly Paradise* (1941), about the paintings of Hieronymous Bosch before exploring in *The Drama of Christ* (1948) the frescoes in Giotto's Arena Chapel in Padua and then *The Legend of St Ursula* (1948) seen through the works of Carpaccio. Other titles included *The Miraculous Brothers* (1949), drawn from the works of Fra Angelico, and, using the paintings of Botticelli, *The Story of Spring* (1949). As these translations into English of their titles suggest, the key to the work of Emmer and Gras was a focus on the narratives revealed in the paintings.

> '[Emmer] was convinced that the cinema had inherited the narrative functions that painting had once exercised', the critic Lauro Venturi wrote, 'and that by reviving those popular legends which were so often recounted in episodic pictures, a new public interest in painting could be created. So he decided to present the world of art on a narrative level which could be understood by a large public'. (UNESCO 1949: 33)

Early French films like René Huyghe's *Rubens et son Temps* (1936–37) and René Lucot's *Rodin* (1941) explored the work of dead masters, but Jean Lods' *Maiilol*, completed just before the sculptor's death in 1944, was one of the country's first films to profile a living artist. Highlighting an issue that has remained a dilemma for filmmakers ever since, Gaston Diehl described another film with a living artist, *Matisse* (1947) directed by François Campeaux, as

> an interesting experiment and a failure at the same time. The sequences relating to the painter's creative processes are, it is true, an invaluable aid in explaining Matisse's work and in demonstrating the secret requirements of his craft. Nevertheless, the rest of the film often needlessly sacrifices the work to the personality. (UNESCO 1949: 52–4)

Curt Oertel's feature-length *Michelangelo, Das Leben Eines Titanen* (1940) is another important precursor to so many later biographical profiles. Oertel was the director of photography on a number of G. W. Pabst's feature films including *Geheimnisse einer Seele* (*Secrets of a Soul*, 1926), and in the mid-1930s he directed cultural documentaries about the tomb of the Unknown Soldier and the sculptures of Naumburg Cathedral. His study of Michelangelo, produced in Switzerland and released in Germany, uses exceptionally-lit images of the sculptor's works filmed mostly in Rome and Florence. 'A diffuse blend of travelogue and art catalogue, distinguished mainly by its sensitive photography', was how *Time* described it. After the war Oertel's footage was re-edited by Robert Flaherty with an English commentary, and released by producer Robert Snyder as *The Titan: Story of Michelangelo* (1950). The film won Snyder the Academy Award for Best Documentary.

Two other early productions from the United States deserve to be noted, although before the 1950s only a handful of American documentaries about the arts were produced. 'None of them yet compares with the work we have been seeing from Europe', wrote Arthur Knight (UNESCO 1949: 45). Knight, however, cautiously welcomed *Henry Moore* (1949), made by James Johnson Sweeney for the American-British Art Center, and Thomas Bouchard's film of Léger living in New York. The Moore film pre-dates John Read's important 1951 profile for the BBC, and begins with the opening of the sculptor's exhibition at New York's Museum of Modern Art before looking in more detail at the works. 'But the commentary', Knight felt, 'is so insistent, so complicated, so disassociated that the spectator is soon forced to choose between listening and seeing – he cannot do both' (ibid.).

Early arts on screen in Britain

In Britain, I cannot identify any documentary film made before 1942 that deals centrally with the arts. The short international catalogue *Films on Art*, produced by UNESCO in 1949, contains extensive listings of titles made in the two previous decades in Belgium, France, Italy and the United States but only eleven titles from Great Britain, five of which are about architecture, one which deals with pottery and one with history in general. *The Apocalypse* (1949) is an intriguing title produced by H. G. Gasparius about 'the engravings of Albert Durer' [sic], but it has eluded my attempts to locate a print. But then there are two wartime productions: *CEMA* (1942) and *Out of Chaos* (1944).

Produced by Alexander Shaw for the National Film Council of the Department of Information, *CEMA* is an introduction to the work of the organisational precursor to the post-war Arts Council, the Council for the Encouragement of Music and the Arts. After an on-screen preface by R. A. Butler, the film showcases the arts and audiences in wartime with a harp trio playing in an English country church and the Old Vic company rehearsing and playing Shakespeare's *The Merry Wives of Windsor*. The critic Eric Newton endeavours to persuade a sceptical public that modern art is 'part of what we're fighting for' and a small orchestra presents the first movement of Tchaikovsky's Piano Concerto to an enraptured audience of Britain's working men and women. The Tchaikovsky concert is strikingly intercut with sequences of armaments manufacture before a closing title outlines CEMA's mission: 'Bringing the best to as many of our people as possible to cheer them on to better times.' Although the film has little in the way of narration or dialogue, Dylan Thomas is among the five credited writers.

The more complex *Out of Chaos* was the first film directed by Jill Craigie who previously had been an actress and a documentary scriptwriter for the British Council. Made for the Rank subsidiary Two Cities Films, the production highlights the work of painters commissioned by the War Artists Advisory Committee to record the war on canvas. Kenneth Clark outlines the role of the committee, but it is Eric Newton again, acknowledged here as 'art critic of the *Manchester Guardian*', who comments on the exceptional scenes of artists in the field. Anthony Gross paints women working with artillery, Paul Nash sketches the twisted wreckage of a crashed plane, Stanley Spencer scrutinises the men labouring in the Clyde shipyards, Henry Moore observes sleeping figures sheltering from the Blitz in the London Underground and Graham Sutherland is seen at work on his painting 'Limestone Quarry'. Each is an iconic glimpse of these painters at this time, and even at this stage Moore's media friendliness was apparent. 'The execution of the work [in the film] was so beautifully timed', Craigie recalled admiringly, 'and adapted to a medium devised for action – it was shot in one take – that Henry's conquest of the film unit was complete' (in Berthoud 1987: 190). At the end of the documentary, visitors to an exhibition say that they find it hard to understand modern art, but Newton reassures them with the response that beauty comes with understanding, and that they must learn about an artist's ideas to appreciate truly his work. His analysis of the Sutherland canvas includes an intriguing use of animated graphics to demonstrate the painting's formal structure. Both the complaint about popular incomprehension and the response are consistent elements from television programmes across at least the next sixty years.

After the war, Jill Craigie combined dramatised scenes with documentary in her study of the rebuilding of Plymouth, *The Way We Live* (1946), but in general film documentarists demonstrated no greater interest in these years in art and artists than they had before 1939.

The next significant project was the series of four films, *Poet and Painter*, produced in 1951 for the British Film Institute and the Festival of Britain by the animation director John Halas. Described as 'an attempt to interpret verse by means of illustrative drawings or paintings by contemporary artists' (Arts Council of Great Britain 1953) these shorts, filmed with an animation camera tracking across artworks, drew on an exceptional range of talents. Michael Rothenstein illustrated the anonymous verse 'The Twa Corbies' read by John Laurie; this was twinned with Peter Pears reading Shakespeare's 'Spring and Winter' with illustrations by Mervyn Peake. John Minton, Michael Ayrton, Henry Moore and Ronald Searle were among the other artists, with poems by David Gascoigne, Thomas Nashe, Kathleen Raine and William Cowper. Mátyás Seiber contributed a strong modernist score.

In contrast to the film documentarists, those working for the new medium of television, which started regular broadcasts to the London area from Alexandra Palace in 1936, were rather more engaged by the arts. Even before the formal opening of the service, the BBC made experimental broadcasts using John Logie Baird's television system between 1932 and 1935, and an early item on 28 September 1932 was Maria Gambarelli dancing her own choreography to music from 'Coppelia'. Numerous ballets were transmitted in this way, and the *Daily Telegraph* enthusiastically reviewed one presentation on 4 July 1935:

> Undeterred by the restrictions of 30-line television Mr Eustace Robb ... presented to the BBC televiewers last night another complete ballet, the classic ballet 'Carnaval' ... To crowd such complex movement on to the narrow screen, capable of showing only two or three figures simultaneously, was a considerable feat. In its adapted form, parts of the ballet actually came to life, and gave a foretaste of the full enjoyment that will come with high definition television. (In Penman 1993: 104)

Ballet broadcasts continued from the larger studios at Alexandra Palace, and from here there exists a fragment of a pre-war film recording from a live studio broadcast by the painter John Piper. Piper stands behind a small Henry Moore reclining figure with a Gainsborough on an easel to his right and a large modernist canvas similarly displayed on his left. Carrying over the conventions of the lecture room to the television studio, as so many figures who followed were to do, Piper introduces the second painting: 'And this is a masterpiece of another kind, by a Spanish artist whose work – although he's over fifty, his reputation is enormous – his name is Picasso.'

Broadcasting to a tiny affluent audience, Piper and others including Robert Medley regularly discussed paintings and sculptures lent by London dealers. Correspondence in the National Gallery archives records the debate among the Trustees of the National Gallery about whether they should loan actual canvases to the BBC for such programmes; it was decided that the dangers of damage were too great, and that in any case since the television image was in black and white, reproductions would suffice. Kenneth Clark, who was Director of the National Gallery through the 1930s, recalled taking part in 1937 in what he claimed was 'the first "art" programme on the new medium'. 'I was chairman of a panel', he wrote in the second volume of his autobiography, 'in which four artists tried to guess who wrote certain lines of poetry, and four poets guessed, from details, who painted certain pictures. The poets won. I suppose about 300 people saw it' (1977: 205). Such were the joys of television from the BBC before the war took the service off the air on 1 September 1939.

The television offerings were framed by the ideas and ideals of public service broadcasting. This foundation to so much of what would follow was developed by and with the BBC radio service after a monopoly of transmissions was granted in 1922 to what was initially the British Broadcasting Company. From this earliest moment, it was decided by the government that funding would come from an annual licence fee for possessing a receiver, at this stage set at ten shillings. In 1923 the government's Sykes Committee began to define public service broadcasting when it determined that, 'The wavebands available in any country must be regarded as a valuable form of public property ... Those which are assigned to any particular interest should be subject to the safeguards necessary to protect the public interest in the future' (Sykes 1923: 6). The state's interests were firmly established, grounded in an understanding that operating so important a national service could not be handed over to an unconstrained commercial provider.

The refinement of the idea of public service broadcasting is recognised as the achievement of John Reith, Director General of the British Broadcasting Company 1923–26 and the first Director General of the British Broadcasting Corporation 1927–38. Reith contributed a memorandum to the 1925 Crawford Committee's deliberations which stressed broadcasting's responsibilities to bring into the greatest possible number of homes in the fullest degree all that was best in every department of human knowledge. The BBC should lead public taste not simply set out to meet it. 'He who prides himself on giving what he thinks the public wants', Reith pronounced, 'is often creating a fictitious demand for lower standards which he himself will then satisfy' (1925: 3). As the historians Paddy Scannell and David Cardiff have summarised, Reith's memo amounted to 'a cogent advocacy of public service as a cultural, moral and educative force for the improvement of knowledge, taste and manners' (1991: 7). Scannell and Cardiff have also located the motivating idea of *service* in the legacy of the Victorian middle class:

> The Victorian reforming ideal of service was animated by a sense of moral purpose and of social duty on behalf of the community, aimed particularly at those most in need of reforming – the lower classes ... One strand in this general concern for the conditions of the poor focused on their educational and cultural needs. A key figure in this development was Matthew Arnold whose definition of culture as 'the best that has been thought and written in

the world' was echoed by Reith in his advocacy of public service broadcasting. (1991: 9)

These ideas dominated the radio and television output of the BBC through to at least the late 1950s, although as the 1977 Annan Report pointed out, 'the ideals of middle-class culture so felicitously expressed by Matthew Arnold a century ago ... found it ever more difficult to accommodate the new expressions of life in the 1960s' (Annan 1977: 14).

With radio from the BBC generally felt to have had 'a good war', the television service resumed on 7 June 1946. The next day's programming included the Victory Parade, but a performance by Margot Fonteyn also featured in the opening presentations. Other early transmissions included *A Midsummer Night's Dream* broadcast from the Open Air Theatre in Regent's Park along with ballet and opera from Covent Garden and Sadler's Wells (see Briggs 1979). Part of a Promenade Concert was shown live in early September 1947. The 1949 series *Grand Ballet* brought companies into the studio for extracts of major works, including recent productions like *Adame Miroir* choreographed by Jean Genet to the music of Darius Milhaud.

Cultural programming was a concern for the BBC as it began in 1949 to prepare for the government's enquiry about the future of broadcasting chaired by Sir William Beveridge. In response to a request from the BBC's Director General Sir William Haley for a forecast of programme development for television, Controller of Television Norman Collins provided a list of items needing attention which began '(a) Science (b) Art (c) Music...' (in Briggs 1979: 287). Months later Collins, writing internally about audience response, warned about 'such programmes as ballet, where viewers feel that they are having Culture foisted upon them' (ibid.). The foisting continued with a few short films about the arts, all acquired from abroad, including in January 1949 a documentary about Van Gogh by Alain Resnais (the *Radio Times* printed the director's name as 'Resnay') and, in February 1950, William Chapman's American film *Lascaux, Cradle of Man's Art*. Also in 1949 the series *The Eye of the Artist* offered *The Chantrey Collection*, which was tied to an exhibition at the Royal Academy. 'Reproductions of some of the pictures', the *Radio Times* for 12–18 February promised, 'are shown and discussed in the studio.' Television in these years remained overwhelmingly a medium of live broadcasts transmitted from central studios using two or three electronic cameras. Among the cultural subjects of these programmes were pub signs and the Elgin Marbles (especially photographed at night for the programme) as well as artworks from the stately homes of England. The producer of many of these early arts broadcasts was John Read.

'A specifically British modernism': the films of John Read

John Read shaped the BBC's presentation of the visual arts throughout the 1950s and beyond. In a dozen or so important films made during the decade with contemporary artists he defined the forms of the filmed profile. The son of the influential art critic Herbert Read, he grew up in what his father called the 'modernist fortress' of Hampstead, where the family's friends and neighbours included Henry Moore, Barbara Hepworth, Ben Nicholson and Naum Gabo. Passionate about film, he turned his bedroom into a 35mm cinema and admired the work of John Grierson and the British documentary filmmakers of the 1930s. He was also impressed by the art documentaries of Luciano Emmer and Enrico Gras.[4]

In 1948 he wrote an article, 'Is there a documentary art?', which argued passionately for a social grounding to documentary – and for the arts to be seen as central to democracy and education:

> The faith that underlies Documentary is the faith of democracy and education. It is the belief that it is for the common good for man to know as far as he can, what he is doing and why ... The greatest in art is often associated with great human issues and the society from which they arise. Much of our learning and knowledge of life is apprehended through our senses moved by poets, actors and painters, arousing in us the sense of pleasure that is also understanding. The highest purposes of documentary can be achieved in a like manner, where the educational is also implicit in the artistic. (1948: 157)

His polemic was printed in *Sight and Sound* and secured him a job as an assistant to John Grierson, researching the Central Office of Information series *This is Britain* (1946–51). He then went to the Talks Department of BBC Television at Alexandra Palace, and it was in this context that he produced a host of live studio transmissions illustrated with stills. He also worked on a weekend magazine series with host Joan Gilbert and, on being directed to appeal to a more up-market audience, he introduced art spots, including one with John Minton discussing his painting 'The Death of Nelson'.

The television service began to make some short films from 1947 onwards, having reassured suspicious cinema producers that it had no interest in distributing them 'as celluloid'. In 1949 the five-reel *Round the World in Eight Days* was produced along with the BBC's first full-length documentary, Robert Barr's *Report on Germany*, which combined studio elements with film inserts. *August Bank Holiday 1949* was one of the first full-length films to be produced for television transmission within a few hours. Yet the EMI electronic scanners used for transmissions struggled to cope adequately with film prints, and Read was aware of cultural reasons too as to why he had to argue for the use of film in documentaries:

> It was oddly difficult to persuade people to let you work in film. The attitude then was: it was the great new electronic medium, the wonder of seeing it as it happens – or, often, seeing it go wrong as it went wrong. I suppose they had to make claims for the new medium. But I saw it as a marvellous method of film distribution. (In Lennon 1983)

Read's decision to use film for his Henry Moore profile also had a pragmatic component. The sculptures were too bulky to bring in any quantity to the studio and Moore's ethos stressed how they should be seen in natural light against the landscape. Moore himself had a keen interest in how his works were photographed – he was also an avid television watcher, especially tennis from Wimbledon, and it is intriguing in the 1951 film to see an early set in his living room at his house, Hoglands. 'I remember learning everything from Moore about photographing sculpture', Read acknowledged, 'and especially about the use of natural light for "modelling"; he taught me, and I think the cameraman too.'[5]

Henry Moore follows the creation of the 'Reclining Figure' that the artist was making for the site of the Festival of Britain. It opens with the artist's hands, working with tools, carving stone and modelling clay. The impulse to capture creation on celluloid is strong throughout the film. A cut from a blank sketchbook page to a close-up of Moore's eyes, underlined as so much of the film is by William Alwyn's music, is intended to suggest 'inspiration'. For the viewer, there is a particular fascination in witnessing those aspects of Moore's working processes, especially the casting of bronze, that he was prepared to reveal to the camera. But this is clearly incomplete – Moore's studio assistants, for example, are only glimpsed in the background – and the creative act inevitably eludes both the filmmaker and the viewer.

The day after the 30 April 1951 transmission the television critic of the *Daily Mail* was unenthusiastic about the film. 'Don't let's have any more, Mr Moore', wrote J. Stubbs Walker. 'I would have been happier to have been told what soap flakes I should use and have it followed by a reasonably entertaining film than this inflexible directive on my artistic taste which I was given last night' (1951).

The advertising of soap flakes and much else on television was a live issue in these months, since although in January the Beveridge Report had recommended that the BBC should retain an unchallenged provision of broadcasting, committee member Selwyn Lloyd had produced a minority report calling for commercial radio and television. It was only in July 1951 that a White Paper accepted that the BBC should retain its public service monopoly. Following its publication, there were vigorous debates in Parliament about commercial broadcasting, and the likelihood of its introduction moved significantly closer once a Conservative government was returned to power in October.

Coinciding, as already noted, with the opening of the Festival of Britain, *Henry Moore* was just one of an estimated 2,700 broadcasts, mostly on radio, made by the BBC about every aspect of the the event (Hewison 1995: 59). The South Bank site of the Festival offered the Telekinema, the precursor of the later National Film Theatre (now BFI Southbank), which showcased stereophonic film sound, 3-D images and other innovations, as well as recognising the achievement of Britain's documentary film tradition. The Festival and broadcasting forged a productive partnership which together constructed an image of the nation that both looked back to the triumphs of the first Elizabethan age of the sixteenth century and anticipated the second that would begin when Princess Elizabeth took the throne. Henry Moore can be seen as an artist who fulfils many of the longings of this moment. Close to the land of England, Moore was known to be (and is portrayed by Read as such) inspired by its rocks and roots, intuitive rather than intellectual, heroic yet determinedly down-to-earth, modern and forward-looking yet at heart profoundly traditional. Here indeed was an artist for the BBC, for the Festival, for the nation and soon for the world. More than three decades later, at a time when the BBC in the 1980s was once again struggling to define its role, the new entrance building to the BBC's Television Centre at White City prominently displayed a sturdy reclining figure by Moore. The match of its values to those aspired to by the BBC at that moment made the choice of the sculpture an apposite one.

After *Henry Moore*, between 1953 and 1957 John Read made twelve films for the BBC, four of which were produced in association with (and distributed as 16mm film prints by) the Arts Council. In addition to profiles of Graham Sutherland and John Piper, released in 1954 and 1955 respectively, these Arts Council co-productions were *Artists Must Live* (1953; discussed in detail in Chapter 3) and *Black on White* (1953), a film essay written by Reg Groves about British cartoonists and caricaturists. The film traces a line from Hogarth to David Low, who appears and acted as script adviser; at one moment, a film image of Low's face cross-fades to a Hogarth self-portrait painted two hundred years earlier.

GRAHAM SUTHERLAND
written and directed by John Read
a BBC Television film made in association with the Arts Council
of Great Britain
28 minutes, 1954

The camera is mounted on the front of a car travelling down a country road overhung with leafy branches. In these first moments of the film we are taken directly, deeply into the landscape of England. Superimposed across the shot is a title card: the artist's name written in his own hand. It is as if Graham Sutherland is signing Nature herself.

'The best of British painting', the narrator's voice asserts as the image cuts first to a single tree and then a wider landscape, 'is that which has kept alive our ancient association with nature and expressed a poetic vision of our surroundings. Interest in the power and mystery of landscape is particularly English and is found in our literature and art.'

Nature and the British Romantic artist's response to it is the first tradition in which Sutherland is located by Read's film profile. Henry Moore's embeddedness in the landscape of England is similarly central to the director's profile of the sculptor from three years before. But whereas that film was scored by William Alwyn, known for the lush harmonies accompanying British feature films like *Odd Man Out* (1947) and *The Fallen Idol* (1948), here another framing for Sutherland is signalled by the modernist music of Mátyás Seiber, a Hungarian composer and teacher much indebted to Bartók and Schoenberg.

Sutherland is introduced in his home nestled in a picture postcard Kent village. As the camera explores the domestic interiors, Rex Warner's narration (written by Read) points to suggestive sources for the artist's paintings: a fishbone, crystals, a cutting of thorns. These he explains are the starting points for Sutherland's art, 'but as his imagination is stirred and he digests their character, a change takes place; the forms assume a new reality, at once familiar and unfamiliar'.

At the Tate Gallery, the artist's retrospective of 1953 offers the chance to look at a range of his paintings, and to discuss both the importance of the Welsh landscape to his work and also Sutherland's experience as a war artist. Sutherland's post-war crucifixion for St Matthew's church, Northampton, is considered by its commissioner Canon Hussey (in the film's first sequence with synchronous sound) against the history of Christian art and its redemptive aspirations.

Close to the halfway point of the film, there is a radical shift to a new landscape, that of a semi-tropical scrub of the hills near Cannes on the Mediterranean coast. From 1947 onwards Sutherland had been spending more and more time in France, and the film feels the need to justify this with the statement that the move was 'a logical extension of his pre-war interest in Wales … His colour already implied the clarity and warmth of the Mediterranean sunlight.'

Next is a sequence shot in a heightened, almost Expressionist style, accompanied by insistent music, of the artist walking in a landscape, catching a grasshopper in his hand and then returning to his studio, making a first mark at an easel, smoking, staring. Gradually, a drawing emerges. For many viewers today, fifty years after the film was made, much of the film seems over-written and off-puttingly earnest, even with the recognition of the historical interest of seeing Sutherland at work. It is the 'creation sequence', however, that appears particularly unconvincing.

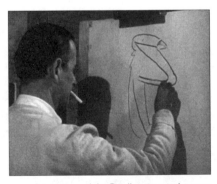

John Read's camera observes Graham Sutherland at work

The archival value of the film is reinforced as we observe Sutherland at work on his well-known portrait of Somerset Maugham, who is seen (in a re-staging, since the canvas is dated 1949) being drawn in front of his villa at Cap Ferrat. Artist and subject are speaking, but again there is no synchronous sound, and Sutherland only gains a voice in a final, extended statement delivered direct to camera, squinting into the sunlight and sitting on a reversed wooden chair in his garden.

'To try to express in words the equivalent of the look that one wants in paint almost invariably ends in failure', Sutherland tells the viewer, 'because words and painting are really separate means of expression.' The camera is obliged to jump around to construct coherence from a number of takes, and Sutherland, speaking with a refined (and obviously rehearsed) upper-class voice, appears uncomfortable. His words, however, clearly demonstrate the interest of an artist's statement of self-image, even in a documentary made right at the start of the tradition of artist encounters with the camera, and as a concluding succession of works is shown, the viewer looks at them anew.

'It has been said', Sutherland reflects, 'that my most typical images express a point of view dark and pessimistic. This is foreign to my mind. The precarious tension of opposites, happiness and unhappiness, beauty and ugliness, so near the point of balance, can be interpreted perhaps according to the needs of the spectator. With delight or with horror, as with the taste of bitter-sweet fruit.'

Read as filmmaker is here, as in many of his other documentaries, entirely at the service of the artist. Yet as is demonstrated by this distinguished film, and by very many artist profiles that have followed, this is far from a dishonourable position to adopt.

Other subjects for Read during the 1950s included Moore again (he made six films with the artist in total), Stanley Spencer and L. S. Lowry, as well as *Discovery of a Landscape: The English Lakes* (1954) which matched images of the landscape with the words of Defoe, Wordsworth and others. Each of these, together with the Sutherland and Piper films (but leaving aside the Lowry) celebrates what the historian Patrick Wright has characterised as 'Deep England', the imagined green and pleasant pastoral landscape that contrasts with the grim realities of wartime (1985: 81–7). Taken together the films can be seen as extending what David Thistlewood has identified as a key concern of the art criticism of John Read's father Herbert, the cultivation of 'a specifically British modernism in continuation of a vital cultural tradition' (1993: 76).

In all of his work Read focuses on a direct encounter with the artist. Critics or presenters rarely appear, and the films aim for only minimal mediation by the camera. There are moments in all of the films where the screen simply shows an artist's work, albeit with the viewer's focus and feelings prompted by framing, camera movement and, often, by music. Yet in comparison with many later documentaries, Read's films can feel strikingly 'open' for the viewer to bring his or her own responses. As the title of his series *The Artist Speaks* (1960) suggests,[6] Read took a similar approach to interviewing his subjects.

On this point he wrote:

I do not myself believe that the art film is a legitimate instrument of criticism. The opportunities for contrived argument are too many and the impact of the screen too authoritative. I prefer to think that sympathetic interpretation and the identification of the audience with the artist are more legitimate objectives. When possible the artist should be in the film to speak for himself and I prefer building up commentary and explanation from the artist's own opinions and statements, leaving the spectator to form his own judgement. (1955)

Read worked for the BBC as a producer until his retirement in 1983, and during these years he made films with Bernard Leach, Arthur Boyd, Naum Gabo, Peter Blake, Patrick Heron, Marc Chagall, Carel Weight and the Brotherhood of Ruralists. He continued to work after his retirement, producing with support from the Arts Council the tribute *Ben Nicholson* (1985) about an artist who had eluded the camera while alive. Made as a co-production with *The South Bank Show*, the film is most notable for a lively interview with painter Patrick Heron, who knew Nicholson in St Ives.[7]

'The basic reason for [making films about artists]', Read stressed, 'is simply that you've got to stand up for the imaginative world, the imaginative element in the human personality, because I think that's constantly threatened. It's a very materialistic society; it's an increasingly technological society, or economic society; and there are other values – people do have imagination and sensibilities, and I think that does need constant exposition' (in Lennon 1983).

Read's concern throughout this immensely distinguished (and too rarely celebrated) work was the expression and exploration of a British tradition of art. His values and concerns are rural rather than urban, individual rather than mass-produced, organic and not technological, modernist but as a critique rather than an embrace of the modern material world. Hence his return time and again to Moore, right through to their last collaboration, *Henry Moore at Eighty*, in 1978. It was to be Read's BBC colleague Ken Russell who would present Pop art for television in his 1962 film *Pop Goes the Easel*, and it was Herbert Read who dismissed this new movement:

> Until we can halt these processes of destruction and standardisation, of materialism and mass communication, art will always be subject to the threat of disintegration. The genuine arts of today are engaged in a heroic struggle against mediocrity and mass values, and if they lose, then art, in any meaningful sense, is dead. (1965: 175)

In 1951, when *Henry Moore* was first broadcast, what many perceived as mediocrity and mass values were about to be unleashed on television.

'What the public wants': ITV arrives

In 1949, recognising that the BBC's current Royal Charter would soon expire, the Labour government appointed a committee chaired by William Beveridge to consider the future of broadcasting. In its evidence the BBC forcefully re-stated its public service commitments, arguing against changes to its monopoly privileges:

> So long as broadcasting is continued as a public service conducted by one independent, impartial, single instrument, that organisation will be free, without any over-riding obligation, to discharge all of the responsibilities to the community that broadcasting involves … They include the responsibility … for the use of broadcasting as an educational medium and a means to raise

the public taste, for the discharge of broadcasting's duty to and in all the arts, for the encouragement of all artistic endeavour whether of creation or performance... (In Briggs 1979: 323)

Delivered in January 1951, the report advocated the continuation of the monopoly, but it also included a cogently argued minority contribution from Selwyn Lloyd warning against the dangers of monopoly. This echoed other influential voices, including that of Sir Frederick Ogilvie, who had succeeded Reith as Director General of the BBC but who had resigned during the war. In a letter to the *Times* in 1946, he wrote: 'Monopoly of broadcasting is inevitably the negation of freedom, no matter how efficiently it is run, or how wise and kindly the board or committees in charge of it ... In tolerating monopoly we are alone among the democratic countries of the world' (1946).

With the support of businesses including Pye Radio, the advertising agency J. Walter Thompson and the *Financial Times*, a Popular Television campaign lobbied effectively for the introduction of commercial or, as it was felicitously named, 'independent' television. Also cheerleading from its pages was the *Daily Mail*, employer of J. Stubbs Walker, the critic who so unsympathetically welcomed the BBC's film *Henry Moore*. With the enthusiastic support of a Conservative government elected in 1951 with a strong commitment to consumer choice, the 1954 Television Act brought the new service into being. Remarkably, Kenneth Clark, former Director of the National Gallery and then Chairman of the Arts Council of Great Britain, was appointed as Chairman of the Independent Television Authority (ITA), the regulatory public corporation with oversight of the networked commercial service that soon became known as ITV. He wrote:

During the long argument that had preceded the passing of the Television Act I had been in two minds [about the worth of television]. It was obvious that Commercial Television would produce a *cloaca maxima* of rubbish, but the television produced by the BBC was often extremely dismal ... I realised that television was above all a popular medium, and believed that commercial television might add some element of vital vulgarity which is not without its value. (1977: 137–8)

The ITA owned the service's transmitters and appointed the companies, mostly consortia representing a range of business and entertainment interests, to make programmes for regionally organised franchises. ITV went on the air, initially only in London, on 22 September 1955. The franchise holders had to invest heavily, and their early attempts to present a schedule representing a range of interests were overturned as they faced significant losses.

'Let's face it once and for all', Roland Gillett, Director of Programmes for the franchise holder Associated-Rediffusion, said in November 1955, 'the public likes girls, wrestling, bright musicals, quiz shows and real-life drama ... We gave them the Hallé Orchestra, Foreign Press Club, floodlit football and visits to the local fire station. Well we've learned. From now on, what the public wants, it's going to get' (in Sendall 1982: 328). Neither comments such as this, nor a schedule packed with quiz shows and acquired American film series like *Dragnet* and *Wagon Train*, did much to endear ITV to those who had resisted its arrival. Nonetheless, it quickly became clear that the public was very happy with this new alternative to the BBC.

Television ownership spread rapidly in the early 1950s. In 1951 there were about one million sets; by 1955 this number was closer to five million. Successful coverage of the Coronation in 1953 gave the BBC's television service a boost, but its output as a whole through most of the 1950s demonstrates strikingly little concern to respond to the challenge of ITV. Studio programmes remained the staple of the service, and these frequently featured music, opera and dance performances. Tours of exhibitions and galleries were also broadcast, including ones hosted by Sir Gerald Kelly, President of the Royal Academy. According to the historian John A. Walker, 'Kelly startled viewers and the press with his forthright opinions and his colourful language' (1993b: 27). *Buried Treasure* (1954–59) was an occasional series 'designed to show how people lived thousands of years ago' (BBC 1962). Sir Mortimer Wheeler presented some of these programmes, as he did three 1960 films under the title *The Grandeur that was Rome*. The previous year BBC viewers had enjoyed *The Glory that was Greece* (1959) introduced by Sir Compton Mackenzie. Studio cameras also transmitted how-to-do-it programming, including a series with the painter Mervyn Levy.

> During the past year or so television has created something like 20,000 non-professional painters. At least 5,000 contributed their work to my recent series of programmes on painting for the amateur, which were given in the afternoon programme for women viewers, *Leisure and Pleasure*, and also in the evening series *Painter's Progress*. (Levy 1954: 12)

In the 'Foreward' to Levy's slim volume of lessons published after the transmission of the series, Mary Adams, Adviser to the Controller of Television Services, identified a key issue for all producers working with artworks. 'In its short history', she wrote, 'television has shown itself a mass medium of great power and potentiality. It has already influenced thought and action. But so far it has not succeeded in making much impression on the viewer's attitude to the visual arts. Why not?' (1954: 5) Her answer was that there is too great a distance between a painting and its reproduction on a black-and-white screen:

> [it] has lost its colour and texture; its emotion ... Too much is left to the imagination ... It is true that sculpture and the crafts suffer less than painting, for objects in the round can be shown more effectively. But even here lighting transforms the subject, scale is often destroyed, and the subtleties of technique are incommunicable. (Ibid.)

Kenneth Clark was soon to face precisely these problems. His term of office as Chairman of the ITA ended on 31 August 1957. At dinner that evening Bernard

Sendall, who was to become the essential historian of ITV's early years but who at that time was working in the industry, suggested to Val Parnell and Lew Grade that they should sign up Clark once he was out of contract since, as he later recorded, 'he could become a great populariser of the arts' (1982: 381). In his autobiography Clark recalled at his farewell banquet being beckoned across to Lew's table. '"It's after midnight"', Clark recorded Grade as saying. '"You're no longer chairman of the ITA. You can come and work for us – we've got a contract for you." ... I agreed, and thus entered a field of activity which was to occupy much of my time for the next twenty years' (1977: 205).

In 1958 a presenter for the ITV company ATV welcomed viewers to what he described as 'a new and exciting exploration'. He introduced Kenneth Clark, but stressed that 'this is not a programme written by experts on art for experts for art at all'. The discussion with Clark which followed was called *Is Art Necessary?* and was built around reflections on the abstract idea of beauty. Clark later described the programme as 'a total disaster', but he learned quickly how to master the medium. In total he made 48 programmes for ATV, including *Should Every Picture Tell a Story?* about Picasso's *Guernica* which features a discussion with John Berger. For the documentary producer Norman Swallow writing about these lectures, the programmes 'were still probably the most effective concentrated attempt by television to treat art seriously and at the same time hold as large an audience as possible. They were illustrated lectures of great charm and subtlety' (1966: 158).

Clark found that the lecture format was far more effective than the discussions in his early programmes, as he discovered that what viewers wanted was narrative rather than abstract musings. *Five Revolutionary Painters* (1958) was the first success which was followed by a celebrated trilogy about Michelangelo. He went on to present outside broadcasts like *Picasso at the Tate* (1960) which remains as an invaluable record of the hang and – to a degree – the experience of the highly significant retrospective. But despite his closeness during the 1930s and 1940s with forward-looking British artists like Moore and Sutherland, he was never comfortable with abstraction and he resisted the full force of modernism. Art historian David Mellor has said:

> Kenneth Clark's vision of how mass culture can be leavened, of how it can be penetrated by a high culture, is essentially that of the Victorian philanthropists. They see their mission as essentially that of educating these broad masses of people, people who now have access through democracy to information, to power itself. So you can see Clark as a kind of cultural broker to these people. I don't think there's any sense in which he's being paternalist in this. He sees his mission to keep alive a high culture but to disseminate that in as many ways as possible, and by seizing hold of television he does that.[8]

Clark's series of lectures were ITV's main arts offering in the early years, but they were not entirely isolated in what by the later 1950s were aggressively populist schedules. In 1959, for example, on Sunday afternoons early in the year, actor

Simon Kester interviewed authors for ABC Television's series *The Book Man*. In February Associated-Rediffusion presented a programme directed by Cyril Coke about the franchise holder's local orchestra, *The Hallé at Work*; in May the same company offered a relay from the Royal Academy's Summer Exhibition. By this stage ITV's programmes were securing an overwhelming majority of viewers, yet they were regularly criticised as little more than 'wiggle dances, give-aways, panels and light entertainment' (Briggs 1995: 16). Recognising that the BBC's Charter was due for renewal in 1964, the same year as the initial ten-year licences of the ITV companies had to be assessed, the Conservative government in 1960 set up the Pilkington Committee to advise on the future of British broadcasting.

The first magazine: *Monitor*

On New Year's Day 1960 Sir Hugh Carleton Greene started work as the BBC's new Director General. He was determined both to demonstrate to the Pilkington Committee the BBC's social and cultural worth and to reverse the ratings decline that between 1955 and 1958 had seen the BBC's share of the audience fall to around thirty per cent overall. By 1962, with an invigorated and far more entertaining schedule, the BBC was winning an equal measure of the audience with ITV and the Pilkington report enthused that 'the BBC know good broadcasting [and] by and large they are providing it' (1962: 46). Among the BBC's most celebrated contributions to 'good broadcasting' was *Monitor* (1958–65).

Conceived in 1957 by Kenneth Adam, then newly appointed as Controller of Television Programmes, this magazine strand from the Talks Department was, as Adams detailed in an internal memo, intended to cover the arts in a 'highly sophisticated type of magazine without necessarily appealing only to Third Programme types' (in Briggs 1995: 167). The presenter and first editor of *Monitor* (although he was not the first choice for the latter role) was Huw Wheldon, who by the time of the Pilkington report was closely identified with the programme's style and achievement. Wheldon had joined the publicity department of the BBC in 1952 having been awarded a Military Cross in the Army, run the Arts Council in Wales and organised concerts for the Festival of Britain. He worked on numerous historical series in the mid-1950s and, between 1952 and 1960, he presented the children's strand *All Your Own*.

Heralding the first broadcast on 2 February 1958, the anonymous writer in the *Radio Times* avoided calling *Monitor* an arts programme, but instead described it as 'presenting to viewers a variety of interesting topics that might loosely be called non-political and non-sociological ... it will cover such subjects as the theatre, films, books, painting, sculpture, music, architecture and entertainment generally'. The 45-minute programmes, shown on alternate Sunday evenings, initially presented as many as five or six items, with the opening show featuring Peter Brook speaking about *musique concrete*; a discussion of a new production of Tennessee Williams' *Cat on a Hot Tin Roof*; Kingsley Amis interviewed about his novel *I Like it Here*; Joseph Cooper at the piano illustrating the musical styles of composers; Jacob Epstein in voice-over discussing a number of his works; and a short impressionistic film by John Schlesinger about Tom Arnold's circus at Haringey. 'Our specific programme aim was this', Wheldon later wrote, 'to say something true, within the limits of our perception, about art and artists; and at the same time, sacrificing neither to the other, to make good television with all that implies' (1962: 13).

Subjects in the first series included the Italian Opera Company at the Theatre Royal, Drury Lane; Yehudi Menuhin interviewed by Robert Robinson; Tyrone Guthrie speaking about Stanislavski; and Paul Robeson playing Othello at Stratford-upon-Avon. Among items about the visual arts were a profile of the Artists International Association, with commentary by painter James Boswell, and artist Michael Ayrton speaking about Masaccio. But the tone was not resolutely highbrow: the third edition featured the two 'Happy Wanderers' buskers entertaining people outside the Warner Cinema in London's Leicester Square, and later subjects included Brighton Pier and a send-up of the Hi-Fi craze with 'the new development of stereo'. Everyone associated with the programme later spoke of Wheldon's effectiveness in building and motivating a talented team. Producers included Nancy Thomas, Peter Newington and Humphrey Burton, and key to the successful creation of many of the filmed items were the cutting-room skills of Allan Tyrer (who later edited *Civilisation*).

'Wheldon's skill in choosing his team resulted in memorable programmes', Melvyn Bragg recalled, 'and the early establishment of ways of making arts programmes: the illustrated interview, the process film, the 'art' film biography (most memorably on Elgar), the quirky/oblique director slot, the overall and undisguised intention to educate through television story-telling' (1982: 41–2).

The series made effective and imaginative use of the television studio, as in a powerful piece in which the singer Lotte Lenya performed Kurt Weill songs including 'Mack the Knife' to back-projected images of the rise of Nazism in the 1930s. But it was the film items that increasingly attracted the enthusiasm of critics. The greater flexibility and focus of film was appealing, especially as 16mm camera and recording technology was becoming lighter and less intrusive. Schlesinger contributed further films on Georges Simenon, literary creator of the Inspector Maigret character, on the imagination of children, and on Benjamin Britten at Aldeburgh. David Jones, later to be a distinguished drama producer with the Royal Shakespeare Company and at the BBC, profiled Lawrence Durrell at his home in the Camargue and E. M. Forster on his eightieth birthday. 'It's for its own films', the critic John Holmstrom noted in the *New Statesman*, 'that *Monitor* is most respected. John Schlesinger made his name here with some very deft satirical pieces … and the current golden boy is Ken Russell' (1964).

Ken Russell: the biggest director in the world

Ken Russell was a feature photographer for *Illustrated* magazine who made three short 'amateur' films in the late 1950s, including *Amelia and the Angel*

(1957), which was partly financed by the BFI's Experimental Film Fund (EFF). From his first films for *Monitor* he demonstrated how liberating and creative the film camera could be. For the series he directed a succession of sideways looks at English life and culture, mostly between ten and twenty minutes long, including his first contribution *A Poet in London* (1959) with John Betjeman, *The Miners' Picnic* (1960) about a brass band competition at Bedlington, and two documentaries about choreographers, *Marie Rambert* (1960) and *Cranks at Work* (1960). His *The Light Fantastic* (1960) is a still-fresh look at ballroom, Morris dancing, rock'n'roll and other kinds of social dance.

For a special Easter programme in 1962, he made the 44-minute film *Pop Goes the Easel*, which observes four young artists just out of the Royal College of Art (RCA) – Peter Blake, Derek Boshier, Peter Phillips and Pauline Boty – living in a London of fairgrounds and street markets, fast cars, parties and American music. Fragments of movies are intercut and quotes from the radio are used on a soundtrack that is largely free from interviews with the artists. The film, shot by Ken Higgins, takes its subjects on their own terms, seeking to find in movement and juxtaposition a form that echoes the bright, brash, quotation-soaked and often collage-based art they were making. Wheldon contributed an on-screen introduction in which he spoke of the film presenting 'a world which you can dismiss if you feel so inclined as being tawdry and second-rate, but a world all the same in which everyone to some degree lives whether they like it or not'. One suspected from his manner as preserved in the recording that this world was not one that filled him with much enthusiasm.

Russell's first portrait of a composer was an early *Monitor* film, *Gordon Jacob* (1959), the subject of which was still living. But the focus of his second, *Prokofiev: Portrait of a Soviet Composer* (1961), had died eight years earlier, leaving behind no archive footage and few photographs accessible in the West. Arguing that he should be permitted to use actors against the opposition of a deeply sceptical Wheldon and the head of the Talks Department Grace Wyndham Goldie, the director was finally allowed to feature shots of an actor's hands playing the piano and of a shadowy figure reflected in a pond. These are combined with effectively re-cut scenes from Sergei Eisenstein's *Oktyabr* (*October*, 1928) and *Alexandr Nevskiy* (*Alexander Nevsky*, 1938) and with newsreel footage of Russian troops in action.

The following year, in the lushly romantic *Elgar* (1962), commissioned as *Monitor*'s hundredth programme, Russell was finally permitted to use actors to portray the composer and his family, although they had to be shown mostly in long shot and they could not speak (see Chapter 4 for a fuller discussion of this landmark film). From here throughout the 1960s, in addition to the two feature films *French Dressing* (1963) and *Billion Dollar Brain* (1967), Russell extended and developed in increasingly Baroque ways the form of an artist's life in drama. *Béla Bartók* (1964) counterpoints images of the isolated composer in New York with lavish stagings of *The Miraculous Mandarin* and *Bluebeard's Castle*, while the feature-length *The Debussy Film* (1965), co-scripted with Melvyn Bragg and made for *Monitor* in its final months, parallels the life of the composer (played

The young composer gallops over the Malvern Hills in Ken Russell's *Elgar*

by Oliver Reed) with events amongst a film crew making a biography of the musician.

The thrilling *Isadora, the Biggest Dancer in the World* (1966) opens with a *Citizen Kane*-like montage reviewing the events of the dancer's life and then dramatises her attempts, in France and then Russia, to found a school of dance for the world's children. The closing sequence, just before a final shot of her face in death, is of Isadora (played by Vivian Pickles) dancing with children to Beethoven's Ninth Symphony. *Song of Summer* (1968) is a more lyrical portrait of Frederic Delius in his last years and of his amanuensis Eric Fenby, while *The Dance of the Seven Veils: A Comic Strip in Seven Episodes on the Life of Richard Strauss* (1970) is derived, although at some distance, from a book by the critic George Marek that deals with the composer's relations with the Nazis. The film, with its self-consciously 'shocking' scenes of dancing nuns and a comic Hitler, provoked a furore and Russell, feeling that the BBC failed to back him, ended his relationship with the BBC:

> I was cocking a snook at the whole dramatised documentary idea, this mess which in a way I had left behind me at the BBC, the assumption that you could dress people up in old clothes and it would suddenly be 'real'. The whole deal had degenerated into a series of third-rate clichés, I wanted to dress people in old clothes and do it in a totally unreal way, and thus make it more real than ever, and in the process send up this new civil service/academic way of doing things which *Monitor* had instigated. (Ken Russell in Baxter 1973: 128)

Back among the civil servants and academics, Jonathan Miller, fresh from the Broadway success of the satirical stage show *Beyond the Fringe*, took over as *Monitor* editor in the autumn of 1964. The series became more intellectual, more ideas-led, but its initial embrace of what one critic sneeringly characterised as 'jeans-and-sneaker culture' (Worsley 1970: 148) was blighted by reactions to an early appearance by the American intellectual Susan Sontag. Sir Hugh Carleton Greene later described her contribution as 'ludicrous ... which embarrassing though it was at the time has become in retrospect almost a lovable symbol of the silly and pretentious' (in Worsley 1970: 10). Speaking of the differences between Wheldon's approach and his own, Miller said: 'He had very much an *ad hominen* view of the arts, and it was a series of great heroes or trophies. Whereas I think I was more interested in what went into the arts, what their social context was and so forth.'[9] But as Miller admitted, 'there were things I thought could be done [on television] and they could not be done ... relatively complicated ideas could not be put across' (in Bakewell & Garnham 1970: 130).

Monitor lasted for just one season under Miller, being replaced in the autumn of 1965 by the eclectic *Sunday Night* strand of single-topic documentaries. Peter

Ustinov offered a monologue about his ancestors, W. H. Auden and Luchino Visconti were profiled, Wheldon chaired the debate *Who Cares about the Arts?*, and in *The Drinking Party* Jonathan Miller staged a modern recreation, set in a school, of a dialogue by Plato. Ken Russell contributed *Don't Shoot the Composer* about Georges Delerue. But the slot failed to establish an identity and after one season, in the summer of 1966, it too was retired. By this point, the BBC's new channel, BBC2, was offering a much wider range of arts programming, but cultural offerings from the main channel were not entirely confined in the early 1960s to Wheldon's strand. The art critic David Sylvester, for example, wrote and presented the series of lectures *Ten Modern Artists* (1964) which profiled, among others, Pollock, Mondrian, Soutine and Matisse. Then, after the failure of *Sunday Night*, in 1967 the new strand *Omnibus* came to the screen, and proved to be far more resilient and a worthy substitute for *Monitor*.

Tempo: 'a swinging *Monitor*'

By the time ITV's programme output was condemned for its relentless populism by the Pilkington Committee's report in June 1962, the companies had begun to offer a more balanced schedule. Central to their response was ITV's first arts magazine programme *Tempo* which, when it began in October 1961, was transmitted fortnightly for fifty minutes on Sunday afternoons. The high-profile theatre critic Kenneth Tynan was asked by ABC Television's Director of Programmes Brian Tesler to be the first editor. 'I remember writing [to Tynan] originally that I wanted it to be a swinging *Monitor*', Tesler said later, 'and that's what we started out to do' (in Bakewell & Garnham 1970: 133). But as his wife Kathleen recalled, Tynan's commitments at the time were overwhelming and he was happier as a small-screen performer (notoriously later as the first person to say 'fuck' on British television) than as an executive: 'Of the fifteen editions [for which he was responsible], Ken was most pleased with an idiosyncratic interview with [theatre designer] Gordon Craig on his ninetieth birthday', she wrote, adding that he was also happy with

> a programme in which Françoise Sagan, Nathalie Sarraute and others were interviewed in Paris about the artist's responsibility during a political crisis, such as the Algerian war; the first performance in England of Isaac Stern's trio; Jill Craigie's filmed critique of contemporary British architecture; an essay on Christ in art, written by John Whiting; Graham Sutherland at work; and Joe McGrath on psychotic art. (1987: 184)

'The faults of *Tempo* are more serious than its timing [2.45pm on Sunday]', wrote Peter Black in the *Daily Mail*, reviewing an early edition in December 1961.

> They go deep into the structure of commercial television ... The programme manages to appear pretentious and anxious, sincere, amateurish and bogus

all at once. There are few signs of a dominant unifying personality, least of all Tynan's ... the programme manages to irritate, disappoint and sadden the eggmass who wishes it well. Yet it would be unkind to assume that ABC doesn't want it to succeed, is only waiting until the Pilkingtons are looking the other way to kick it to death. (1961)

The series in its first three years was primarily studio-based and made on a tiny budget; the presenters included the Earl of Harewood and Clive Goodwin. *A Vision of England* (1963), with Trevor Howard and Leo McKern, was a homage to Shakespeare; Jacques LeCoq performed mime; the Hungarian conductor Laszlo Heltay demonstrated that *Carols Mean Christmas* (1963); and *Postscript to the Ballet* (1964) paid tribute to Dame Ninette de Valois. But there were more adventurous outings also, including *The Medium-Sized Cage* (the title, taken to refer to television, was courtesy of Samuel Beckett's *Murphy*) for which students from the Film and TV Design course at the RCA were invited to make a 'comment' specially for the series. 'The programme took the audience from the devising of the programme to the presentation itself', one of the creators, Trevor Preston, later wrote, 'the portrayal, internal and external, of an art student "moving digs" ... A single set with a single actor, the man and his things; his self-mocking stream of consciousness voiced over' (2007: 6).

Tempo: The Medium-Sized Cage ponders the mysteries of life and boots

Film documentaries were increasingly featured in the series, including *The Bundle* (1962) about kids in a drama class at a secondary modern school in Tottenham, north London and, later, the well-regarded *A Tale of Two Talents* (1966) directed by Jim Goddard, about the Canadian dancer Lynn Seymour working with the Royal Ballet and pop star Tom Jones recording the film songs 'What's New Pussycat?' and 'Thunderball'. In 1965 the series was refreshed under producer Mike Hodges, who had been working for Granada's *World in Action* current affairs series and who would later make feature films including *Get Carter* (1971). Hodges encouraged experiments with cinematic tricks, leading the way with a programme about Richard Lester's feature film *The Knack* (1965). Documentary profiles followed, including features on Harold Pinter, Jean-Luc Godard and fashion designer André Courrèges. 'Gone were the studios, the front man, the dinosaur cameras, the static presentation, gone was television theatre', wrote Preston, who after *The Medium-Sized Cage* was offered a job on *Tempo*. 'We were on the move, outside in the world, on 16mm; and it was like a breath of fresh air to a drowning man. Programmes started to have a political edge: a film on the built-in obsolescence in society was particularly powerful' (ibid.).

In early 1967 eight films under the title *New Tempo* explored fashionable themes of the time, including *Stimulants*, *Heroes* and *The Information Explosion*. Not everyone, however, was enthusiastic. 'So far out as to be barely comprehensible as a communication', was Peter Black's verdict on the series under Hodges (1967). But he welcomed *Tempo* back for its last series in the 1967–68 season when producer John Irwin returned the series to the studio with groups of programmes under the titles *Performer and Composer* and *The Actor and the Role*. Daniel Barenboim discussed Beethoven in the former, while Edith Evans, Donald Pleasence and Michael Hordern (on Prospero) featured in the latter.

To ensure that the ITA and others noticed its commitment to culture, in 1964 ABC Television produced an elegantly designed book about the series written by the novelist Angus Wilson. Wilson suggested:

> To recruit not only intelligent but sensitive and imaginative people to work for television [they] will want to feel that television can create new forms, make statements in ways that no other medium can ... *Tempo* is always at its best when exploring the processes of creation, finding out exactly how a new production of a play comes into being, how a ballet is imagined and set going, how a choir is brought into unity and so on ... It is in fact by examining the act of creation that television most successfully exalts the finished work of art; it is also in probing and presenting the creative imagination at work that the television producer seems to come nearest to producing something original of his own, a work of art. (1964: 9–10)

Post-Pilkington, the Television Act of 1964 gave the ITA powers to 'mandate' certain programmes and to require all the companies to show them at prescribed times in the schedule. Among the types of programmes included in these provisions was a weekend arts special, to be shown before 10.40pm, which *Tempo* and, later, *Aquarius* (1970–77) and *The South Bank Show* provided. The ITA also paid particular attention to the regional offerings of the contractors, and many of these produced arts strands with a particular focus on local activities. 'One interesting aspect of the 1960s', Bernard Davies wrote, 'was the number of excellent arts programmes made locally: the ambitious *Kaleidoscope* in which Border, Grampian, Scottish and Ulster (the Gaelic fringe?) all took part; Ulster's own programmes, including the later *Spectrum*; Anglia's investigations into its past in *Romany Rye* and similar programmes; [and] the coverage by TWW of ebullient Welsh culture' (1981: 12)

BBC2's new line-up

In its evidence to the Pilkington Committee, the BBC had explained that in the newly competitive environment 'it is inevitable that the problem of scheduling for one network only leads to a situation where cultural programmes suffer most' (in Pilkington 1962: Appendix E, 225). The committee members were persuaded by this argument and the report, as already noted, was largely laudatory about the BBC's television service. As a reward, the BBC was 'authorised forthwith to provide a second programme' (in Briggs 1995: 295). BBC2 launched to the London area on 20 April 1964, broadcasting a 625-line UHF transmission (which just over three years later would allow colour broadcasts). Viewers needed to convert their 405-line sets or purchase new ones to watch the channel, which was in any case only gradually available across the whole country. The costs of changing to 625-line sets, as well as the commitments that Hugh Carleton Greene had made to Pilkington, meant that the BBC did not want to restrict BBC2's offerings to minority programmes or education. The new channel's head, Michael Peacock, devised a schedule that he called a 'seven faces pattern': Mondays would feature 'straight family entertainment', education would dominate on Tuesday, Wednesday would be repeats night and so on. But the difficulties under this scheme of planning complementary programmes with the main channel meant that it was abandoned within three months.

Three days after opening the channel showed a profile of Russian ballerina Olga Spessivtzeva written and directed by Ludovic Kennedy for one of the earliest independent production companies, Television Reporters International. Other programmes in the first month included a masterclass with Paul Tortelier; *Writer's World*, with author interviews produced by Melvyn Bragg, and *Quintet*, an original ballet for television (the first of five) choreographed by Peter Wright and featuring Anthony Dowell. Early music and opera presentations included a broadcast of the Sadler's Wells' production of Benjamin Britten's *Peter Grimes*, Aaron Copland conducting the London Symphony Orchestra, five Prom concerts from the Albert Hall and a German television recording of *The Magic Flute* from Salzburg. Judging solely from the schedules in yellowing copies of *Radio Times*, despite the concerns to appeal to a wide group of new viewers the channel adopted – in the arts at least – a rigorously 'highbrow' agenda, with a modern but hardly contemporary focus: Britten and ballet, Klemperer conducting Beethoven's Ninth Symphony and, taking up eighty minutes of an August evening, 'an impression of the 1964 Festival at Aix-en-Provence'. Studio operas were also a part of the BBC2 schedule, with eight shown in 1966, including Benjamin Britten's *Billy Budd*, and four more in 1967. Yet this musical menu was leavened by *The Artist in Society* (1967), which set out to examine different aspects of the role played by the artist in society during a thousand years of European civilisation, by a series of profiles of French New Wave directors and by the short films *Canvas* (1966–70) each of which featured a different expert offering personal reflections on great paintings.

From 12 September 1964 (following a previous outing in the early evenings as *Line Up*), BBC2 offered in *Late Night Line-Up* at the end of each weeknight evening an open-ended review of the arts and culture (including, often controversially, responses to the BBC's own output). Regular presenters on the show, which ran until December 1972, included Denis Tuohy, Michael Dean and Joan Bakewell, who later recalled: 'Looking back, the freedom we enjoyed was just extraordinary. Essentially we were allowed to create a programme that we enjoyed presenting. The sense was that if we found something interesting, then it would be interesting to the viewers' (in Kinnersley 2007: 8). Listings for the show, which are for many editions all that survive, promise interviews with everyone from Ralph Richardson and Willy Brandt, Tony Hancock to Juliette Greco, Cecil Beaton to Gloria Swanson. An edition in 1972 featured Malcolm Muggeridge and Bernard Levin discussing pornography, censorship and sex. Another from 1970 included a spoof report by Willie Rushton from the World Cup in Mexico; at the end of the item, which was shot in a taverna, the camera followed Rushton out into a London street. A weekend version, *The Look of the Week* (1966–67), was one offspring, the regular *Film Night* (1970–76) was another, *One Man's Week* (1971–75) was a third, and a fourth was *Colour Me Pop* (1967–68), a rock music strand that featured Frank Zappa, the Moody Blues and the Nice amongst others. Much of the extensive output was presented live and not recorded. Many items, either from the studio or shot on film, do remain, but it is hard to form a historical sense of its achievement. Yet it is still a vivid component of memories of the 1960s, and the valedictory words in 1972 of the *Television Mail*'s critic Bernard Davies remain valid: it was 'inseparable from, and symbolic of, one's concept of BBC2' (1972).

The other series on the BBC that offered regular coverage of the arts was *New Release*, which ran from October 1965 to March 1967. In a magazine format it presented reviews and short features including a film portrait of director Federico Fellini, Jane Arden interviewing Salvador Dalí in New York, a day in the life of the pantomime dame Clarkson Rose and Robert Hughes questioning whether the Royal Academy's Summer Exhibition had outlived its usefulness. In a July 1966 edition Alex Glasgow interviewed the Minister for the Arts, Jennie Lee, who revealed that she wanted to entice young people into museums. *Plus ça change*. Returning in colour and as *Release* in the autumn of 1967, the series continued to offer a thoughtful and usually topical menu, including Alexander Walker interviewing Fritz Lang, choreographer Glen Tetley working on his ballet *Ziggurat*, and an interview with Coleman Hawkins. Among the regular presenters were Robert Hughes, Irving Wardle and John Donat. 'BBC2's brief, as far as I was concerned', said the channel's Controller David Attenborough of these years, 'was to cover all those aspects of human activity that BBC1 didn't.'[10]

Regular transmissions in colour began on BBC2 on 1 July 1967, just in time for the final week of that year's Lawn Tennis Championships at Wimbledon. Having been used for test transmissions for months beforehand, *Late Night Line-Up* became the first regular colour programme in Europe. But it was 18 months before one of colour television's great triumphs, the 13-part *Civilisation*, made its way to the screen. It began, as many things on television did and still do, with a lunch. David Attenborough extended an invitation to Kenneth Clark, who had been working on a joint BBC/ITA film about Royal Palaces ('a total failure', according to Clark (1977: 209)). Attenborough suggested that Clark might like to tackle 'civilisation'. 'I was munching on my smoked salmon rather apathetically when I heard [the word]', Clark later wrote, 'and suddenly there flashed across my mind a way in which the history of European civilisation from the dark ages to 1914 could be made dramatic and visually interesting' (1977: 210). There exists in the Clark archives, held at Tate Britain, a note – seemingly written that afternoon – outlining the titles and subjects of the 13 films. The audience figures for the series were modest but its impact was remarkable. The *Times* thundered its approval not on the arts pages but in a first leader encomium titled 'How Like an Angel' (1969). In its wake, *The Ascent of Man* (1972) with Jacob Bronowski and Alistair Cooke's *America* (1972), both made as 13 one-hour programmes, were among the first non-art series bearing its influence to reach the screen. But for our story (considered further in Chapter 4) the line that runs from the final frames of *Civilisation* through to *Power of Art* (2006) with Simon Schama, takes in *Ways of Seeing* (1972) with John Berger, Robert Hughes' *The Shock of the New* (1979) and *This is Modern Art* (1999) with Matt Collings, as well as many less distinguished offerings.

Towards the end of 1972, as *Late Night Line-Up* was winding down, BBC2 experimented with a new studio-based arts and entertainment programme. Hosted by actor Joe Melia and produced by Tony Cash, *Full House* ran live for over two hours on a Saturday evening, and aimed to bring together in front of a studio audience an eclectic mix of performers, commentators, sketches and short films. The opening programme, on 14 October, included rock group Humble Pie; drummers and dancers from Ghana; American sociologist Paul Goodman analysing body language; *The Musical Pig*, an animation from Yugoslavia; a film report about a Tate Gallery show of Caspar David Friedrich; Cathy Berberian singing songs by Saint-Saëns, César Cui and Gilbert & Sullivan; the drama *The Punishment* by E. A. Whitehead, plus sketches by Adrian Mitchell and an audience discussion of issues raised by the play.[11] Most editions were broadcast from Television Centre in London, but one was transmitted from Tyneside and another from Glasgow; in February 1973 one programme was devoted to the work of West Indian writers, artists, musicians and filmmakers, and included a short film directed by Horace Ové of Russell Henderson and his band as well as the television drama debut of Mustapha Matura.

Strands of the *Full House* idea survived in *Second House* (1973–76) which superseded it in the autumn of 1973. The presenter was Melvyn Bragg; the live audience was banished, the running time trimmed and increasingly the items were themed. 'More of a sense of *Monitor* than last year's fun palace and none the worse for that', was the verdict of the *Guardian*'s critic Peter Fiddick; 'A bit aggressive, uptight even, in its political commitment, but going for the right subjects and a good tough mix' (1973). But the mix never quite gelled and from August 1976 BBC2 changed its weekend cultural offering once again. *The Lively Arts in Performance* presented a major opera, ballet or concert on Saturday evenings, and these transmissions were complemented by documentaries, often on a related subject, on Sundays.

The age of *Aquarius*

In the 1967 round of ITV contract awards, a new consortium, widely recognised as containing an extraordinary assortment of creative talent, made a bold and successful bid for the weekend franchise in London. To provide the weekday service in London, the Authority created a new company, Thames Television, from a forced merger of ABC Television and Associated-Rediffusion. The weekend programming, traditionally a home for arts broadcasts, was to be produced by London Weekend Television (LWT), which began with promises to elevate public taste. The ratings at its start were disastrous, and the general economic recession and poor internal management exacerbated the problems. In the spring of 1971 Rupert Murdoch's News of the World Organisation offered to buy the ailing company. Although the ITA vetoed Murdoch taking the chair of the new company, on monopoly ownership grounds, it had little choice but to approve his bid. LWT was duly restructured and relaunched successfully.

Humphrey Burton, once a producer on *Monitor* (where he made a delightfully human film about the Allegri String Quartet) and from 1965 to 1967 the BBC's first Head of Music and Arts, was one among that greatest concentration of talent running LWT. The BBC, he thought, had become smug and set in its ways. In 1970, to fulfil the consortium's promise to provide quality programming and to meet the ITA's mandated arts programme requirements, he launched *Aquarius* as a fortnightly Sunday evening arts strand. *Aquarius* was, in Burton's words, to be 'an experiencing rather than a critical programme' (in Bakewell & Garnham 1970: 120), but he was unable either as editor or the first presenter to give it a strong personality. Subjects included the filmmaker Denis Mitchell (*Television's Master Film Maker*, 1970) and – now that the *Omnibus* film *Cracked Actor* (1970) about David Bowie had brought pop music into the arts programming canon – singer Elton John (*Mr Superfunk*, 1971). Burton's great discovery, however, was the flamboyant presenter and producer Russell Harty, who with director Charlie Squires was responsible for many of the more memorable editions of the series, including *Derby Day* (1971), *Hello Dali!* (1973) and a film about two distinguished residents of the island of Capri, Gracie Fields and William Walton.

Despite running the not-yet-opened National Theatre, and regularly directing plays, Peter Hall accepted the job as the presenter of *Aquarius* (working with editor Derek Bailey) from the autumn of 1975. Among his first contributions was an interview with fellow theatre director Peter Brook. Other editions included National Theatre architect Denys Lasdun speaking about the Greek amphitheatre at Epidaurus. But as Hall's published diaries revealed, he was soon assailed by doubts. '*Aquarius* is all wrong from me', he recorded; 'I am somebody who *works* in the arts, and the programme should reflect this. It's no good at the moment. I was wrong to do *Aquarius* at all. Too late now' (1993: 187). Later editions included Lynn Seymour dancing Frederick Ashton's choreography to a Brahms waltz, a film about the painter Euan Uglow ('I wanted to own [his 'Summer Painting'], to live with it. Easy if one had £3,000 to spare. I don't' (Hall 1993: 208)), a Russell Harty film about Edna O'Brien and a film by Jeremy Marre on British reggae. Hall's final verdict on his performance applied also to the series as a whole. 'It's been passable; but that isn't enough', he decided in November 1976. 'The commercial companies don't expect arts programmes to get ratings, but they do expect them to get attention – which means press – and *Aquarius* has been getting next to no attention' (1993: 270). Early the following year the show was cancelled.

The golden years of *Omnibus*

For 35 years, between 1967 and 2002, BBC1's schedule included the *Omnibus* strand as the capacious catch-all for full-length arts programmes. Given its name and mission by Head of Music and Arts Humphrey Burton, just before he left the BBC to join LWT, the series went on air with dramatist Henry Livings as its first presenter. At different times during its long run, which was supervised by at least eight editors, *Omnibus* offered coverage of the Academy Award ceremonies from the United States, numerous concerts from the Proms, tributes to the recently deceased, including Huw Wheldon in April 1986, and extended interviews with major figures like Margot Fonteyn and Gene Kelly. Acquisitions from outside the BBC, including a number funded by the Arts Council (discussed in Chapter 3), also featured in the strand, along with performance such as Kurt Jooss's ballet *The Green Table* produced by Swedish Television, shown in June 1976, and documentaries like Johanna Demetrakas' film *Judy Chicago's Dinner Party*, presented in January 1981. There was also a period in the early 1980s when, as Laurence Marks later wrote,

> Bill Cotton, controller of BBC1, brought in Christopher Martin as editor to turn it into a snappy magazine programme, fronted at different times by Barry Norman and Richard Baker. Cotton then learned what his 1960s predecessors had discovered by experiment: that a full-length arts programme makes a greater impact on viewers than a ragbag of disparate items. (1992: 63)

Omnibus as a strand never attracted the affection that its BBC2 sibling *Arena* was later to achieve, in large part because it failed to develop a clear identity. Its value was as a showcase for individual films, and when the choice of filmmakers was strong then so too was the series. This was particularly the case under its editors Barrie Gavin and then Leslie Megahey in the 1970s. Before the richly imaginative runs produced by these executives who were themselves imaginative directors, the series' first editor Christopher Burstall wrote and directed an early *Omnibus* classic in 1967 with *Tyger, Tyger. An enquiry into the power of a familiar poem*. The film draws on performance, natural history footage and the contributions of an eclectic cast list to understand the enigma of William Blake's poem. A taxidermist, the poet Robert Graves, schoolchildren, a zoo-keeper, a teacher of English literature, a man identified only as 'a psychiatrist', together with Stuart Hall and Richard Hoggart, are among those who submit the verse to close readings. The film reaches no conclusion but the conflicting contributions deepen both the religious mystery and the power of the poem.

Other distinctive directors who contributed in the early years included Ken Russell, whose *Dante's Inferno* (1967), *Song of Summer* (1968) and *Dance of the Seven Veils* (1970) were all screened in the series, and Tony Palmer whose controversial *All My Loving* (1968) cleverly juxtaposed interviews and performances by musicians of the day (including Frank Zappa, Jimi Hendrix and Paul McCartney) with news footage of demonstrations, police brutality and the Vietnam War. The former Controller of Programmes at BBC Television, Stuart Hood, cautiously acknowledged the force of the film in the *Spectator* where he wrote: 'I have no doubt that wherever it is shown the film will win professional acclaim. Remarkable for its virtuosity, its impact is inescapable. No wonder it has been the subject of passionate argument in the corridors of the BBC for months' (1968). *Omnibus* also showcased dramatisations including Jack Gold's adaptation of three A. E. Coppard short stories (*The World of Coppard*, 1967) and the gloriously spooky ghost story *Whistle and I'll Come to You* (1968), directed by Jonathan Miller after a M. R. James short story.

The most significant documentary director who contributed to *Omnibus* in its first decade and more was the Hungarian émigré Robert Vas who, working as both producer and film editor, made among other films *East of Bedlam* (1967) about Victorian melodrama, *The Golden Years of Alexander Korda* (1968) and *Mr Laurel and Mr Hardy* (1974). In 1970 Vas directed *Heart of Britain*, a profile of Humphrey Jennings with whose film work his own shared many characteristics. Lindsay Anderson memorably described Jennings as 'the only real poet the British cinema has yet produced' (1954: 181) but his epithet could be applied to Vas in the context of television. Vas's films operate with precise, often surprising, combinations of sound with image, with poetic uses of archival sources, and they develop their subtle politics in parallel with a unique mastery of metaphor. Vas directed his best-known films in other contexts within the BBC, including his 1974 study of the General Strike, *Nine Days in '26*, but *Omnibus* offered him a sympathetic context for his oblique and revealing explorations of film history and popular culture. He died in 1978 and his films today are almost forgotten, yet in the archives of arts programmes and elsewhere there is a major figure awaiting rediscovery.

In 1975 Barrie Gavin took over as series editor and he encouraged a more adventurous approach to subjects and to the filmic approaches adopted by directors. The series had already begun to feature studies of popular culture of the kind that became more closely associated with the later *Arena*. A 1970 film looked at the life of Ian Fleming, the creator of James Bond, and *Morecombe and Wise: Fools Rush In* (1973) observed an edition of the *Morecombe and Wise Show* in rehearsal. But it is Alan Yentob's film *Cracked Actor* about David Bowie that is mythologised as having opened up mainstream arts programming to rock culture. Gavin encouraged other imaginative engagements with music, including Leslie Megahey's delightful study of the composer Ligeti, *All Clouds Are Clocks* (1976). Having been production assistant on Ken Russell's *Béla Bartók* for *Monitor*, Gavin directed documentaries about music and cinema for the BBC through the 1960s and early 1970s and later his career would include numerous films about classical music. At *Omnibus* he encouraged Robert Vas, but he also offered opportunities to Mike Dibb, who made a rich film about cricket and society with C. L. R. James, *Beyond a Boundary* (1976); to Philip Donnellan, who directed *Pure Radio* (1977), a wonderfully inventive film about the work of BBC Radio Features between 1936 and 1964; and with *Marevna and Marika* (1978) to Jana Bokova, whose only previous full-length documentaries were *Just One More War* (1977) for ATV, about photographer Don McCullin, and *Love is Like a Violin* (1977), made for the Arts Council.

ONE FOOT IN EDEN
directed by Barrie Gavin
a Platypus Films production for the Arts Council of Great Britain
50 minutes, 1978

'A Film about Orkney' reads the first title card, and there is a pause before the words are completed by 'and the Music of Peter Maxwell Davies'. The film then quietly suggests its distinctiveness with a long, long pan around a grey, featureless seascape in which the sea and the sky are but barely distinguishable while Maxwell Davies, off camera, speaks about the importance of new music experiences.

Barrie Gavin's film poem presents images and sounds of the island on which, when the documentary was made, the composer Peter Maxwell Davies had lived and worked for almost a decade. We see the landscapes and traces of Neolithic habitations, we look into the faces of people, and we hear the sounds of gulls and everyday speech. We recognise the island as a place

Performance of 'The Martyrdom of St Magnus' from *One Foot in Eden*

with a deep past but also, with the natural gas industry, a modern future. And even before the music begins we sense what Maxwell Davies (who is only briefly glimpsed in performance) describes in voice-over as the 'rightness of the sound of the place'.

Music and performance emerge from the weave of the film and, until the final credits, the works given (including 'Ave Maris Stella', 'O Magnum Mysterium' and the chamber opera 'The Martyrdom of St Magnus') are not individually identified. The composer collaborates closely with the people who live on Orkney and with their musical traditions, fusing these with his own modernist concerns. Yet none of this is made explicit in the film. Rather a tapestry of impressions and quotations is laid out for the user to encounter and experience. The invitation is rare but most welcome.

Central to the film's aural patterns are poems and legends from the ancient Orkneyinga Saga and the writings of, among others, Edwin Muir, Robert Randall and George Mackay Brown, whose work introduced Maxwell Davies to Orkney. These fragments and myths become layers in a film that often suggests the strategies of Humphrey Jennings: precise visual perceptions accompanied by a complex of sounds, tradition recognised in the ways of the world today, community created by a film portrait.

From the early 1960s, Barrie Gavin has worked imaginatively with music and film, often finding striking ways of engaging television audiences with contemporary music. Remarkably, for a 1972 *Aquarius* film he presented Harrison Birtwistle's 'Down by the Greenwood Side' suggesting in the programme's title that this was *A Pantomime with a Difference*. He produced *Vive a Venezia*, a 1978 film for the BBC about the Italian composer Luigi Nono, which I recall as so strange in its use of avant-garde techniques that it was buried by a puzzled channel controller in an afternoon slot. His other subjects have ranged across Pierre Boulez, Percy Grainger and Hans Werner Henze.

In *One Foot in Eden*, over an extended image of an avenue of prehistoric stones, a key quotation is offered: 'Poetry, art, music thrive on these constants. They gather into themselves a huge scattered diversity of experience and reduce them to patterns so that for example in a poem all voyages past present and future become *the* voyage ... the symbol becomes a jewel, flaming throughout history. Men handle the jewel and know themselves enriched.'

Only one of Jana Bokova's *Omnibus* films between *Marevna and Marika* (about the 84-year-old onetime mistress of Diego Rivera and her daughter) and *Dallas: The Big Store* (behind-the-scenes at the city's department store Neiman-Marcus, made in 1981) engaged with a subject that might have been expected from an arts strand. *Quinn Running* (1980) is about the Hollywood actor Anthony Quinn as he journeys from Italy to New York, but Bokova's intimate and indirect approach – as in each of her films from this time – explores his character in surprising ways. She often holds on the screen a self-consciously framed interview for a second or two after a more conventional director would have cut away, and she quietly suggests the distances between what her subjects are saying and what they are thinking. *Living Room* (1978) and *I Look Like This* (1979), as with all of her films, are about how people present themselves, about how they construct their identities, and how fragile the necessary dreams and deceptions often are. *Blue Moon* (1980), which gets to know the topless dancers at the Paris nightclub Concert Mayol as it faces closure, is more explicitly about performance and show business, as is *Sunset People* (1984), made for the BBC's *Arena*, which travels along Los Angeles' Sunset Boulevard learning about the dreams and disappointments of those who live and work there. These are all quiet, unflinching, direct but warm films, with not a trace of cynicism or superiority towards those who appear in them. Only slowly do they reveal their charms, but made as they are at unconventional lengths they demonstrate better than any other group of work from these years how arts programming could sustain a totally distinctive filmmaker working right at the boundaries of the genre.

'I had absolute freedom in the whole BBC series', Bokova reflected in a 2006 interview:

The only thing we discussed was the length of the film, which sounds ridiculous today. Today they give you 52 minutes and that's that. Filmmakers would get complete trust at the time, just based on their reputation. I had an absolute *carte blanche*. That golden age is over. And it is a terrible misunderstanding. Today the author is forced to thoroughly explain the whole film within the first three minutes. The viewer is about to reach for the remote and TV networks just don't want to be switched. (Institute of Documentary Film 2006)

Bokova's later films were one component of *Omnibus*'s output during its best years, when Leslie Megahey was series editor between 1978 and 1981. Megahey's own *Schalken the Painter* (1979; considered further in Chapter 4) and *Landseer – A Victorian Comedy* (1981) were also part of this, together with contributions from Barrie Gavin on Stockhausen (*Tuning In*, 1980); David Wheatley profiling Ray Bradbury (*The Illustrated Man*, 1980); Mike Dibb and Christopher Rawlence working with critic John Berger on *Parting Shots from Animals* (1980); and Phil Mulloy's dramatised *Mark Gertler: Fragments of an Autobiography* (1981; made with the Arts Council) with Antony Sher as the painter. Even in the brief *Radio Times* billing (1–7 March 1980) for *Parting Shots from Animals*, Berger's distinctive voice and the unconventional approach can be heard: 'We animals are disappearing. We have made a film, not so much about us the animals, but about you, the people ...'.

Under its later editors Christopher Martin, Andrew Snell, Nigel Williams and Basil Comely, the series was never as adventurous, constrained by the increasing expectations that a BBC1 series should deal with the mainstream and, at least on occasions, deliver audiences. Yet in a further twenty or so seasons there were numerous notable successes, including *Made in Ealing* (1986), produced by Roly Keating; Christopher Swann's *Leonard Bernstein's West Side Story* (1985); Andrew Piddington's dramatised *George Grosz: Enemy of the State* (1987); Diana Lashmore's ground-breaking trilogy *The Arts and Glasnost* (1987) about writers, artists and filmmakers in the disintegrating Soviet Union; Peter Adam's two-part *Art in the Third Reich* (1989); and Kim Evans' *Don DeLillo: The Word, the Image and the Gun* (1991). *A Vision of Britain* in 1988 offered Prince Charles a canvas on which to paint his view of the blighted architectural landscape of the nation and Nadia Haggar's *Behind the American Dream* (1990) explored the image of the singer Madonna. This was intelligent and accessible programming, presented for a mainstream audience.

Celebrating the series' 25th anniversary in 1992, Laurence Marks wrote: '*Omnibus*'s strength is that it has usually managed to combine a similar spirit of adventurousness [to *Arena*'s] with intelligibility and a consistent scale of intellectual and aesthetic values' (1992: 63). His assessment is correct but his measured enthusiasm indicates how the series failed to inspire critics, filmmakers and audiences (while *Arena* unquestionably did) and how it lacked the clear identity that over a comparable time-scale Melvyn Bragg was able to impart to *The South Bank Show*.

Arts from the south bank

During the 1960s, having been taken on as a production assistant on *Monitor*, Melvyn Bragg worked on the BBC2 series *New Release* and the books strand *Read All About It* as well as writing feature films including Ken Russell's *The Music Lovers* (1970) and *Jesus Christ, Superstar* (1973). In 1977 Head of Features at London Weekend Television, Nick Elliott, brought him to the ITV company to create the arts strand to replace *Aquarius*. With a title that references the location of LWT's offices and studios, *The South Bank Show* went on the air in early 1978, initially as a magazine series. 'It is for *Monitor*, for which I worked during Huw Wheldon's last couple of years, that I feel most affinity as we set up this new show now', Bragg wrote in 1978. Aiming to be 'serious and entertaining, rigorous and accessible', Bragg set up the series with three principles: to respect the integrity of the subject; to respect the audience; and to be professional and skilful in the use of the medium. He was both editor and presenter of the show, and almost every film was built around his interview with the subject.

The opening show, much like *Monitor*, featured a number of items of varying lengths, but the series moved quickly towards a model of either a single 50-minute documentary or, on occasions, two half-hour films. Specials for showcasing in prestige prime-time slots could occupy more airtime, as in the later celebrations *Laurence Olivier – A Life* (1982) and *Michael Flatley – Lord of the Dance* (1997). Subjects in the first year included Martin Amis and Ian McEwan, Dennis Potter at the time of his television masterpiece *Pennies from Heaven* (1978), and the young film director Stephen Frears. Early on, Bragg was proud of the first television portrait of Herbert von Karajan, the first British television interview with Ingmar Bergman, a programme about Kenneth MacMillan's 'Mayerling' for the Royal Ballet and a commissioned film *Hullabaloo* by James Ivory.

Bragg recognised that television's dealing with the arts involved losses – of scale, of presence, of immediacy – and of the viewer's attention being able to engage with the aspect of an artwork that most interests them at a particular moment. But he has always been a singular proponent of the added value that the screen can bring. 'The gains can be very remarkable indeed', he wrote in a celebration of the first decade of the series.

> In [Francis] Bacon's case, the visual admission of his stark credo, the intercutting of violent action photographs with his violent paintings, the purgatorial social milieu of this painter of screaming Popes, the bleak but grand overview of art history – nothing between the Egyptians and Goya! All this was pure gain. (1988: 43)

Francis Bacon – The Brutality of Fact (1985) was directed by David Hinton, the most imaginative filmmaker to have been nurtured by the strand. The film begins with monochrome images looking down on London street scenes as Bragg reads the introductory narration. Blocky red arrows, in a shape familiar from the artist's canvases, are superimposed over freeze-frames, picking out Bacon walking through the world of Soho. Newsreel images – of horses, of trains, of animals, of wrestlers – are rapidly intercut with details from the artist's work before Bragg and Bacon begin to discuss slides of his work and masterpieces from art history. These move from a Tate Gallery storeroom to his studio to a restaurant where with the red wine their speech becomes progressively more slurred and more revealing. Hinton's other subjects for *The South Bank Show* include Elvis Costello, Karole Armitage, Bernardo Bertolucci and, most memorably, director Michael Powell, in a film full of delightful and surprising tricks that mirror Powell's ideas and images.

Across its thirty years, the programme-making approach of *The South Bank Show* has encompassed a range of strategies, including films that are illustrated interviews, authored polemics, portraits of process, the occasional studio lecture (including contributions by Kenneth Clark and Ernst Gombrich), in later years an annual awards show and, mostly, film profiles directed by a stalwart team of in-house directors. Yet throughout its three decades, and unlike, for example, *Omnibus* in the late 1970s and early 1980s, the series has only rarely been distinguished by truly imaginative filmmaking. For a time the strand worked with Tony Palmer who contributed thoughtful, measured essays about two of the great composers of the twentieth century, *A Time There Was...* (1980) with moving footage of Peter Pears speaking about his long-time companion Benjamin Britten, and *At the Haunted End of the Day* (1981) about William Walton. Ken Russell directed a clutch of increasingly eccentric films about composers, including Arnold Bax, Vaughan Williams and Anton Bruckner. As the critic Michael Brooke has noted, 'His 1960s films featured the occasional Russell cameo … but *The South Bank Show* would be much more openly autobiographical, with Russell himself presenting most, and three even featuring his name in the title' (2006). The flamboyant and breathless *Ken Russell's ABC of British Music* (1988) is distinguished both by a manic energy and shameless self-indulgence.

The South Bank Show successfully surveyed the modern and, on occasions, the modish. But it concentrated on established reputations and rarely took risks with the truly edgy. However, one notable programme was commissioned from director Ken Loach in 1984. An anthology of striking miners' songs and poems, *Which Side Are You On?* was inspired by the bitter pit dispute being played out as the Thatcher government orchestrated the endgame of the trade unions. Just before transmission, the film was withdrawn by LWT because of what the company's press office described as its 'highly partial view of a controversial subject'. Acknowledging that he made the film from a position of engaged sympathy with the miners, Loach reflected publicly that it appeared as if only 'approved' people could make comments about a decisive struggle like that of the miners. *Which Side Are You On?* was eventually screened by Channel 4 in January of the following year.

That the programmes are invariably congratulatory in tone, and that the series has failed to develop a critical voice, are among the criticisms that have been persistently laid against *The South Bank Show*. Lamenting the small number of slots for the strand (and for arts programming in general), Bragg wrote that 'lack of space tends to inhibit the employment of a critical approach: as there are so few slots, the thinking goes, it is simply a waste not to use most of it on revelation and illumination' (1982: 40). The series has also been attacked for its perceived trivialisation and for its fascination with subjects from popular music and comedy. Editions devoted to Dolly Parton, Cliff Richard and Moby, among others, attracted particular opprobrium. Yet Bragg has had a host of other subjects with which to respond, figures that outside of *The South Bank Show* would never feature on mainstream television, whether they be Emir Kusturica or Akram Khan, Albert Camus or Jane and Louise Wilson. He has effectively defended his engagement with both 'high' and 'low' art, at the same time as acknowledging the necessity of seeking occasional large audiences as the ITV environment, and television as a whole, becomes ever more focused on audience numbers.

Once Channel 4 offered a new outlet for programming from the ITV companies, Bragg's teams made numerous contributions, including the regular books series *Book Four* (1982–5) and *The Modern World: Ten Great Writers* (1988). These series, and *The South Bank Show* in particular, have undoubtedly been enormously significant in LWT retaining its franchise and in ITV as a whole continuing to demonstrate, even as the series was moved into later slots on Sunday evenings, a residual commitment to the public service ideals of Reith, John Read and so many more. Indeed, when Michael Grade took over as Chief Executive of ITV in early 2007, his first public statement confirmed that *The South Bank Show* would remain on the air for at least a further three years. Melvyn Bragg has had a central role in keeping broadcasters focused on the importance of the arts on television and his dedication to the arts documentary, formed during the *Monitor* years, has continued to carry a quiet authority.

'Just as *The South Bank Show* was the first series to include television dramatists – Potter, Welland, Bleasdale – on an equal footing with stage dramatists', he wrote,

> so the quality of arts films has convinced more and more people that they can
> have a value comparable with that of a play or a novel. Indeed, in my opinion,
> there are at least as many well-made and stimulating arts films to have come
> out of television over the last ten years as there are British feature films or
> stage plays. (1982: 41)

Nearly thirty years after its first transmission, *The South Bank Show* demands respect for longevity and for its honest commitment to values in broadcasting that, as the last quarter of the twentieth century unfolded, began to look threatened from all quarters.

Before continuing the story of television arts programming with the founding of Channel 4 in 1982 and the events that followed, I want to end this chapter with a further personal reflection. Towards the end of 1978 I had been Television Editor for *Time Out* magazine in London for just over a year and I was regularly writing previews of editions of *The South Bank Show*. At LWT's offices on the South Bank one day I watched an almost finished version of Tony Cash's film *Anatomy of an Opera: Jonathan Miller's Figaro*, a polished documentary for Bragg's series about Miller directing a new production of Mozart's master-piece for English National Opera. '[The] film is lively and cleverly-constructed', I wrote, 'but undoubtedly it's Renaissance man Jonathan Miller who makes it compulsive' (1978: 24). Engaged and intrigued, I bought my first opera tickets to see the production – and the artform has been central to my life ever since. The anecdote is both trivial and, in true Ken Russell style, self-indulgent but such a simple acknowledgement of the direct effect of arts television is one expression of advocacy for its continuing value.

CHAPTER 2
'A CRISIS OF CONFIDENCE': ARTS TELEVISION INTO THE TWENTY-FIRST CENTURY

Among the television memories that I hold dear are running home from school each day to catch the regional travelogue that opened Southern Television's transmission; watching the first episode of *Doctor Who* (1963–) the day after President Kennedy's assassination; and as a neophyte critic previewing the first two episodes of Dennis Potter's *Pennies from Heaven*. Nestled alongside these is the recollection of sitting before a screen one November afternoon in 1982 and thrilling as a clutch of computer-generated blocks formed into a multi-coloured numeral. 'Good afternoon', the presentation announcer said after David Dundas' four-tone theme. 'It's a pleasure to be able to say to you: Welcome to Channel 4.'

I had been writing about and lobbying for this new service for nearly five years. I believed that the fourth television service would change the shape of broadcasting as we knew it, as, for a while, it unquestionably did. Like many friends and colleagues, I was even beginning to make programmes for it. But although the tone of these opening paragraphs may suggest otherwise, it is not nostalgia that motivates my personal, partial judgement that terrestrial television in Britain was overall at its richest, most diverse and most challenging during the 1980s – and that Channel 4 was the single most important factor in making it so. Extraordinarily, Channel 4 had a statutory mandate to 'encourage innovation and experiment in the form and content of programming' (Broadcasting Act 1980: clause 3 (c)), which is what it achieved across the widest range of genres, including the arts as well as some – like multicultural programming and independent film and video – which it effectively invented.

The arts on 4 – Peter Greenaway's *Four American Composers* (1983), performance films from Peter Brook and the National Theatre, documentaries from Mike Dibb, Gina Newson and others, even my own company's *State of the Art* (1987) – made a key contribution to the cultural richness and diversity of television in the 1980s. There were other arts broadcasting highlights, not least the BBC's essential *Arena* series that hit its stride during the decade. Also, in early 1989 *The Late Show* began transmissions four nights a week, with an unrivalled mix of discussion, review and imaginative arts filmmaking. But already there was a sense that the good times could not last.

BBC Head of Music and Arts Richard Somerset-Ward told a conference at London's ICA in 1983:

> Up to now [arts programme-makers] have been relatively well-cushioned against the rough winds of competition and the demands of schedulers. Some of us have come to believe that we have a divine right to make programmes. But arts programmes, I suspect, are going to be seen increasingly by schedulers and planners as a luxury – a very expensive one … I have a suspicion that our time is running out.[1]

Time has never quite run out for arts programmes, and they have never disappeared from British television. But in 2001, less than two decades on from Somerset-Ward's warning, Channel 4's founding Chief Executive Jeremy Isaacs was moved to write: 'There is less space for the arts on TV today than there ever has been, in my recollection' (2001). To adapt Virginia Woolf's words about the end of Victorian England, on or about 1 January 2000 broadcasting changed. Then or thereabouts multi-channel television really began to bite into the audiences of the terrestrial services. That was when the mainstream broadcasters hastened their retreat to the middle ground, when audience share became the dominant factor in decision-making, and when certain previously central subjects, including the arts, were marginalised. This chapter traces that history for the arts on terrestrial television, from the new dawn of Channel 4 to an early twenty-first century twilight.

The account, however, is not intended simply as a lament, as a chronicle of ruins at which today we can only stare and despair. Exceptional programmes continue to be made, the digital channels BBC Four and Sky Arts (previously Artsworld) have extended viewers' choices and (as Chapter 5 considers) there are numerous new forms of production and distribution for the arts on-screen, including DVDs, the Internet, mobile systems and more. Original media forms are emerging, some of them exciting extensions of the values and concerns that have been central to filmmaking and broadcasting about the arts. The present is simply a different country, and our maps of the terrain are still only tentative. But for open-minded viewers and producers, critics and contributors, the future has much to offer.

What's this Channel Four?

Since the mid-1950s it was understood that the spectrum allocation for broadcasting across Britain could accommodate only one more national television channel. As early as their 1957–58 Annual Report the Independent Television Authority suggested that it would soon be entrusted with a second commercial service. But Pilkington, fearing that another commercial channel would lead to less diversity, rejected the ITA's proposals. The 1964 Television Act, taking into account that any new service would broadcast in UHF on 625 lines to what would initially be a restricted audience, authorised just a second service from the BBC. Only with the return of a Conservative government and an upturn in commercial television's profits in the early 1970s was the question returned to. In December 1971 the ITA formally proposed to the Minister for Posts and Telecommunications that the vacant spectrum slot should be occupied by ITV2, a commercial service run in a complementary manner to the existing offerings of the franchise holders.

Opposition to the idea of ITV2, however, was focused in the hastily formed but highly effective TV4 pressure group and the government postponed the allocation of the fourth channel. Once Labour had been returned to power in February 1974, a committee was reconvened under the chairmanship of Lord Annan to consider the future of broadcasting, including the decision on any new service. Published in March 1977, the Annan Report reviewed a host of topics, but crucially it recommended that the fourth channel be established under a new body, the Open Broadcasting Authority (OBA). The world had changed and broadcasting had to catch up. The report proclaimed:

> Our society's culture is now multi-racial and pluralist. That is to say, people adhere to different views of the nature and purpose of life and expect their own view to be expressed in some form or other. The structure of broadcasting should reflect this variety. (Annan 1977: 30)

The OBA's channel, the Report recommended, should act as a publisher and encourage a plurality of viewpoints from a plurality of programme sources, including those from a range of independent producers, as well as other bodies such as the Arts Council.

In July 1978 the Labour government endorsed the idea of the OBA in a White Paper, but before this could be realised the Conservatives returned to power. The Queen's Speech for Margaret Thatcher's incoming government promised that 'subject to strict safeguards' responsibility for the fourth television channel would be given to the Independent Broadcasting Authority (IBA, formerly the ITA). Throughout the next nine months of intensive debate, Annan's recommendations remained influential, especially on the question of independent production, and the IBA's eventual authorisation of the Channel Four Television Company carried through many of the report's key ideas. What gave it added impetus was the new government's determination to promote a market economy and to dismantle or destabilise as far as possible the large public bodies of the post-war state – including those of broadcasting. Leftist imperatives towards access and diversity, expressed through Annan, became uncomfortable bedfellows with the ideas of Tory free-marketeers. Home Secretary William Whitelaw told a gathering of executives in Cambridge:

> What the Annan Committee had to say about the prospect which a fourth television channel could afford for innovation, to give new opportunities to creative people in British television, to find new ways of finding minority and specialist audiences and to add different and greater satisfactions to those now available to the viewer – all of this has commanded a remarkably wide measure of agreement and support. (In Lambert 1982: 93)

The BBC and the ITV companies were defensive in their responses to the idea of a fourth channel and perhaps unsurprisingly sceptical about the prospects of non-broadcaster production. 'It has taken thirty years for the combined weight of both the BBC and ITV to fill the screens with a mere three choices', even that most enlightened BBC executive Brian Wenham wrote; 'there is already evident nervousness about the sturdiness of programming to be offered by the fourth' (1982: 23–4). That programmes could, however, be created and owned by 'independent' producers working outside the broadcasters was demonstrated as early as 1962 with a company formed by a number of disaffected correspondents from the BBC's *Panorama* (1953–). Robert Kee, Ludovic Kennedy, Malcolm Muggeridge and others set up Television Reporters International. Despite an initial arrangement with ATV, however, they struggled to find buyers among the ITV contractors and the venture collapsed.

Three years later, in 1965, a trio of *Tonight* (1957–79) editors, including the future BBC Director General Alasdair Milne, established a similar enterprise, but this too was wound up after only two years when Milne returned to the BBC. Allan King Associates, a company formed by four Canadian and two British filmmakers, found a way to work independently (making, among other films, the highly-regarded documentary *Warrendale* (1967)), but much of the company's revenue came from sales to Canadian television. As the next chapter will demonstrate the Arts Council through the 1970s also provided funding and a creative context for filmmakers to produce arts documentaries away from the broadcasters. A handful of hardy individuals, including the former ATV documentary head Peter Batty and the distinguished director of music films Christopher Nupen, were also able to establish themselves as lone independents.

'The BBC has resolutely refused to relinquish even a small part of its stranglehold [on production and distribution]', Nupen wrote in frustration; 'this is not only arrogant and unjustified but counter-productive – as has been demonstrated by the successful relationships between the television networks and independent producers in other European countries' (1979: 43). Once Channel 4 was established, Nupen made a number of exceptional documentaries with support from the service, including *Johannes Brahms 1833–1897* (1984) featuring the composer's violin and viola sonatas, three films with Pinchas Zukerman and *The Language of New Music* (1985) on the music of Schoenberg and the writings of Wittgenstein.

Following on from William Whitelaw's Cambridge speech, the 'Channel Four Group' published an open letter signed by almost four hundred individuals and organisations underlining their concern that 'the Fourth Television Channel must accord with the Government's stated view that it should "extend and enhance" the range and quality of British television' (1979). The radical Independent Film-makers' Association (IFA) made the argument that safeguards at the channel must exist for 'innovative and experimental work' (1980: 1). All of this, and much more, shaped the IBA's blueprint for the channel published in November 1979, which proposed that the channel's budget would be raised from the ITV contractors, who in return would be given the right to sell the channel's advertising. Finally, by the Broadcasting Act 1980, Channel 4 was brought into the world. Confidently taking its Parliamentary place as clause 3 (c) was the provision that the new service must 'encourage innovation and experiment in form and content of programmes'.

'Here were riches': Channel 4's first five years

'A high priority to the arts' was one of nine commitments outlined by Jeremy Isaacs in his letter of application for the job of the new channel's Chief Executive. BBC2's interest in the arts, he felt, had by that time peaked 'and seemed to me slack and quiescent' (2001). Once the channel was on air, Isaacs, with his Commissioning Editor for Arts Michael Kustow, ensured that culture was central to the channel's output. Among Kustow's principles, as expressed in an internal paper written in January 1982, was the intention to achieve

> a closer and more mutual relationship with a wider range of artists and arts institutions than previously in television. To affect, and not only reflect the arts, by co-planning and cooperation on things that might not have happened, or not so fully, if we had not 'gone in with' the theatre, ensemble, or artist.

Such an attitude differed markedly from the position adopted as appropriate by other broadcasters in their dealings with arts organisations.

'The arts on Channel 4 began with performance', Isaacs recalled in his memoir of these years. Given the regular presence of *Arena*, *Omnibus* and *The South Bank Show* on the other channels, 'it did not seem a good idea to me to offer a regular single-subject format at the same length and in the same slot each week … However hard to schedule, we would find space for the major event' (1989: 168). These major events included a lavish version of the Royal Shakespeare Company's stage hit *Nicholas Nickleby* (1982); *King Lear* (1983) with Laurence Olivier; Aeschylus's *Oresteia* (1983) translated by Tony Harrison, staged for the National Theatre by Peter Hall and presented on one night in a four-and-a-half-hour broadcast; Peter Brook's *Tragedy of Carmen* (1983), filmed in Paris in three versions with three sets of principals, plus his epic *The Mahabarata* (1989); Bill Bryden's *The Mysteries* (1985); plus twelve operas a year, including new commissions for Kent Opera's version of Michael Tippett's *King Priam* (1985) and a studio version of *The Midsummer Marriage* (1989). The channel even found a space in the schedule for Jean-Marie Straub and Danielle Huillet's rigorous and austere film version of Schoenberg's *Moses and Aaron* (1973; shown in 1986). Perhaps most extraordinary of all were transmissions from Sadler's Wells of Pina Bausch's challenging contemporary performances with the Wuppertal Dance Theatre, *1980* (1984) and *Bluebeard* (1984).

The channel also commissioned dance films for the screen, with productions of Tom Jobe's *Run Like Thunder* (1984) with London Contemporary Dance and Christopher Bruce's *Ghost Dances* (1984) with Ballet Rambert. Charles Atlas's disturbing dance film with Michael Clark, *Hail the New Puritan* (1986), remains one of the strongest visions on film of London's cultural world in the 1980s. The series *Sinfonietta* (1986) explored chamber music of the twentieth century in films made by six directors with contrasting styles, and *Deep Roots Music* (1982) traced the development of reggae from its Jamaican origins. The live music show on Friday evenings, *The Tube* (1982–87), was one of the channel's early successes. There were extended debates about ideas in *Voices* (1982–88) and oblique explorations of the cinema in the magazine strand *Visions* (1982–85). Many of these programmes were made by newly-founded independent companies, a number of which including Landseer, Large Door and Illuminations Television started out with a commitment to finding new forms for arts programmes. Reporting on the arts also found a regular home on the nightly hour-long *Channel 4 News* (1982–) from ITN. After Channel 4 had been on the air for 15 months, in the introduction to a brochure about early programmes Michael Kustow, who was Director of the ICA for four years in the late 1960s and had been working as an associate director at the National Theatre, outlined his philosophy:

> The channel's arts programmes share certain qualities: a search for originality and immediacy, a fidelity to artistic intentions and standards, and a reluctance to take the more obvious and damaging short-cuts in the name of mass appeal ... I believe that they represent an important commitment to the arts as a vital part of television and of life. (1984)

UNESCO recognised Channel 4 with its Camera Award for the best cultural policy of the year in 1984 and by 1986 the arts department was spending around ten per cent of the channel's programming budget.

In the run-up to the channel's launch, the ITV companies proposed a number of large-scale series, with Thames offering *The Renaissance* and Granada suggesting *The History of Western Music*, which lumbered onto the screen in 1986 as *Man and Music*, with Alan Bennett narrating. Isaacs and Kustow embraced the grand statement on occasion, as with the unconventional six-part series about contemporary ideas and images *State of the Art* (discussed in Chapter 4), but on the whole they preferred to look to individual projects by imaginative directors working on less obvious topics. Mike Dibb had been part of the production team of the BBC series *Ways of Seeing* with John Berger and had made a number of allusive and poetic documentaries with the BBC, including *Seeing Through Drawing* (1978), an essay about imaginative expression with the critic Peter Fuller and, also with Fuller, a richly inventive profile of the American painter Robert Natkin, *Somewhere Over the Rainbow...* (1981). Now for Channel 4, and working again with Fuller, he made the two-part *Memories of the Future* (1983), about the legacies of John Ruskin and William Morris. He also collaborated again with Berger and others on the series *About Time* (1985). This, the press pack promised, 'explores the way in which our modern sense of time, with urban and industrial acceleration, the revolutions of new physics and our awareness of the potential end of time in nuclear destruction, co-exists with more ancient time schemes, related to religion, architecture, folklore and the cycles of the body'. 'Argument is turned into compelling narrative with minimal commentary', wrote the critic Geoff Dyer celebrating the distinctive poetic tapestry of the series. 'Ideas are enacted rather than explained. Sound and vision tug at each other, coaxing extra significance out of one another ... You watch in a state of perpetual expectancy which is simply another phrase for active absorption – following clues instead of being led by the nose' (1985).

Gina Newson, who made the witty and surprising film *Have You Seen the Mona Lisa?* (1981) for the BBC's *Arena* strand, directed *Joan of Arc* (1983) for the new channel; with the cultural critic Marina Warner, she examined the myths and realities associated with St Joan. *Imaginary Women* (1986), developed the arguments of Warner's book *Monuments and Maidens* which explored why abstract virtues are invariably represented by statues of naked or minimally clothed women. The subtle but hard-edged film is built around a dinner party with six women, including Toyah Willcox, Katharine Hamnett and Susan Hiller, discussing the way in which they work with symbols. Newson also made three films for the much admired series *Open the Box* (1986) about how we *watch* television, which was produced by Michael Jackson who would later create *The Media Show* for Channel 4 and *The Late Show* for BBC2. With her partner Jeremy Newson, Gina Newson went on to make a number of further memorable series for BBC2 including *The Look* (1992), about the fashion business, and *The Music Biz* (1995).

Dibb and Newson were among the many accomplished arts directors for whom Channel 4 in its early years provided a sympathetic context. Others included Dennis Marks and Geoff Haydon, with the *Repercussions* (1985) series; Jeremy Marre who directed a clutch of distinguished world music films; Paul Joyce, with profiles of directors Nagisa Oshima and Nicolas Roeg; dance film specialist Terry Braun; and Geoff Dunlop, my partner at Illuminations, who with David Hinton made a glorious early film with the American band Talking Heads. But the dominant figure from those years is Peter Greenaway, who worked as an editor for the Central Office of Information in the 1970s while he was developing his unique personal style in films like *A Walk Through H* (1978) and *The Falls* (1980). Obsessive cataloguing, deadpan humour, images of landscape, language, structural film, the body and bird-watching are just a few of the concerns of his work that he carried across to the films, including the feature film *The Draughtsman's Contract* (1982), that he made with and for Channel 4. *Making a Splash* (1984) and *26 Bathrooms* (1985) are short hymns to the pleasures of water, each accompanied by the flowing music of Michael Nyman. However, his masterworks for the channel are the four-part *Four American Composers* and his collaboration with the painter Tom Phillips, *A TV Dante* (1985–88).

Robert Ashley, John Cage, Philip Glass and Meredith Monk are the composers whose portraits Greenaway created in what was one of Channel 4's earliest commissions. In each filmed encounter he searches for a distinctive film language, most successfully in the profile of John Cage which is built around the stories from Cage's work 'Indeterminacy'. These stories, Greenaway recalled,

> each occupied exactly one minute, although some consisted of eight words and some of three paragraphs. So the stories which consisted of eight words were to be read v...e...r...y s...l...o...w...l...y. To fill the time. The ones that were three paragraphs had to be run terribly fast. A nice idea. And it seemed to me a way of coping with narrative in cinema. By overloading a film with thousands of bits of narrative, hundreds of events and millions of characters, you were negating narrative. (In Auty 1983: 64)

A TV Dante, an adaptation of the first cantos of the 'Inferno', began as a lavishly illustrated book by Tom Phillips. In a pilot made in 1985 and then in eight 12-minute episodes produced in 1988, Phillips and Greenaway collaborated with their committed video editor Bill Saint to exploit the electronic post-production techniques of the time to create a strikingly original visual language. Greenaway had also trained as a painter, and both artists were intrigued by the possibilities of combining graphic composition with poetic visuals. 'In the way that medieval monks illuminated texts', Phillips explained, 'we are illuminating an old work with a new, more modern quill – television' (in Dugdale 1990: 26).

The sense of the screen as a graphic canvas was a key component of the work of Mark Lucas and Jane Thorburn of the independent producers After Image, whose strand *Alter Image* (1983–88) presented a diverse range of talent from the avant-garde, including Station House Opera, Michael Clark, Bow Gamelan Ensemble, La La La Human Steps and Michelle Shocked. The American composer Robert Ashley collaborated with video artists John Sanborn and Dean Winkler on the seven-part 'opera for television' *Perfect Lives, Private Parts* (1984), which also exploited early forms of image manipulation. And *Ghosts in the Machine* (1986, 1989) and other series presented the work of British and international artists exploring video as a creative medium. Channel 4's openness to the cutting-edge of the moving image was also apparent in its commitment to what came to be called 'independent film and video'. As Chair of the BFI Production Board Jeremy Isaacs had been exposed to the work of radical filmmakers and groups who through the 1970s had initiated a fundamental reassessment of cinema, politics, social practice and representation. It was these ideas that at the time informed the ideas of 'independence' and 'innovation' put forward by the Independent Filmmakers' Association and others, although in the years since these associations have largely drained away. While this work is mainly tangential to the story of the arts in British television, it is important to recognise the achievements of Alan Fountain and Rod Stoneman in nurturing on Channel 4 a wide range of truly independent work, much of which was presented in the early strand *The Eleventh Hour* (1982–88).

A quarter of a century on from Channel 4's founding, and with the service pre-occupied by *Big Brother* (2000–) and attention-grabbing stunts like a group of programmes announced under the rubric of 'Wank Week', the service's early output is often dismissed as amateurish, elitist (a word that will recur in other debates), of interest to only tiny audiences, and, at best, patchy. Channel 4 continues to offer some exceptional programmes, and it is unquestionably the case that in its first decade it showed some dreadful programmes. In those years, however, its output overall demonstrated an openness, an excitement, a commitment to difference and an edge that no channel has since approached. There was a strong sense of trusting the vision of programme-makers rather than, as has become the norm in twenty-first-century television, subordinating this to the identity of a channel and the concerns of a host of commissioners. In the arts, Channel 4's programming was underpinned by a sense of commitment to the central value of culture in all of our lives. It presented an exceptional range of international work, when the agenda of most arts broadcasters was, as it remains, parochial. It believed that creative directors could make allusive and ambiguous art directly for the small screen. It showcased truly contemporary artistic creation, and it celebrated art that was often difficult and complex and hard to pin down.

SHADOWS FROM LIGHT
a film by Stephen Dwoskin
produced by (Stephen Dwoskin) Urbane Ltd for the Arts Council
of Great Britain
50 minutes, 1983

Few films are as insistently yet as elusively about space. But the explicit subject of *Shadows from Light* is the photography of Bill Brandt, and many of his most famous images are here. Brandt, who died in December 1983, is also present, seen in profile, blinking in the light, recalling in voice-over the creation of some of the photos. About the famous portrait of Francis Bacon with a lighted lamp and glowering sky behind, he remembers that it was hard to get Bacon to turn up at the right time.

The film begins by taking us into a room. The camera relentlessly explores the space of this room, its boundaries, its openings. On its walls, tucked into its window frames, on the floor, we discover Brandt's photographs. Portraits, landscapes (like Stonehenge in the snow), more portraits, city scenes by moonlight, nudes. The photographs are objects, not simply images, and they carry their physical presences. They are outside too, propped up in the grass, and in other spaces, and in no space. The camera zooms at these photographs, flits past them, casts light across them and withdraws. The camera moves constantly in space while the images remain still.

The space of the film is neither logical nor consistent, There are mirrors, reflections and frames, juxtapositions of different depths and distortions of perspective. Brandt explains that he started late in life to take his famous

Photographer Bill Brandt caught by Stephen Dwoskin's camera in *Shadows from Light*

nudes because he wanted to make photographs of rooms, but he felt the need to have something in the rooms. *Shadows from Light* is a film of a room, and of many rooms. Female nudes come and go within them, the camera at times capturing equivalents of Brandt's images.

Then there is the film's surface, a succession of glistening, high contrast monochrome frames, echoing Brandt's style and blurring the boundary between the photographs and the film's photography. On the soundtrack is music and the background 'silence' that filmmakers call atmosphere, and often the film simply lets the viewer look, with the voices of two narrators supplying only the titles of the images. There are quotations too, about photography, from Man Ray, Susan Sontag, Edward Steichen, plus a child reading fragments of *Alice Through the Looking Glass*. *Shadows from Light*, like Lewis Carroll, is mysterious and haunting, innocent yet rewardingly complex.

Stephen Dwoskin began making films in New York in 1959. His experimental cinema often combines the modernist and materialist concerns of structural film with images of the body and performance. All of these interests are strongly present here, as they are in his other Arts Council-funded documentary, *Ballet Black* (1986), about the Ballets Negres dancers in Britain in the 1940s and early 1950s. But there Dwoskin is working with only minimal traces of performance. Although the film features interesting attempts to recreate the impact of dances by animating photographs and reconstructing movement, *Ballet Black* is a distanced study, somehow lacking in empathy for its subject. *Shadows from Light*, in contrast, and perhaps because of the adamant immediacy of Brandt's images, is a richer and, while demanding, more accessible film, a personal statement by a filmmaker and yet a warm and wholly distinctive tribute to a major artist. Unsurprisingly, it was one of the first films purchased from the Arts Council for screening on Channel 4.

Shadows from Light, a narrator says at the start, is 'a cinematographic journey through the photographic atmospheres of Bill Brandt'. At the end Brandt is filmed setting his camera and taking an image of Dwoskin the filmmaker. 'This is me', Brandt's voice says, 'during the making of this film.' He stares at the camera, staring from the space of the film. He scrutinises

Dwoskin as he makes an exposure, then winds the film on; back to the look, and to looking at us. 'Well, it could be better.' He chuckles.

Here were riches, as Jeremy Isaacs celebrated in his memoir of his years at Channel 4. 'Television spread our bounty', he wrote, 'out of London, far and wide. Viewers living in Wick and Worcester, Ambleside and Argyll wrote in gratitude for the feast we were able to put before them' (1989: 170). But at the end of 1987, having failed to secure the position of Director General of the BBC, Jeremy Isaacs left Channel 4 to become General Director of the Royal Opera House. Michael Grade, at that point Director of Programmes at the BBC, was chosen as Isaacs' successor, a choice that the channel's founding Chief Executive opposed. 'I said [to the Channel 4 Board] that he was a competitive and commercially-minded television executive', Isaacs wrote later, 'who would seek to take the channel down-market, make it more popular, prepare it for privatisation.' He also publicly informed Grade that he was handing on a sacred trust. 'If you screw it up', Isaacs challenged him, 'if you betray it, I'll come back and throttle you' (1989: 197).

Their way: *Arena*

There were once three *Arenas*, and then five. When the strand began on BBC2 in October 1975, it was a topical magazine show which cycled weekly through *Art and Design*, *Cinema* and *Theatre*. *Television* and *Rock* then joined the scheduling roundabout in 1978. In its sedate early months the series trod a comparatively conventional path, following the lead of previous BBC2 strands like *Review*. Roger Graef and Simon Jenkins considered European Architectural Heritage Year for an early *Arena* and there was an obituary of painter Michael Ayrton. One of the few occasions when the series strayed from the mainstream was in March 1976 when it devoted an edition to British television's first presentation of artists' video, with works by David Hall, Peter Campus, Peter Donebauer and others. A decade later, however, *Arena* was home to a bunch of self-styled maverick filmmakers who were making many of the most distinctive and delightful documentaries of the 1980s.

Arena's editor Alan Yentob first shifted the series away from a multi-item format and from the nominated weekly focus. By early 1979, the show was making single-edition films about punk singer Poly Styrene and Australian maestro Barrie Humphries, but the accrued mythology ascribes *Arena*'s true genesis to Nigel Finch's documentary *My Way* (1979). Made with throwaway insouciance, this is an expert, frequently hilarious montage of an unlikely cast, including George Brown, Welsh rugby star Barry John and Sid Vicious, performing Frank Sinatra's song and talking about its significance in their lives. Anthony Wall, who was the film's researcher and whose original idea the film was, acknowledged the inspiration of Christopher Burstall's 1967 *Omnibus* about William Blake's poem, *Tyger, Tyger*. 'There was some sense of a magical world that the television had enabled you to visit', he said in a broadcast interview marking *Arena*'s thirtieth anniversary, 'and I began to see the television as a wonderland.' Its familiar subject and casual approach, he recognised, 'negated the preciousness which is what people say they dislike about arts programmes.'[2]

Although rock musicians, television dramatists and music hall stars had featured in *Omnibus* and *The South Bank Show*, and although discussions of popular culture had been a staple of *Late Night Line-Up* and other strands, no series before *Arena* entered this territory with such energy and panache. 'We found ourselves in this bloody great verdant plain where nobody else was', Wall said, before cuffing the ear of Ken Russell's celebrated *Elgar*. 'At the time most arts documentaries consisted of people riding around on bicycles with classical music playing in the background. We were trying to escape from those clichés and do something more arresting' (in Clarke 1998: 19). So Nigel Finch took a close look at the eccentric inhabitants of the *Chelsea Hotel* (1981) and with comedian Alexei Sayle he celebrated *The Private Life of the Ford Cortina* (1982). Wall directed *Desert Island Discs* (1982), films about Jerry Lee Lewis and the Everly Brothers, and the exceptional *The Life and Times of Don Luis Buñuel* (1984). All of these were irreverent, imaginative films colliding great characters with submerged skeins of cultural theory, boundless curiosity with a delight in every kind of surprise.

At the same time, *Arena* had a grown-up side that was at least as important both to its healthy audiences and to its remaining on-screen. A fortnight after *My Way* in 1979, the series presented *Let Us Now Praise Famous Men* about the writing of James Agee and the photography of Walker Evans in Depression-era America. Subjects during 1980 included the architecture of Richard Rogers, theatre in Soweto and painter John Hoyland. The irrepressible sensibility of director Nigel Finch was balanced by the more cerebral offerings of a director like Mike Dibb. His film *Somewhere Over the Rainbow...* (1981), made with critic Peter Fuller about Robert Natkin, psychoanalysis and the well-springs of art, remains a vividly unconventional engagement with a painter's work. There were also occasional attempts at arts journalism, such as *How Glorious is the Garden?* (1985), responding to the Arts Council's report 'The Glory of the Garden'. In 1982, Alan Yentob and Leslie Megahey produced the compelling, compendious *The Orson Welles Story* and this initiated *Arena*'s exploration of the life stories of major figures, some made with the subject's involvement, some not. *George Orwell* (in five parts, 1983–84), Evelyn Waugh (*The Evelyn Waugh Trilogy*, 1987) and Graham Greene (*The Graham Greene Trilogy*, 1993) were in the latter category, while the film director Billy Wilder granted to Volker Schlöndorff one of the very few extended conversations about his work for the series in 1992.

In the mid-1980s *Arena* also began to programme thematic 'nights' for BBC2. The idea looked back to the scheduling patterns of the first months of the channel but these occasional offerings proved influential in loosening up the schedule. After a special *Blues Night* presentation in 1985, *Arena* co-ordinated *Caribbean Nights* in June 1986, with contributions from Linton Kwesi Johnson, Carlos Fuentes and Ruben Blades. December 1989 saw the five-hour *Animal*

Night compilation with films about the gorilla John Daniel I and about trials of animals in medieval Europe, plus links from the puppets of *Spitting Image*. *Food Night* followed for Christmas 1990. In 1985 *Arena*'s editor Alan Yentob became Head of Music and Arts, and subsequently Controller of BBC2, and the strand was jointly edited by Anthony Wall and Nigel Finch until the latter's death in 1995. In addition to the japes of *My Way* and *Chelsea Hotel*, Finch had made many other distinguished films for the series, including profiles of Robert Mapplethorpe and Louise Bourgeois, and in his final months he was completing work on *Stonewall*, a drama about the riot involving drag queens and the police in New York in 1969.

The 1990s were a less glorious decade for *Arena*, but the series continued to seek out subjects unlikely to find a home elsewhere and for certain creative filmmakers it remained a congenial and supportive environment. Jana Bukova directed a richly textured portrait of *Havana* (1990) and Leslie Woodhead made *The Incredible Case of Comrade Rockstar* (1992), a remarkable film about the life and strange death of the Eastern bloc's rock superstar Dean Reed. Writing in 1988, as *The Late Show* was about to go on air, the critic John Dugdale pinpointed the loosening of genre boundaries as an important reason for the series' significance:

> When editing *Arena*, [Alan Yentob] called that programme 'a collection of cultural essays', and frequently saw the art or artist in a given film as a 'way into' the American South, Catholicism, the Thirties, Brixton, etc. Holding on to the flexible key notion of 'culture', *The Late Show* sustains a process of encroachment into the domain of other forms of programming, comparable to the way that drama, through 'faction', has taken up documentary and current affairs subjects. (1988: 33)

By the end of the 1980s, however, *Arena* was faced with numerous other series, including youth magazine strands like *Network 7* (1987–88), trampling across Anthony Wall's 'bloody great verdant plain' of pop culture. The series began to look occasionally fatigued and self-indulgent, too often developing a riff on an established success and no longer capable of startling the viewer. These were also years when, as the *Arena* filmmaker Robert McNab said, 'the scene at the BBC was pretty ugly [with its] Murdoch-driven frenzy'[3] and the times were not propitious for an oddball arts series that could occasionally appear to be past its prime. Yet there were biographical trilogies about Peter Sellers (in 1995) and Noel Coward (1998) and the sprawling but revealing *Stories My Country Told Me* (1996) in which human rights activist Eqbal Ahmad, historian Eric Hobsbawn, writer Maxine Hong Kingston and Archbishop Desmond Tutu explore the contemporary meanings of nationhood.

Taking *Arena* into the new century, Wall re-invented the series as a showcase for occasional, high-profile 'specials' in the BBC Two and BBC Four schedules. High-profile documentaries co-produced with the strand, increasingly with extensive festival screenings and even theatrical releases, included James Marsh's stylish and allusive *Wisconsin Death Trip* (2000) and Vikram Jayanti's dark, obsessional *James Ellroy's Feast of Death* (2001). The series also continued to poke around in the most interesting parts of Britain's culture during the twentieth century, with the two-part *The Private Dirk Bogarde* (2001) and Adam Low's complex biographical film *Francis Bacon's Arena* (2005). In 2005 *Arena*'s triumph was its international co-production with American public television's *American Masters* series on *Bob Dylan: No Direction Home*, Martin Scorsese's glorious examination of the singer's early years.

> I really do think it's one of the best films about that time, if not the best, I have ever seen. It takes you on a ride through the twists and turns of these quite extraordinary years from 1961–1966 in the most comprehensive, stylish and engaging way. It's beautifully edited. The archive footage is to die for, so it has a general historic appeal independent of its primary subject. (Wall 2005)

Like the very best of *Arena*, the film offers an experience, framed and contextualised but yet direct and powerful. Few arts documentaries are as rewarding.

Art as the new politics: *The Late Show*

'Television', said Mark Lucas of the independent producer After Image, 'has been brow-beaten by the government and other external forces into its most conservative mode to date – falling back on a conventional journalistic approach to programming. People are not making committed programmes any more and broadcasters will soon admit their relief at being excused their public service obligations' (in Carter 1989: 37). Working with artists and leading-edge video techniques, Lucas had made experimental programmes for Channel 4, and his sense of the increasing constraints on such work chimed with a broader perception that by the end of the 1980s mainstream broadcasting was retreating from the cultural high tide of the mid-decade.

In the same month as Lucas's interview, January 1989, a series began that appeared initially to exemplify what he dismissed as 'a conventional journalistic approach'. In fact, *The Late Show* proved for the next half-decade to be a stimulating and imaginative context for the arts on-screen. The series was broadcast for 45 minutes from Monday to Thursday in the 11.15pm slot on BBC2, immediately after the channel's current affairs strand *Newsnight*. The first edition on 16 January 1989 included an interview with Salman Rushdie about the furore prompted by his novel *The Satanic Verses* (1988), a report on the sacking of Daniel Barenboim from the Opera de la Bastille in Paris, a review of the Royal Academy's exhibition 'Italian Art in the Twentieth Century' and a live performance by the band Fairground Attraction.

One defining influence was BBC2's *Late Night Line-Up* from more than two decades before. Like that series, *The Late Show* was studio-based and hosted by a rotating team, including Sarah Dunant, Kirsty Wark, Michael Ignatieff, Tracey MacLeod, Paul Morley and Matthew Collings. Broadcast live from the BBC's studios in Lime Grove, it offered a diverse menu of items and formats, including interviews and discussions, pointed and occasionally vituperative reviews and responses to cultural events, film reports and performances from rock musicians and dancers. One-on-one extended interviews in the *Face to Face* format from the 1950s had Jeremy Isaacs taking the interrogator role once incarnated by John Freeman. As the strand developed, films both short and long became more prominent and confident, and full-length documentaries were soon part of the mix. In its tone, *The Late Show* incorporated elements of the irreverence, the playfulness and the ironic knowingness that had come to be associated with *Arena*, but at the same time it could shift gear and deal straightforwardly and seriously with subjects that required such treatment.

Innovation came with the embrace of a new agenda. In part, this recognised a spreading sense of culture that, as *The Late Show* editor Michael Jackson noted, included 'media, architecture, design and style'. Jackson accepted too that the arts were increasingly shaped by the forces of the marketplace. 'No longer can you make a cultural programme', he said, 'and not be very interested in issues of money and power, of who owns what and how it affects what is produced' (in Marshall 1989: 13). Then there was the idea that the old distinctions between high and low culture had all but disappeared, as the critic, *The Late Show* presenter and soon-to-be Commissioning Editor of Arts at Channel 4 Waldemar Januszczak celebrated: 'The new arts programmes have no difficulty at all in mixing the Pogues with Paganini, Modigliani with magazines, literature with film, music with dance, art with A-ha, in ways which the fastidious old arts broadcasters of the wireless, keen on categories, would not have tolerated (1989: 19).

His optimism, however, about the general acceptance of this proposition proved to be misplaced. In an article marking the closing of *The Late Show* in 1995 Mark Lawson recalled an important debate 'initiated by [David Hare on] the programme on whether Dylan's lyrics were better than Keats's poems [which] was viewed by detractors as typical of its style (bearded men and pale-faced women talking arty rubbish) and its ethos: a wilful refusal to distinguish between high and low culture' (1995). 'The argument', Matthew Norman recalled, 'which ran for weeks, was intelligent, passionate and utterly fascinating. The question of how we make cultural value judgements lies at the heart of our culture itself' (1992: 37).

Another vibrant component of *The Late Show*'s agenda was the belief that the arena of culture was where many of the political debates of the time were now being played out. Margaret Thatcher's Conservatives had been in power for a decade, rampantly changing every aspect of British society with a determinedly free-market agenda. The conventional left, at least in the form of a deeply divided Labour party under Michael Foot and then Neil Kinnock, appeared to have no cogent or effective response to the energy of the Tories. In an elegant contribution to *New Socialist* the cultural critic Judith Williamson pondered the question of why the left in these years had developed such an interest in soap operas, pop music and images of Princess Diana.

What I want to ask is, how is it that we [leftist intellectuals] have become so peculiarly uncritical? What are the shifts in society at large that have pushed the left to grovel before a popular culture we would once have tried to create an alternative to? ... One explanation for current attitudes must be the left's post-79 awareness of the right's successful populism, known to many as 'Thatcherism' ... In the 'Thatcherite' era the left has been demoralised (in real, political terms, I mean) with little actual power. Many left intellectuals are not only fed up; they are, in a sense, bored. (1986: 14)

The producer Roger Graef extended this analysis to television: 'Where the left-of-centre opposition is blocked, there's a diversion of energy into other areas. And for some time politicians have been discredited as sources of insight about the world. Nobody recognises their own experience in politics any more, so people turn to art for descriptions which are more complex and contradictory' (in Dugdale 1988: 33). Art was the new politics, it was suggested, and most obviously this was where contemporary questions of race, gender and identity were forcefully being played out. Art could offer us understandings of our society and our world that parliamentary debate and representative democracy no longer appeared capable of encompassing.

In its 919 editions *The Late Show* tackled a remarkable range of topics, but the crystallising issue was Salman Rushdie's novel *The Satanic Verses* and the *fatwa* calling for the author's assassination, issued by Ayatollah Khomeini in response to what was seen as an inappropriate depiction of the prophet Muhammad. On the day Ayatollah Khomeini proclaimed his ruling, 14 February 1989, Hanif Kureishi was interviewed on *The Late Show* about events. A week later an entire programme was devoted to the issue with contributions from Norman Mailer, George Steiner and others, and in May Michael Ignatieff travelled to Bradford for the series to talk to British Muslims. In September, the series reported on the bombing of bookshops selling the novel.

There were numerous other issues with which *The Late Show* engaged where the domains of art and of politics were woven together. Jonathan Miller, for example, robustly defended an artist's right to exhibit jewellery decorated with human foetuses against an outraged protest by the anti-abortion campaigner Victoria Gillick. The impact of AIDS was a subject to which the series returned on numerous occasions, and in the series' first year there was the debate about Section 28 of the recent Local Government Act which banned the promotion of homosexuality in schools. Images of the Falklands War were pored over in an early edition. These were the years too when the Eastern bloc was breaking apart, and *The Late Show* dealt with the fall of the Berlin Wall and, especially in the 1990 season of programmes *Tales from Prague*, explored a host of reflections on the political and cultural changes in Czechoslovakia and elsewhere. Towards the end of the run, there was the fall-out from the war in Bosnia to consider.

The series demonstrated an impressive internationalism, with reports from across Europe and, especially, the United States. A monthly American edition started in December 1991, in a joint venture with the New York Public Broadcasting Service station WNET. There were mutterings, however, that the show was less enthusiastic about the culture of the regions and nations at home, and in 1993 a regular Scottish edition was introduced in part to counter such concerns. In February 1990, as a recognition of its critical success (and despite limited audiences), *The Late Show* became a distinct unit within the BBC Music and Arts department producing other programmes apart from the four-nights-a-week magazine. A modest but interesting collaboration with the Arts Council of Great Britain saw the co-commissioning of a series of *One Minute Television* by artists. As Matthew Norman enthused in the *Mail on Sunday* in March 1992: 'Just by being there, *The Late Show* says something important: that BBC2 is making precisely the commitment to public service broadcasting we have every right to expect. By being so good, it plays an active role in setting as well as covering the cultural agenda' (1992: 37).

I was an enthusiastic viewer of *The Late Show*, although not an uncritical one. I was frustrated that, *pace* Matthew Norman, it seemed too often to chase after cultural agendas set elsewhere rather than attempt to establish its own. The series' failure to speak with sufficient authority at times annoyed me, as did the over-use of an ironic stance. The idea of authenticity was difficult in a decade framed for many in the media by the ideas of postmodernism, and irony always was an easier position to adopt. Yet I was convinced then (as I remain) that authentic responses could be communicated without the mysticism or the ideological baggage that had accompanied so many critical pronouncements of the past. 'You can't achieve authority or authenticity with the smug, the superficial, the vacuously stylish', I presumptuously told the production team when, with others, I was invited in for a session of self-criticism. 'But you can achieve them with more rigorous thought, tougher self-questioning, bolder formal invention, greater critical engagement and, indeed, more rigorous thought.' I, however, did not have to turn out three hours of television and more each and every week.

Roly Keating, then Janice Hadlow and finally Mike Poole succeeded Jackson as series editor, and they responded to criticism that the series was not sufficiently interested in engaging with what continued to be seen as the 'high' arts. In part, this involved finding increasingly imaginative ways to tackle traditional subjects, as director Anand Tucker achieved with an item linked to a retrospective of the work of John Constable. He concentrated on the artist's studies of clouds and shot interviews with a distinguished range of contributors with each of them lying on their backs on grass as if staring into the sky, as Constable did, from Hampstead Heath. Yet the series remained driven by journalistic impulses rather than those of creative or poetic filmmaking. Increasingly, however, the series produced stylish full-length television essays, including *The New Middle Ages* (1994), Benjamin Woolley's ruminations, made with producer David Stewart, arguing that the twenty-first century was shaping up to look just like the fourteenth; Ian MacMillan and Matthew Collings' *Big Art in a One Horse Town* (1995), about the artist Donald Judd in the Texas town of Marfa; and Roger Parsons' *Thinker, Painter, Scholar, Spy* (1995), a compelling study of Poussin and Anthony Blunt.

The series ended at the end of 1995. It was no longer drawing the press attention or sparking the dinner-party 'buzz' that had made it valuable for the BBC. Moreover, its substantial annual budget of £11 million could no longer be justified in a context that Alan Yentob, who had initiated the series and was now Controller of BBC1, outlined in a July 1993 speech to the Radio Academy Festival. 'The BBC clearly looks after the ABC1 audience', he said, 'but there is a sense from our research that we perhaps look after them too well. We do believe that we need to talk to the whole audience and address them all in different parts of the schedule. That other audience is not so well served' (in Leapman 1993: 1).

In the jargon of the time, with *The Late Show* as with other offerings, the BBC was seen to be 'super-serving' the ABC1 audience. Yentob was also one of the co-ordinators of a substantial consultation exercise that in 1995 produced the weighty report 'People and Programmes: BBC radio and television for an age of choice'. Among its many observations, there was the thought that arts programme makers were out of touch with their audiences. The report reflected:

> Specialist producers tend to think of [arts progamme making] as rooted in the cutting edge of contemporary artistic endeavour and the business of serious cultural interpretation and criticism. Although some members of the audience strongly agree, many others seem to regard the arts first and foremost as a leisure activity for which the prime requirement is a less ambitious sort of consumer information and advice. (BBC 1995: 69)

Whatever else it was, *The Late Show* was not about 'less ambitious ... consumer information and advice'. Its moment had passed, and although the BBC made the argument that its resources would be diverted to more arts programming in prime time, the regular nightly commitment to culture was lost.

'Few other programmes', the critic and *The Late Show* presenter Mark Lawson wrote in a valedictory tribute, 'have had such influence on the style and staffing of other BBC programming. Few series at their death have been survived by so many offspring' (1995). *Late Review* (1995–2000) was spun off as a regular Thursday night review strand, and this was later integrated into Friday's edition of *Newsnight* to become *Newsnight Review* (2002–), an analytical discussion of current arts and culture events by a panel of semi-regular contributors, including Mark Kermode, Julie Myerson and Hari Kunzru. The excellent music performance show *Later with Jools Holland* (1993–) was another progeny, offering a range of international artists performing live in the studio. *The Works* (1995–96) was a series of single documentaries that took forward personnel and ideas from *The Late Show*, with subjects including the Unabomber, architect Berthold Lubetkin and ex-Fleetwood Mac musician Peter Green. Another reinvention of the prime time BBC2 series came with *close up* (1998–2000) with Komar and Melamid, Patrick O'Brian, Dennis Potter and Bob Hope among its subjects. For individual careers, association with *The Late Show* proved to be a positive addition to many people's CVs. Michael Jackson became successively Head of Music and Arts, Controller of BBC2 and then BBC1 before moving to become Chief Executive at Channel 4. In mid-2007 Roly Keating is Controller of BBC Two and Janice Hadlow, who was the third editor of *The Late Show*, is Controller of BBC Four. Numerous other alumni of the series are producers and executives throughout British television, and *The Late Show* directors Mary Harron, Anand Tucker and Sharon Maguire have gone on to make successful feature films.

Art is dead: Michael Grade's Channel 4

Michael Kustow, who was soon to be eased out of the new regime at Channel 4, gave a speech in October 1988 at the launch of a new arts strand, *Signals* (1988–90). He said:

> Those who are concerned with quality fear that television may be driven down-market by deregulation and a multitude of channels. Arts programmes would probably be among the first casualties. They probably wouldn't disappear ... More likely they would be pushed into blandness, made middle-of-the-road, severed from the danger and struggle and challenge that are at the heart of creativity.[4]

Two decades later, neither the words nor the qualities of danger, struggle and challenge feature in either arts broadcasting or the too often desultory discussions attached to it. Nor were danger, struggle and so forth anywhere apparent in the consistently uninspired *Signals*. One of Michael Grade's early decisions at Channel 4 when he arrived there in early 1988 was to corral the arts into this weekly slot. Co-ordinated by the independent production company Holmes Associates, *Signals* was edited by the distinguished documentary director Roger Graef. 'We are seeking intimacy, energy and spontaneity', said the briefing notes to producers. 'Try to fold in the public, and let them speak directly as possible [sic]. The caretaker, usherette or box office attendants, the stage hands and musicians may have interesting reactions.'

An early programme covered a street dance competition in Leeds. Programmes followed on the persecution of Soviet artists under Stalin and the heritage industry. 'It had to appeal to *Daily Mail* and *Mirror* readers', The series co-ordinator Andrew Holmes was quoted as stressing that the series had to appeal to *Daily Mail* and *Daily Mirror* readers as much as to those who read the *Independent* and the *Guardian*. The series quickly demonstrated how Channel 4's commitment to the avant-garde had now been replaced by a cheery and unconvincing populism. Channel 4's discovery instead of 'popular culture', which was in part at least the result of Grade's first year as Chief Executive, could also be recognised in *Halfway to Paradise* (1988–94), a smart-looking series about music, film, sport and comedy from Scotland, Ireland and the North of England.

For the ITV companies, the 1990 Broadcasting Act replaced the IBA with the Independent Television Commission (ITC). Top of the new body's in-tray was renewal of the franchises. In line with the government's free-market expectations, the ITC awarded these to companies that entered the highest bid, albeit with the proviso that the applicants had to pass a quality threshold. In London, Carlton TV outbid the holder Thames, paying £43 million for the franchise, while Central Television was able to renew its licence for just £2,000. Many of the companies now had the additional burden of the franchise cost, at a time when advertising revenue was being eaten into by competition from cable and satellite channels. Direct competition would also soon come from Channel 4, which from 1 January 1993 was no longer funded by a subscription levied on contractors (at the end of the arrangement 13.6 per cent of the previous year's advertising revenue from both commercial channels) but had to sell its own advertising. With monies tighter and programming expectations looser, the arts documentaries and performances that had been offered to the main network by companies such as Granada dropped away. On occasion, however, the ITV companies created productions for Channel 4, including in the run-up to the franchise renewal the remarkable *Una Stravaganza dei Medici* (1990), produced by Thames at a cost of £1.1 million. This early use of Hi-Definition image technology presented a spectacular performance of sumptuous musical interludes written for a wedding in Florence in 1589.

In addition to network offerings, most of the ITV companies had also been presenting regular arts programming for their region. Granada had *Celebration* (1979–94), Anglia *Folio* (1980–6) and Central *Contrasts* (1987–90). But these too would fall victim to cost-cutting and ratings expectations. Suddenly, there seemed to be a saviour for the conundrum of continuing local coverage: the listings show. Starting in October 1987 for Thames Television, the independent producer Mentorn Films made *01-for London* (1987–90, then when London area telephone codes changed simply *01*, 1990–2), a bright, brash and, above all, fast-moving half-hour drawing its inspiration from the cultural guide to the capital, *Time Out*. 'I accept that a three-minute item on an opera may do the production a serious injustice', said Thames Television's executive Alan Horrox, who commissioned the show; 'but if the three minutes are well done and set alongside a three-minute review of a popular film, it may draw a broad audience for both' (in Ure-Smith 1990: 33). Local versions were soon being produced in at least five ITV regions, including Anglia, TVS and Central, but the criticism that the show was patronising continued. 'I defy anyone to remember a listings programme after it's been broadcast', Roger Graef told *Broadcast* on 6 October 1989. 'It signifies what I see as the gradual erosion of commitment to arts programming. I'm very concerned that the auction of the ITV franchises is drying up money that would otherwise be spent on arts programming' (in Tobin 1989:18).

Following Michael Kustow into the arts commissioning chair at Channel 4, Waldemar Januszczak arrived at Channel 4 with an outsider's eagerness to shake things up. Previously the literary editor at the *Guardian*, he told *Broadcast*,

> The kind of films I would like to see made are the kind that needn't be made by arts broadcasters. You and I both know that there are 18.5 people in this

country who've been making the arts films for everybody for the last ten or twenty years. I personally want to hear from other people. (In Gill 1990: 16)

He was soon working in a world where Channel 4 sold its own airtime, which inevitably began to inflect the schedule with an expectation of ratings success. Januszczak's replacement for *Signals* was *Without Walls* (1990–97), a weekly slot most often featuring two half-hour films. The breadth of what could be included in the arts was taken beyond even that of *The Late Show* agenda, and early programmes in the series offered films about men crying and satellite dishes, car design and banned books. The key innovation of *Without Walls* was the sub-strand *J'Accuse* (1991–96), a series of 'combative criticism' conceived by the independent producer Jeremy Bugler. His aim in these half-hour essays, authored and presented by prominent figures, was to counter the perceived sycophancy of arts television. Bugler wrote in *The Listener*:

> Let's celebrate, and evangelise to television's large audiences, hungry for enlightenment – so the Reithian tradition says … But the success of that approach has mined out the vein. Now we are left with television which is a superbly edited, lovingly shot extension of public relations for the arts … Arts television is usually film-led, and the filmic leads more naturally to celebration than cerebration. Hostile criticism is hard to achieve on film … The arts world has actively conspired to promote adulation-by-television. (1990: 14)

George Melly took on Henry Moore, scriptwriting expert Robert McKee dismissed *Citizen Kane* (1941) and Tom Sutcliffe opined that Benjamin Britten's work was 'flawed', but the programmes failed to find a satisfying form – they are mostly scrappy compilations of archive sequences and photographs built around the presenter speaking to camera – and too often they are either a shrill cry of Don't-Like-This or a more nuanced piece (like Griselda Pollock's considered deconstruction of the myths surrounding Van Gogh) that fails to justify the strident strand title.

Another notable offering from *Without Walls*, driven by the same populist iconoclasm of *J'Accuse*, was Muriel Gray's four-part series *Art is Dead, Long Live TV* in June–July 1991. This set out, as its presenter claimed, 'to discover if the avant-garde has any real relevance to twentieth-century life' or whether contemporary art 'is just a pile of horse dung churned out by people who know the art of the market to be full of buffoons with considerable wealth and little reasoning power' (1991). Graced with interview contributions from well-known critics and commentators, the series profiles the sculptor Kenneth Hutcheson, architect Janna Patrizio, film director Richard Bradley-Hudd and experimental novelist Laura Mason. Hutcheson, the film claims, works with smell, mashing up the carcasses of dead animals and smearing them on wood. In the film, he resists Gray's larky questioning and apparently throws the heart of an ox at one of the camera crew. Damien Hirst first showed his sculptures with the heads of dead animals in 1990, starting with the work 'A Thousand Years', and Hutcheson might be a Hirst acolyte, or even the figure from whom the emerging king of the young British artists stole his ideas. But in fact, like the other artists in the series, he is a fiction, although this was revealed only after a number of critics had taken him for real. 'I ache for artists to be better than they are, art to be more profound than it is, and television to ignore it unless it screams genius', wrote Muriel Gray (1991). It was not entirely apparent how *Art is Dead, Long Live TV* would help fulfil any one of these.

The series was perceived by commentators as symptomatic of a television time that had lost confidence in the traditional values of the arts. Andrew Graham-Dixon wrote:

> It is (its makers might argue) an appropriately postmodern television programme made for an era that has lost faith in quaint concepts like 'truth', which prefers to suspend conflicting opinions in a world where fact and fiction merge … so *Art is Dead* eschews commentary and strands the viewer in a desert of semantic ambiguity; this is TV for the age of the floating signifier. Or at least it pretends to be: in reality, the statements that it makes are abundantly clear, and terribly familiar. (1991)

In the 1990s Channel 4 commissioned a number of arts programmes that were more substantial than *Without Walls*, including the four-part series *Hidden Hands* (1995) about the darker by-ways of modernism: the role of the CIA in promoting abstract expressionism internationally, for example, and the collaboration of modern artists with fascism during World War Two. *Skyscraper* (1989), made by Karl Sabbagh, intelligently documented every stage of making a Manhattan office tower. But too many of its offerings, like the magazines aimed at a youth audience *Club X* (1989) and *Big Mouth* (1996), were blighted by the attitudes identified in *Art is Dead, Long Live TV* by the academic Andrew Clifford:

> …a kind of closing off of serious analysis, replacing genuine insight with jokes, irony, cynicism, self-referentiality. *Civilisation* … is regarded as passé, belonging to an elitist Leavisite past; postmodernism and deconstruction seem to propose that, as language is relative, partial, biased, the only strategic discourse is indirect: allusive, self-ironic and playful. Isolated from a broad framework or history, postmodernism and deconstruction soon become excuses for an unwillingness to comment, to expound, to be brilliant… (1991: 38)

Or as Stuart Cosgrove, Channel 4's Controller of Arts and Entertainment, acknowledged uncomfortably in 1996, 'I don't think Channel 4 has made significant gravitas films on the arts' (in Considine 1998: 18).

DANCE FOR THE CAMERA
a BBC/Arts Council co-production
various producers and lengths, 1993–2003

Ballet was a staple of BBC broadcasts right from the earliest days of television. As noted in Chapter 1, numerous excerpts were included in the live broadcasts of the experimental transmissions made between 1932 and 1935, and the medium's enthusiasm for the artform continued during the transmissions from Alexandra Palace from 1936 until 1 September 1939 when the war closed the television service. Marie Rambert's company, the Vic-Wells Ballet, Anthony Tudor's London ballet, de Basil's Ballets Russes and even Kurt Jooss's company all appeared before the cameras, although all but a very few fragments of this went unrecorded.

Ballet was equally a part of broadcasts from 1946 onwards, with major presentations in the series *Grand Ballet* (1948–49) and the series *Ballet for Beginners* (1949). Kenneth MacMillan choreographed work especially for the screen on children's television in *Punch and the Child* (1953). Margaret Dale, who had been a leading dancer with the Sadler's Wells Ballet, joined the BBC in 1954 and over the next two decades produced numerous dance programmes, including with the visiting Bolshoi Ballet in 1960–61 and from 1961 onwards with the Royal Ballet. Even ITV showed occasional works, including Granada's presentation of the full-length ballet *Cinderella* (1960), choreographed by Frederick Ashton. Modern dance too began occasionally to enter the schedules, with MacMillan choreographing *Dark Descent* for *Tempo* in 1963 and the Paul Taylor Dance Company performing *3 Epitaphs* on *Aquarius* in 1970. By 1978 the BBC was programming *Dance Month* with a slate of programmes and performances, an initiative repeated in 1980. But the dance historian Robert Penman has described the moment at the end of the 1970s as 'the peak of dance programming ... By 1982 the number of complete programmes and dance items broadcast by the BBC had slipped back ... and the low level of investment and output continued throughout the 1980s (1993: 118–19)

Channel 4 arrived with a strong commitment to imaginative dance, and the channel was soon working with the Arts Council to co-fund works translated from the stage or, increasingly later in the 1980s, especially created for the screen. The Arts Council supported two disappointing films with dancers from Ballet Rambert in the 1970s: *Imprint* (1974) by Clive Myer and John Chesworth, with bodies in a box writhing interminably, and *Dancers* (1978) with the over-tricksy direction credited to John Chesworth, Derek Hart and Yutaka Yanazaki, and supposedly developed from the daily life of two dancers. The choices of projects made with Channel 4 was rather more felicitous, with *Freefall* (1988), which paired director Bob Bentley with choreographer Gaby Agis and company, and DV8 Physical Theatre's *Never Again* (1989), also directed by Bentley. *Freefall*'s fluid camera tracks the dancers across rooftops, across a building site and into a wooded grove, while *Never Again* is an intense study of sexual relationships, inflected with an awareness – although this is never made explicit – of AIDS. DV8 have made perhaps television's most visceral dance films, including *Dead Dreams of Monochrome Men* (1991), a collaboration with director David Hinton produced for *The South Bank Show*.

Dance for the Camera developed from the 1992 Arts Council/BBC collaboration on *Dance House*, in which ten short dance films had been commissioned from contemporary choreographers. Best of the bunch here is Davin Hinton's film made with choreographer Jacob Marley, known for his work with the Pet Shop Boys. To the Arts Council's executive Rodney Wilson and the BBC commissioners Bob Lockyer and Dennis Marks, it was clear that short dance films worked best when they had a talented television director involved, and so each film in what became *Dance for the Camera* and a total of 52 'dances' for the screen involved a close collaboration between a director and a choreographer. The first two quartets of films are each 15 minutes long, but later programmes, many of them co-financed with the Dutch broadcaster NPS, ran for between five and ten minutes.

In the first quartet the tedious and faintly absurd *The Rime of the Ancient Mariner*, choreographed by Anthony Dowell, is compensated for by the distinctive beauties of *Duets with Automobiles*, with Shobana Jeyasingh's choreography and dancers and film direction by Terry Braun. In the third series, produced in 1995, the films that stand out include *Boy*, by Peter Anderson and Rosemary Lee with a young boy playing out a fantasy game on sand dunes and mudflats, and the hard-edged *Man Act*, choreographed by Man Act and directed by Mike Stubbs. The dance company V-TOL made the energetic, highly physical piece *The Snowball Effect* (1997) with director Brett Turnbull for series 4, and series 5 has the clever visual storytelling of *R.I.P.* (1997) written and directed by Annick Vroom with the Hans Hof Ensemble.

The 'documentary choreography' of penguins in *Dance for the Camera: Birds*

Series 5 is also distinguished by perhaps the most radical film in the whole 52, David Hinton's *Birds* (1997). This features only archive material of feathered creatures with no dancers or even humans in sight. Hinton described the film as 'documentary choreography', which he also explored in the later *Dance for the Camera* film *Snow* (2003). Documentary choreography, he explained later, 'means that when you edit the film, you think of it as a choreographic process. What you are doing in the editing is making a dance ... fragments of found movement on film can be choreographed into a legitimate dance because film editing gives you complete control over that movement ... Using found movement and.film editing you can create form, rhythm, structure, meaning or any other quality you might want in a dance.'[5]

The series could also accommodate projects that incorporated research with new moving image technologies, most especially with the film *Motion Control* (2002) in series 6. This was devised, choreographed and performed by Liz Aggiss, with music and choreography by Billy Cowie, collaborators on *Beethoven in Love* (1994) in the first *Dance for the Camera* series. Working with an eclectic range of film and tape stocks, and with animation and a complex motion control set-up (which allows the movements of a camera to be mechanically, and therefore precisely, determined and replicated), Aggiss and Cowie create a poetic exploration of the body moving through, as well as fixed in, trapped in space. Both *Birds* and *Motion Control* in very different ways perfectly demonstrate how collaborations in these short-form films could produce innovative work of the first order.

'The arts programme is not dead': the BBC in the 1990s

Riding the success of *The Late Show*, Michael Jackson took over as the BBC's Head of Music and Arts in the summer of 1991. His aims were threefold, he told Stephen Phillips, who authored a strategy document about arts broadcasting for the Arts Council's Film, Video and Broadcasting panel: 'making what is generally available in London available to all; acting as a cultural patron, particularly of contemporary art; exploring the medium of television itself and using it imaginatively.' His immediate goal, however, as Phillips noted, was 'to take on the centre ground in a lively and intelligent way and look again at the big things' (1991). Lesley White, profiling Jackson for *Vogue*, a magazine in which his predecessors in the post had rarely made an impact, noted a professed interest in the traditional arts that was perhaps surprising from the former editor of *The Late Show*. 'Citing the increasing attendance at art galleries and museums', she wrote, 'the high ratings for TV opera, the doubled sales of classical music, [Jackson] perceives in the hunger for traditional arts a longing for security as we approach the millennium' (1991).

Jackson's strategy embraced extended seasons, such as BBC2's Rembrandt project in 1992 with documentaries about the painter's life, including one with Simon Schama, and three distinctive short films including John Berger's thoughts on the artist's obsession with the human body and Ken McMullen's exploration of Rembrandt and blindness. In February 1994 programmes across twelve days were linked to the Tate Gallery's exhibition 'Picasso: Painter/Sculptor'; 21 brief *Talking Picasso* shorts featured comments from critics and celebrities about a single work. There were major series like *Relative Values* (1991), a six-part enquiry into the economic and institutional factors shaping the worlds of the visual arts, and *Naked Hollywood* (1991), which revealed tales from the city of angels including an inside view of agents and the story of Joe Roth as studio head at Twentieth Century Fox. There was also continuing support for programmes about literature, including the consistently strong strand *Bookmark* (1983–2001), from which a number of distinctive filmmakers emerged including the director Pawel Pawlikowski. Pawlikowski's contributions included dark studies of central European and Russian culture, including *From Moscow to Pietrushki* (1990), about Benedict Yerofeyev's study of alcohol in Soviet society, and *Dostoevsky's Travels* (1991) featuring a journey made by the Russian author's great-grandson, a tram driver from St Petersburg. The director subsequently made the acclaimed feature films *Last Resort* (2000) and *My Summer of Love* (2004). As feature films from Anand Tucker, Mary Harron and others also demonstrated, the imaginative freedom of arts television in the 1980s and 1990s proved to be a productive seedbed for creative directors.

One of Jackson's later initiatives was *A History of British Art* (1996), Andrew Graham-Dixon's chronological story of painting and sculpture from the iconoclasm of the Reformation to the local authority vandalism that in early 1994 destroyed Rachel Whiteread's cast of a domestic interior, 'House'. But not everything was conceived on a large scale. A co-production with the Arts Council sustained the short collaborations between choreographers and directors in *Dance for the Camera*. From their second season in 1994, these distinctive films exploited niches in the BBC schedule, as did the delightful *Building Sights* (1988–96). An eclectic cast of contributors chose a favourite building to explore and enthuse about for just ten minutes. Among the most memorable of these was the architect Norman Foster's paean of praise to the lines, volumes and expressive functionality of a Boeing 747 aircraft.

Building Sights was one of a host of programmes contributing during the 1990s to a BBC2 schedule that was often dotted with short programmes – and that, when compared to the rigid structures and the endless trailing, tagging and branding of a decade later, appears strikingly 'loose' and open. Channel 4 had embraced shorts from early on, with series like *Hey Good Looking* (1982), with 15-minute films stripped on each night of a week. But it was BBC2 that made the form its own, creating strands like *The Great Picture Trail* (1993), with a wide range of people talking about favourite pictures (in which Neil MacGregor made his presenting debut) and *Bard on the Box* (1994), in which celebrities including Prince Charles, and members of the public read their favourite lines of Shakespeare. Series of shorts could be used to try out new presenters, such as the eccentric Sister Wendy Beckett, who first appeared in the strand of 10-minute films *Sister Wendy's Odyssey* (1992) before becoming one of the more unlikely television stars of the decade. The Arts Council collaborations on *Dance for the Camera* and subsequent projects took advantage of such opportunities for risk-taking and experiment.

As is explored further in Chapter 3, throughout the 1990s the Arts Council developed a number of co-funding relationships with television, and both the broadcasters and the Council tussled with the issues involved. From the late 1970s, if not before, the BBC in particular (although the other broadcasters were hardly immune from this) required co-production funding from abroad to finance many of their major projects in the arts. In the late 1970s and 1980s a number of high-value, high-cost series, including the Margot Fonteyn project *The Magic of Dance* (1979) and Robert Hughes' history of modernism *The Shock of the New* (1980), were made with the help of foreign financing often secured by producer Reiner Moritz. Such collaborations have been important throughout the development of arts programming, but they have rarely been unproblematic. Leaving aside disputes about funding, contracts and editorial control, the expectations of cultural television vary markedly in different countries at different times. The work that tends to be most acceptable in most territories is, unsurprisingly, the most straightforward and the most traditional. Comparatively little challenging or contemporary work has come from such partnerships.

The most significant foreign venture in arts broadcasting during the 1990s was the launch in 1992 of the French-German channel ARTE with an initial annual budget of £120 million. Owned by ARD and ZDF in Germany and by France's La Sept, the channel has continued to offer a bold and demanding schedule of documentaries, performance and feature films, as well as 'theme evenings' with a linked group of programmes offering sidelights on a particular topic. Through the 1990s, Channel 4 was a frequent co-producer with the channel, and certain BBC productions, including a performance version of *Richard II* (1998), directed by Deborah Warner starring Fiona Shaw as the king, were also financed as collaborations. But in line with the broadcasters' interests elsewhere, especially in costume drama, most arts co-productions have been with the United States, including the Robert Hughes series *American Visions* (1996), co-financed with PBS. Attempts both formal and informal have been made on the part of ARTE to interest either Channel 4 or the BBC in a more structured relationship, including perhaps a British version of the channel, but these have come to nothing.

If Michael Jackson, like his peers, demonstrated little enthusiasm for ARTE, he was keen to see British television acting as a patron of the arts. The BBC had long supported a number of orchestras, and in 1927 Director General John Reith committed to provide a financial guarantee for the annual Promenade Concerts from the Royal Albert Hall. The Proms have been a key component of cultural broadcasting ever since, and as historians Paddy Scannell and David Cardiff wrote, they 'have remained the most successful single attempt at the democratisation of music in this country' (1991: 198).

On a more modest scale, other broadcasters embraced occasional support for the arts, such as Channel 4's sponsorship of the Tate's Turner Prize for contemporary art from 1991 to 2004. The BBC Billboard project in May 1992 was a proactive initiative organised with Mills & Allen, a company that controlled poster sites across the country; 18 artists, including Richard Hamilton, Howard Hodgkin, Damien Hirst and Helen Chadwick created original posters for 150 locations, a process that was documented in the film *Outing Art* and in a dozen short follow-ups. 'Our starting point', Jackson wrote, 'was ... what happens if you replace the reassuring frame which the museum gives art with the everyday frame of the billboard? Can art compete with the images of advertising? Is the value of art reduced or increased by making it more accessible? Have some of art's best ideas been stolen by advertising anyway?' (1992).

Kim Evans, a producer with *Omnibus* and before that *The South Bank Show*, took over from Jackson as Head of Music and Arts in the summer of 1993. She continued the focus on big issues with landmark series fronted by prominent critics and practitioners: Simon Schama explored the themes of his book *Landscape and Memory* (1995); *Painting the World* (1995) focused on paintings at the National Gallery with its director Neil MacGregor; and Robert Hughes related the story of art in the USA in *American Visions*. Such series, along with

Andrew Graham-Dixon's *Renaissance* (1999), were examples of what the critic Mark Lawson dubbed 'canary shows'. Claiming that the appellation came from 'one of the grand old men of the business', he explained that canary shows were ones with serious aspirations but low audiences which 'as long as they remained chirping in the schedule, would prove that the coal-mine of television had not become totally poisoned by the gasses of greed' (1999). These birds have shown few signs of expiring, as was demonstrated perfectly in 2006 by Simon Schama's *Power of Art*, but continued existence is not enough. Each one needs to be examined to consider the value and distinctiveness, the originality and as it were the sweetness, of its song. Certainly there were many who were disappointed by the weightiness of *Renaissance* which comes off the screen as largely dutiful. The critic Richard Dorment was even less forgiving. Watching the series straight through, he decided, was like 'a marathon viewing of *The Travel Show* lightly dusted with a thin coating of colour-supplement culture … Graham-Dixon substitutes a glib prurience about works of art which both covers over his unfamiliarity of the period he is supposed to be celebrating, and betrays his contempt for the audience he is addressing' (1999).

One of Evans' other commissions was far from a canary show. Taking its name from broadcasting's abbreviation for 'transmission', *Tx.* (1996–2000) was a strand of single films that I edited for four seasons. I set out to construct a context for creative filmmaking about the contemporary arts, encouraging – as I said in my pitch document – 'a diversity of new visions both from distinctive filmmakers and from unconventional collaborations'. The series commissioned a number of elegant films, including *Children of the Revolution* (1996), David Hinton's involving story of a group of young musicians at the Beijing conservatoire caught up in the Cultural Revolution of the 1960s and forbidden for more than a decade to play Western music. *Tx.* also brought to the screen some truly experimental work, including John Maybury's bizarre electronic fantasy *Museum of Memory* (1999) and photographer Richard Billingham's *Fish Tank* (1998), a collaboration with Artangel, which uses the artist's home-video footage of his family in a council flat in the Midlands to create a non-narrative, disturbing but ultimately human portrait of a couple and their sons. The film extends and explodes earlier depictions of working-class people that stretch back to the 1930s but it also suggests the poetic intensity of a situation imagined by Samuel Beckett. (Other productions in the series are discussed in Chapter 4.)

'Let's get serious' was the title of a speech delivered by the BBC's Director of Television Mark Thompson to the Royal Television Society in November 1997. 'I certainly don't think the arts programme is dead', he reassured his audience. But he identified a serious crisis of confidence:

> The dumbers down will tell you that it's just a result of our hunger for ratings and for those elusive younger viewers who are said not to care much for serious arts programmes. For me it's more a question of what happened to arts programmes themselves. Because in the late '80s and early '90s, I think they did go through a revolution in identity and purpose.

Thompson's words had been pre-echoed by an article earlier in 1997 from Nigel Williams, outgoing editor of *Omnibus*:

> There is a crisis of confidence about whether we are even allowed to use the word 'art' on television. A recent *Omnibus* programme about Schubert, narrated and presented by Andras Schiff, was trashed by colleagues in the arts department ... The drift of my colleagues' objections seemed to be that it wasn't quite enough to have a great pianist playing some of his music and recounting the simple facts of Schubert's life. They seemed to want a bit more sex and violence. Their lack of enthusiasm for what might be called the High Art approach has, in recent years, become worryingly prevalent. (1997: 16)

Thompson's analysis was that arts programmes had had to absorb the deconstruction of the classical arts agenda, the embrace of popular culture and the increased interest in submitting the arts to journalistic enquiry. The casual relativism epitomised by Channel 4's output had also proved less productive than perhaps imagined, so that, as he said in his speech to the Royal Television Society, 'the great postmodernist experiment began to run out of steam rather sooner than expected'. His solution was a return to first principles, the re-engagement with 'our cultural bearings' and a renewed commitment to substance, enthusiasm and eclecticism.

These qualities would be evident in the cultural critic Patrick Wright's journey down the Thames in *The River* (1999), in a personal view of British theatre presented by director Richard Eyre in *Changing Stages* (2000), and in Neil MacGregor's return to the screen with *Seeing Salvation* (2000) considering images of Christ in art. Each series was conceived in a more-or-less conventional lecture format (discussed further in Chapter 4), often with additional elements of a travelogue. But new programme formats had also been developed for the arts that revealed exactly the confidence crisis that Thompson identified. Early in the decade, in his Arts Council strategy document, Stephen Phillips identified an aspiration that drove many of these developments. 'The best buzz word that the '90s can come up with', he said, 'is "access". This is intended to mean wide availability of experience (many viewers), as well as being unthreatening in form' (Phillips 1991)

In early 1993, for the *Off the Wall* series, the BBC bussed six residents of the Byker estate in Newcastle, together with presenter Muriel Gray, around the English art world. After meeting curators and others, they chose artworks, including paintings by Warhol and Lucian Freud, for an exhibition organised back home. This early form of what a decade on we have learned to call 'formatted documentary' was reprised two years later for *The Art Marathon* (1995) in which another group of 'ordinary citizens' toured galleries for loans to a show that they organised in Derry. A rather different approach to an arts subject in a mainstream television form was the revealing six-part observational documentary *The House* (1996), about the goings on at London's Covent Garden during the 1993–94 season under the General Director of the Royal Opera, Jeremy Isaacs. Director Michael Waldman brought a dispassionate yet merciless eye to show what the *Sunday Times'* media correspondent Nicholas Hellen described as 'embarrassing events, disputes and bad language far removed from the sophisticated public image of one of Britain's most prestigious institutions' (1995: 3). Isaacs, who was responsible for granting permission, was rueful about the films. 'It was naïve of me to think we would get a measured picture of our work', he said. 'I don't think it is that at all' (ibid.).

In 1998, in one of the last co-productions with the Arts Council, the BBC produced *Date with an Artist*, six programmes in which contemporary artists produced a work for the home (or in one case, the prison cell) of someone who did not normally collect art. The model here, if rather a distant one, was the makeover series like *Changing Rooms* (1996–2005) where two families transform parts of each other's house. The climactic moment in such formatted films is the 'reveal' when a person is confronted with their changed living space. In *Date with an Artist* the 'reveal' comes after the commissioner and artist have each spoken of their expectations, then met, and the artist has worked away. But in most of the twelve films (each episode featured two pairings) the moment of unveiling is either forced or flat. Several of the artists, including Cornelia Parker, Chris Ofili and Sam Taylor-Wood speak clearly about their ideas and reveal something of their process, but the demands of the format fit uneasily with the complexities of making and responding to art, and the works themselves are destined to be simply decorative objects for a hallway or bedroom. As in later applications of existing formats to the arts, the programmes come to be far more about the medium of television and its expectations than about the artist and their creative process. Refreshingly, both the artists Jake and Dinos Chapman and their date, Justine Frischmann, the singer with Elastica, refuse to take the project seriously. When the Chapmans bring her their first idea for her bedroom – a wall panel of earth, with blood oozing into a trough of plants – she is unfazed. 'I don't find it aesthetically very pleasing', she says. 'I'd rather have something that reminds me of sex rather than death … I think it's crap.'

A PORTRAIT OF ARSHILE

written and directed by Atom Egoyan
a Koninck production for BBC and the Arts Council of Great Britain
4 minutes, 1995

A Portrait of Arshile lasts for only four minutes. Its images are a close-up home-video shot of a child and a painting, together with a drawing and a photograph linked to the painting. Yet it is a rich, moving and revealing film about an artist, about the past and the future, about exile, about parents and children, and more.

A Portrait of Arshile was commissioned for *Picture House*, along with *Dance for the Camera* and *Sound on Film* another of the BBC/Arts Council co-productions to create inventive short films for spaces in the BBC2 schedule. Unlike the others, this initiative, produced by Keith Griffiths, engaged international feature film directors, who were asked to find an imaginative way to present a single painting.

The responses are nothing if not heterogeneous. Krystov Zanussi acts as a tourist guide asking whether the figure in Leonardo's 'Lady with an Ermine' (a painting housed in a Krakow gallery) is more beautiful than the 'Mona Lisa'. Guy Maddin conjures up a characteristic epic fantasy, with George Méliès-like toy trains, spontaneous combustion and self-administered teeth extraction, in response to Odilon Redon's 'The Eye Like a Strange Balloon Mounts Towards Infinity'. Raul Ruiz creates a similarly bizarre animation from cutouts of Velasquez's 'Las Meninas' and Chinese scrolls with an English, Spanish, Chinese and Arabic soundtrack. Paul Schrader muses on a canvas he owns, 'New Blue' by Manny Farber, and on what Farber – an influential film critic as well as a painter – identified as 'termite art'. 'Termite art', a caption informs us, 'goes always forward with no sign the artist has any object in mind than eating away the boundaries of his art.'

In such company, Egoyan's *A Portrait of Arshile* has a welcome simplicity, yet both an allusiveness and a humanity that mostly elude the other films. It begins with a close-up video image of a young boy. We hear that his name is Arshile and, because of the informal, domestic qualities of the shot, we assume that he is the filmmaker's son. A woman's voice speaks in a language that we will discover to be Armenian before a man's voice, Egoyan's presumably, translates. 'You are named after a man', he says quietly to the boy, 'who painted a portrait of himself and his mother.' The portrait, the two voices explain, was based on a photograph taken in Armenia in 1912 when the boy was eight years old.

The image of Arshile in Atom Egoyan's *Picture House: A Portrait of Arshile*

The video camera tightens on the boy's eyes as he reaches out to play with the camera. 'You are named after a man who adored his mother and was inspired by her love of nature and her pride in Armenian culture and language.' But in 1919 the mother, cradled in the boy's arms, died of starvation. The boy went to America, changed his name, and began to paint.

Now we see the 1912 photograph, a still, monochrome image after the dancing pixels of the video. The quiet rhythms of the poetic text, backed by a piano, continue. 'You are named after a man who would look at his mother's face staring back at him and be afraid of disappointing her, of bringing shame to his name.' Unspoken, but perhaps known to the viewer, is the knowledge that the director's parents were Armenian refugees in Egypt who changed their family name when they emigrated to Canada.

Finally, the painting, 'Portrait of the Artist and his Mother' (1926–36), is shown. 'You are named after a man who changed his name because of what he felt when he remembered his mother's face. His mother's face now stares from a gallery wall into a land she never dreamed of.' Arshile Gorky's painting, the end credits inform us, is in the collection of Washington's National Gallery of Art.

The multi-channel new world

'The citadel is surrounded, and the walls are already being chipped away' is how Controller of BBC2 Brian Wenham characterised his television world in 1982. 'Britain is on the brink of a Third Age of Broadcasting', he wrote in a prescient foreword to a volume of essays, 'in which the expansion of the means of distribution will permit an explosion of television programming beyond the wildest dreams of early pioneers' (1982: 13). This was the moment when only the fourth terrestrial channel was about to go on air, when cable offered little apart from the main channels (and then only to small markets) and when just one home in ten possessed a video recorder; 25 years on, and the overwhelming majority of viewers can choose from a multitude of channels and programmes delivered by satellite, online, to mobile telephones and more. Although the shift to a multi-channel world took longer perhaps than Wenham envisaged, it is the single most significant factor to have shaped television in Britain across the past decade and more.

In 1982 cable television was the focus of the Hunt Committee's report about the feasibility of a national infrastructure, and the following year eleven regional franchises were offered, eight of which were operational by 1985. Britain's first cable television systems were in place in the early 1950s (Gloucester opened the first city-wide one in 1951), but these operated essentially as relays for locations which could not receive good broadcast signals. An early form of pay TV was tried in London and Sheffield in 1966, but before Hunt – and indeed for many years afterwards, given the slow growth of subscribers – cable was marginal to television in Britain. A satellite television service from mainland Europe was carried in Britain by some cable operators from October 1981. The following year this became the Sky Channel, offering just two hours of general entertainment each day. Purchased by Rupert Murdoch's News International, the channel began a more substantial service for transmission by cable in 1984. Five years later, and operating outside the regulatory framework in Britain, Sky started direct broadcasting by satellite (DBS) to homes with special aerials and decoders. A rival 'official' DBS service was initiated by the Home Secretary in 1982, at first envisaged as two channels from the BBC, one for feature films and a second offering the best of international television. The BBC later abandoned these plans for financial reasons.

Even in the uncertain and no more than nascent environment for cable and satellite in 1982, both Brian Wenham and Melvyn Bragg were optimistic about what these services could offer to the arts. Wenham envisaged a subscription satellite channel offering the best from the major orchestras, opera houses and national theatres of Europe, and Bragg similarly saw a means of evading the problem that the terrestrial channel's mass audiences consistently demonstrated little real enthusiasm for the arts:

> Lack of space [on the broadcast channels] inhibits experiment and the taking on of more obscure work, for arts programmes have almost always felt, with good cause, that as the present system is organised, they are merely tolerated and have to prove their reliability without fail … Cable could change this … If the cable systems do spread as widely and as remorselessly as is sometimes anticipated, the effect will be not unlike that of the decentralisation and deregulation of book publishing (1982: 40, 43).

Two models from the USA were frequently introduced into the debate: ABC/Hearst's Arts Channel and Bravo. (Neither in fact made a success of operating as a specialist arts channel.)

The reality of cable and satellite television in Britain has largely failed to fulfil these promises. The IBA-authorised British Satellite Broadcasting package of five DBS channels went on air after significant delays in April 1990, but the service (and the IBA) was effectively out-manoeuvred by Sky. Sky executed a 'merge-over' to gain control of their rival and from April 1991 it was British Sky Broadcasting (BSkyB) offering initially five channels, and then an increasing number. An arts channel, however, was not one of these. In its early months BSB programmed some arts offerings on their NOW channel, but as Claire Burnett reported, 'Initial promises from British Satellite Broadcasting and Sky Television to launch dedicated arts services have so far proved hollow' (1990). Graham King, a consultant to Sky on the arts project, said that the proposed Sky Arts channel was abandoned because Rupert Murdoch had his hands full with four channels and losses running at £2 million per week.

'In the early days of BSB there was some arts programming', Stephen Phillips informed the Arts Council in 1991; 'what remains is a depressing pointer to the new de-regulated future. In the week of writing I can find no single programme on satellite which could by any stretch of the imagination … be described as an arts programme. Unless there is a geometric increase in the numbers of subscribers, satellite and cable cannot afford to originate their own programming in the arts field' (1991). His analysis held good for the best part of a decade. Performance, initially owned by the *Daily Mail* and General Trust, was the first independent channel to explore the feasibility of making a return from cable and satellite revenues, and in January 1999 the *Financial Times* critic Chris Dunkley was enthusiastic about its schedule: 'Like much on this network, [its programme *Authentically Baroque*] provided a poignant reminder of what grown-up television used to be like' (1999: 14). Digital Classics TV was another entrant into the market, initially operating on a subscription model but forced by the arrival of BBC Four and Artsworld to go free-to-air on cable and satellite systems in 2002 before shutting its operations entirely.

Artsworld was the brainchild of Jeremy Isaacs after he had moved on from running the Royal Opera House. The belief that he had given to Channel 4 in its early years about the importance of the arts in the lives of everyone, coupled with the sense that by the millennium many broadcast arts programmes were imposing too many layers of mediation between artist and viewer, led him to found a new channel for digital distribution. Artsworld, which started transmissions on Sky Digital as a premium subscription service in December 2001, was backed by private investors and the Guardian Media Group. Its first schedule, Isaacs recognised, 'draws on the programme libraries of the world … But it also features a high proportion of specially commissioned work celebrating what happens here' (2001).

Artsworld struggled to establish itself, especially when BBC Four came on air in 2002 with a strong arts component. In his June 2004 contribution to the Independent Review of the BBC's Digital Television Services initiated by the Department for Culture, Media and Sport, Artsworld Chairman John Hambley argued that 'BBC Four's impact has been catastrophic on those cultural channels already in the market when it was launched.' Hambley recorded:

> Digital Classics TV has gone out of business. The Performance Channel has cut its budgets to almost zero and become part of a shopping channel. And in our own case, our channel has been teetering on the brink of extinction after losing its principal shareholders as a direct result of BBC Four's creation. (2004)

Perhaps surprisingly, Sky took a fifty per cent interest in the channel in 2003, saving the service from closure, and in 2005 acquired it outright, taking it free-to-air for Sky subscribers. Cynical souls saw its place in Sky's (and thus Rupert Murdoch's) bouquet of channels as a kind of cultural fig-leaf to off-set against the remorseless commercialism of its sister channels, but at the time of writing it consistently offers a wide range of high quality documentaries and performances acquired from both Britain and abroad that are unavailable elsewhere. Even though its budgets are tiny when compared to the terrestrial channels, it undertakes some commissions and is an active co-producer. From May 2006 it was also broadcast in HDTV, well before the BBC or Channel 4 made any arts programming available in this format. In February of the following year it was rebranded as Sky Arts, reviving a channel name from Sky's early years. Sky Arts may not entirely fulfil the fantasy envisaged by Wenham and Bragg 25 years before, but it is nonetheless a valuable offering in the diversified media world of the moment.

Dumb and dumber?

Around the millennium, arts programming became one particular focus for a wider debate within and beyond broadcasting about the perceived retreat by the mainstream broadcasters, most especially the BBC, from public service values.

Voices were raised in protest at the falling away of a commitment to the arts across the terrestrial channels, a shift that was seen as symptomatic of the dilution of Reithian values. Such a debate seems always to be with us. 'There is a crisis in public service broadcasting', producer Phillip Whitehead wrote back in 1984. Noting even then that the mass audience had started to shrink, he identified 'the compulsion [within the broadcasters] to grab as much as possible of it' (1984: 6).

Just as perennial as the expressions of concern is the defensiveness of broadcasters on this issue. Responding to Whitehead, BBC Television's Director of Programmes Brian Wenham wrote, seemingly without irony, 'there is no ratings war' (1984: 2). No executive would offer such an opinion some twenty years on, yet the refusal to accept criticism on the subject remains much the same. In the context of arts programming, when I contributed an article to the *Guardian* in 1999 about the disappearance of single documentaries each of the mainstream broadcasters responded pointing out how misguided I was. I suggested:

The channels which have traditionally nurtured individual arts documentaries, BBC2 and Channel 4, have quite suddenly lost almost all interest in them. BBC2 has been made over to look like a leisure-oriented cable service, and Channel 4 wants finally to grow up to become a focused 'young-at-heart' brand ... The arts documentary is now central to neither the BBC's public service responsibilities nor to Channel 4's encouragement of innovation and experiment. (1999: 7)

Channel 4's Janey Walker was one of those who responded. 'I agree that the cultural consensus has gone', she wrote, 'but it is patronising to argue that this simply leaves us with rag-rolling not culture' (Walker 1999: 7). For the BBC Alan Yentob maintained that 'far from losing interest in arts programmes, we are determined to make more impact with them on our channels' (Yentob 1999: 7). Just under a year later, however, the BBC executive John Willis acknowledged that 'in the intervening months, everything has pointed to Wyver being right. Other genres may have problems but arts programmes are in a major crisis from which they may never escape' (2000: 7).

My critical voice was hardly a lone one. In the years 1998–2002, the critic Christopher Dunkley developed in his *Financial Times* columns a consistent attack on the debasing of values within broadcasting, blaming 'the broadcasting executives who, in less than one generation, have ceased to be keepers of the culture, and have become instead slaves to audience figures and focus groups' (1999: 14). 'What has to be recognised', Hugh Hebert wrote in the *Guardian* in November 1995, 'is the extent to which arts coverage generally has been cut, trivialised, or cold-shouldered' (1995: 12). 'Nobody at the top gives a fig', lamented former BBC executive Sir John Drummond in the 1998 Royal Philharmonic Society Lecture. 'Nobody at the top of the BBC cares for culture.' Alan Rusbridger, editor of the *Guardian*, was another who contributed to this extensive chorus of criticism. 'There has, until very recently, been a terrible failure of corporate nerve over the televising of serious arts programmes for mainstream audiences', he said in a 2003 speech at the Royal Philharmonic Society Music Awards. 'How on earth did it happen that, for so many barren years, the BBC governors nodded on the job while the arts output all but withered away.'

Analysis of the number of hours of arts output supported such concerns. Ofcom reported an eleven per cent decline in total output of arts programmes (including classical music) across the five major channels from 11.5 hours a week in 1998 to 10.2 hours a week in 2002. The reduction in peak time programming across the same period was even more marked, from 3.9 hours to 3.2, a fall of 18 per cent.[6] Even before this decline, in the summer 1998 *BBC Annual Report*, the Governors recorded their concern that 'for the second year running there is still work to do to strengthen overall impact and commission more landmark arts programming' (in Donovan 1999: 6). *Omnibus* had been cut from 25 to 14 programmes a year, *Arena* reduced to six or seven and *Bookmark*'s two runs a year had been reduced to occasional one-off specials. The *close up*, *Tx.* and *Arthouse* strands all disappeared, and the thoughtful and much-admired series about the cinema, *Moving Pictures*, which was spun out of *The Late Show* in 1990, had also gone by 1996. A strikingly personal acknowledgement of the shift came from the former editor of *Omnibus*, Nigel Williams:

> There is absolutely no doubt that the volume of serious arts or science programmes on the Beeb is less than it was. I know this principally because I only have to go down the lists of current projects commissioned out to the arts department, in which I work and have worked for thirty years. I only have to count up the numbers of talented people who have left or been driven away or drunk themselves to death to know that, now, as ever, it isn't easy for serious culture. (2000: 3)

Among the most interesting and symptomatic responses to criticism of declining standards in arts television and more broadly, was a 2002 speech to the Westminster Media Forum by Gavyn Davies, chairman of the BBC, in which he focused on the charge of 'elitism' that was frequently employed by broadcasters as a riposte to criticism. 'The criticism for dumbing down will not go away', he recognised. 'Typically, this criticism comes from a particular group of people in the UK. They tend to be southern, white, middle class, middle aged and well educated. Strangely enough, they are already the type of people who consume a disproportionate amount of the BBC's services – people who get more out of the licence fee than they put into it. In some cases, the criticism of dumbing down is simply a respectable way of trying to hijack even more of the BBC's services for themselves.' Davies argued that 'the Asian teenager on the streets of Leicester' had as much right to be served by the BBC as anyone, but that he might not want what 'a member of the House of Lords' might want. It was the BBC's duty to ensure quality and enrichment for all. Richard Hoggart was among those who responded angrily to what he described as Davies' 'soundbite sloganising' attempting to defend what Reith had described as 'the shoddy, the vulgar and the sensational'. Just before unleashing his most barbed comment, Hoggart concurred with Davies:

> Of course everyone has a right to receive a wide range of broadcasts, and the broadcasters themselves have the duty to give them the best programmes they can conceive ... That does not include silently – or blatantly – saying: 'Many people can only appreciate garbage, so let's give them plenty of that, well honed, and call it good democratic broadcasting.' (2002: 3)

Arts and broadcasting at the millennium

If even the survival of arts programmes on the terrestrial channels had seemed uncertain early in the new century, by 2005–6 the arts had found new niches in each of the main channels' propositions. Overall, the focus was on traditional, mainstream figures and forms and the opportunities for engaging with contemporary work, for being exposed to unfamiliar names and, most especially, for true innovation were limited. Nonetheless, arts programming retained its place, and a survey commissioned by *MediaGuardian* in 2003 pinpointed the turnaround. Maggie Brown suggested:

> The low point followed the BBC's blunt strategy (outlined in 2000) for an entertainment and drama driven BBC1 and a popular, middlebrow, factual BBC2. This has now been disowned, and as a consequence BBC governors have ordered arts back into the mainstream. There are now signs that the BBC intends to increase its commitment to the arts. (2003)

By 2006 there were three regular strands for arts programming: the continuing *The South Bank Show*; *Imagine*, the replacement for *Omnibus*, launched in 2003 with Alan Yentob as presenter; and a weekly BBC2 magazine series, *The Culture Show*, which started in 2004. In its first season *Imagine* profiled Stella McCartney, Carlos Acosta and Sir John Mortimer at the same time as BBC1 sought, not always with success, to secure main channel ratings (in excess of five million viewers) for a handful of other offerings. These included *Rolf on Art* (2001–5) with Rolf Harris offering a mix of cheery how-to-paint-like-Van-Gogh advice along with thoughtful discussions of a major artist's works. Two biographical projects, *Leonardo* (2003) and *The Divine Michelangelo* (2004) dramatised (with some absurd excesses) elements of these artists' lives, while presenter Tim Marlow, with director Ed Bazalgette, energetically attempted to engage a large audience with a profile of *Turner: The Man Who Painted Britain* (2002). Yet the perils of this approach were detailed in the *Guardian*. 'Art is the new rock'n'roll of factual television', the paper's critic Jonathan Jones wrote, lamenting 'the desperation of this weirdly hybrid programme's attempt to find a popular format for an art documentary-drama-thingy ... What is missing is any intellectual and critical core to the programme' (2002: 4).

The big idea at BBC2 in 2001 was the launch of the Arts Zone on 19 March. BBC2 Controller Jane Root had organised programmes into a History Zone on Saturday evenings and into a Friday Night Comedy Zone, and now this innovation, she claimed, would be 'the home of arts on terrestrial television' (in Kinnes 2000: 33). The first group of programmes included *Review* with Mark Lawson; an unremarkable film authored by Alain de Botton, *How Proust Can Change Your Life*; and a foreign buy-in originally acquired for the *Storyville* strand, *Picasso Days*. Subsequent editions included the straightforward but intelligent Neil MacGregor lecture series, *Seeing Salvation*, about portrayals of Christ in art. 'The time and space given to the zone is giving the best possible message to audiences and programme-makers of what the BBC intends to happen', claimed Arts Zone editor Peter Maniura; 'this is only the beginning' (ibid.). But it was the end too, for the idea lasted for only a single season. The following year, in the *Financial Times*, Graham McCann wrote that

> BBC2 – which was meant to serve both as a home to the less commercial arts and a haven to experimentation – has all but abandoned its core cultural components ... in favour of more ratings-friendly life-style, gardening and comedy shows. (2002: 16)

BBC2's next big idea was, well, big ideas. In the autumn of 2002 the channel presented *Great Britons* which, using the Internet and a host of related activities, ran a poll for the nation's greatest individual. The next year *The Big Read* (2003) collected three quarters of a million votes in its search for the best-loved book. Documentary films hosted by personalities made the case for 21 short-listed candidates, and Jane Austen's *Pride and Prejudice* emerged as the runner-up to J. R. R. Tolkien's *The Lord of the Rings*. These projects, and the heritage follow-up *Restoration* (2003–5) generated a lot of buzz and participatory activities across the country, even if the on-screen programmes were often undistinguished. Elsewhere on the channel, *The Culture Show* contributed its reliable if frequently breathless coverage of current arts events, and architecture programming continued to prove popular, especially as it crossed over into lifestyle formats. Theatre and opera were largely banished to the new BBC Four but *The Private Life of a Masterpiece* series (2001–6), with each film tracing the tale of a major painting or sculpture, proved consistently stimulating, and retained an occasional foothold in the terrestrial schedules.

Across London at Channel 4's new Richard Rogers-designed office building, Michael Jackson had replaced Michael Grade in May 1997. In his first interviews he promised to reinvigorate the output and return the channel to basic values of innovation and difference. The *Guardian*'s Maggie Brown offered some advice. 'Top of his list', she wrote, 'should be a commitment to reinvent its coverage of the arts, in their broadest sense ... After the eclectic, inconsistent and often annoying *Without Walls* was hastily abandoned a year ago, the channel promised a re-think and a replacement, but nothing has emerged to take its place' (1997: 13). In October 1997 the channel brought back the one-hour arts documentary in *Arthouse* (1997–99); the eclectic subjects included advertising director Tony Kaye trying to prove that he was a 'real' artist and a profile of hip-hop musician Tricky. Yet neither this series, nor a subsequent half-hour strand, *The Art Show* (2002–4) that followed, was able to establish itself. Jacques Peretti, series editor of the latter strand, explained his thinking. 'One thing we're trying to do is to make smaller, quirkier programmes', he said;

> one thing that was very striking about Michael Jackson's parting speech when he left Channel 4 [he left in October 2001 for employment in the United States] was that he thought TV had become more attention-seeking, more noisy. And that was particularly true of arts programmes – they aren't very significant, ratings-wise, so you're compelled to make more extreme programmes to get press interest. What we're trying to do is to make more muted, thoughtful programmes. (In Jeffries 2002: 16–17)

Peretti employed interesting directors, a number of whom had worked on *The Late Show*, and sometimes they were matched with significant subjects. Ben Lewis, for example, made the clever and funny *Gursky World* (2002) which involved, among other things, his attempt to create his own version of an image by the art world's favoured photographer. There was, however, little consistency to the runs of either *Arthouse* or *The Art Show*; neither series had a discernible agenda and, most importantly, neither was able to create that elusive signature (as long before *Monitor* had managed, and more recently, *Arena*). Perhaps the identity crisis brought on by trying to produce intelligent programming in a ratings-dominated environment proved too much. Or perhaps there were no great cultural causes left any more, or at least none that could be compellingly captured in occasional films contributed by disparate filmmakers working in the absence of a defining idea.

Channel 4 continued to score an occasional hit, like the three-part comprehensive biography *Andy Warhol: The Complete Picture* (2002), but in the visual arts at least the channel's saviour proved to be another refugee from *The Late Show* – critic, former *Artscribe* editor and occasional painter Matthew Collings. Collings wrote and presented *This is Modern Art* (1999), and with its irreverent, casual approach underpinned by a true understanding of its subject, and supported by imaginative filming from director Ian MacMillan, the series demonstrated that the lecture form still associated with Kenneth Clark could feel contemporary and relevant. 'The series is about providing a framework for a general audience to think about up-to-date art', Collings wrote in the *Observer* (1999: 14). Exploring themes like genius, shock, humour and nothingness, Collings brought together of-the-moment British artists like Martin Creed with a range of historical figures. Andrew Billen's *New Statesman* critique of the series gives a strong sense of its self-referential filmic rhetoric:

> [Collings] mentioned Picasso, and tasteful music struck up. 'The trouble', he said, 'is when you mention Picasso, tasteful music strikes up.' Later, over

shots of a supermarket, he told us that as a student he had enjoyed Andy Warhol's book of philosophy *A to B and Back Again*: 'I expect I'll be coming round one of these aisles reading from it, if this ironic easy-listening soundtrack is anything to go by.' And blow me, the next thing he did was just that. So where we sought art criticism, he delivered television criticism, gazumping this reviewer's criticism, which was that, beneath the larkiness, Collings hadn't really found a new way to do an arts programme at all. (1999)

Collings developed the approach in his annual hosting of Channel 4's coverage of the Tate's Turner Prize ceremony and in further series for the broadcaster. *Hello Culture* (2001) was less well-achieved and more confused than *This is Modern Art*, but *Matt's Old Masters* (2002–3) and a two-hour film about Courbet and the Impressionists, *Revenge of the Nice* (2005), were among the very best television programmes about the visual arts in the new century. Under new Arts Commissioning Editor Jan Younghusband, Channel 4 also produced several series with composer Howard Goodall who employed a rather more conventional style to explore classical music in series including *Howard Goodall's Big Bangs* (2000), *Howard Goodall's 20th Century Greats* (2004) and *How Music Works* (2006). Among Younghusband's other successes was a remarkable run of contemporary operas adapted for or, on occasion, conceived directly for television. The most acclaimed of these (and justifiably so) was Penny Woolcock's film *The Death of Klinghoffer* (2003) from John Adams' 1991 work about the hijacking of the cruise ship Achille Lauro. Woolcock rethought the opera for the screen, shot it aboard a boat in the Mediterranean and created one of those rare productions that is convincing, and indeed compelling, both musically and on-screen.

From its start in March 1997 Five (initially Channel 5), Britain's fifth terrestrial channel, was mandated by Ofcom to produce a small percentage of arts programming. These productions were traditionally buried in a slot on Sunday lunchtimes, but in 2002 the channel's Director of Programmes Kevin Lygo moved them to a regular weekday evening slot. 'I wanted to put the arts on prime time', Lygo explained, 'particularly at a moment when the BBC seemed in a state of confusion. This helped Channel 5 to establish itself as a serious competitor with the other terrestrial channels' (in Jeffries 2002: 16).

In slots against guaranteed ratings-winners on other channels, the channel's Controller of Arts, Religion and Daytime, Kim Peat, successfully scheduled exhibition tours with Tim Marlow; visual arts films about traditional subjects; and series with art critic Brian Sewell. This initiative attracted extensive press and regulatory approval. Fivearts Cities, a partnership with Arts Council England, showcased arts in a different city each year through the mid-2000s, and the 2006–7 focus on Oxford included *The Singing Estate* (2006), a delightful series following conductor Ivor Setterfield training a choir from the Blackbird Leys Estate. The series was one of those that attracted up-market viewers who might not otherwise come to the channel; this compensated for small total audiences, and the channel gained a new respect within the industry and beyond. 'We were doing this at a time when Channel 4 seemed to have given up the ghost', Lygo enthused, 'and the BBC had been glaringly devoid of new ideas on its terrestrial channels' (in Jeffries 2002: 17). Only after first Lygo and then his successor Dan Chambers had moved on from the Director of Programmes position (in the latter case, unwillingly so) and after a more commercial focus for the channel was introduced in early 2007, was Five's commitment to the arts in prime time questioned.

Fivearts Cities was one of a number of initiatives in the middle of the new century's first decade to take arts programming 'beyond the broadcast'. Convinced that both scale and activities alongside but outside the screen could help the arts attract both attention and audiences, commissioners increasingly sought to collaborate on projects like *Big Dance* in July 2006. A partnership between Arts Council England, the BBC and other agencies, *Big Dance* was a celebration of dance across England, with a host of classes and performances plus *The Big Dance* on BBC One with world record attempts and mass choreography hosted by Bruce Forsyth and Zoe Ball. Over at Channel 4, *The Big Art Project* (2005–) was an initiative to involve people in commissioning public art for six sites across Britain. Only at the culmination of the process was the project featured in broadcast programming. But one thing was clear from the titles alone, when you went beyond the broadcast, size mattered.

'Everybody needs a place to think': BBC Four

On 2 March 2002, with words having replaced numerals in the designated branding of channels, the BBC launched BBC Four. Outlining his vision of 'a new, world-class cultural centre', the channel's Controller Roly Keating claimed this digital channel was 'the biggest innovation in cultural broadcasting for a generation' (in Thorpe 2002: 7). From November 1997 the BBC had been a partner with Flextech Ltd in a commercial joint venture to provide digital channels, including the arts channel UK Arena. The take-up for this, however, was disappointing and in 2000 the service was relaunched with a more general remit as UK Drama. The BBC also operated a public service digital television channel (available on cable and satellite as well) called BBC Knowledge from June 1999. BBC Knowledge began as a specifically educational channel but in 2000 its remit had been broadened to a documentary and arts channel. Its ratings, however, were tiny and BBC Four took over both its multiplex slot and its mission, along with a greatly enhanced annual budget of £30 million. On the new channel's launch night, Knowledge became the first BBC channel to close down.

BBC Four's opening night schedule (simulcast during prime time on BBC2) was dominated by the arts, with a documentary about artist Michael Landy, Robert Hughes' film essay *Goya: Crazy Like a Genius*, the comedy drama *Surrealismo* about Salvador Dalí, a spoof arts magazine *The Gist*, and Baaba Maal in concert. The tagline of the channel's print and poster campaign was 'Everybody needs a place to think', and a brochure issued for the launch promised creative documentaries from around the world; theatre and drama including a version of *Hamlet* directed by Peter Brook from his recent stage production; international cinema; and world music, opera and jazz. A lavish launch party took its theme from Vanessa Engle's smart and gossipy three-part history *Britart* (2002) which chronicled for the channel the rise and rise of the young British artists across the previous decade. Another early highlight was the series *Painting the Weather* (2002) which was accompanied by a 'red button' interactive digital exhibition (discussed further in Chapter 5).

Fundamental to the success of BBC Four was Freeview, a digital terrestrial service launched in October 2002. Owned by the BBC, BSkyB, Channel 4, ITV and National Grid Wireless, the Freeview bouquet of channels could be received not only across cable and satellite (to which subscription-based services digital channels had previously been restricted) but also by set-top boxes, available for a one-off cost of less than £100, which effectively converted analogue sets to receive digital signals. By March 2006 more than ten million Freeview-enabled digital boxes and digital televisions had been sold. Among the other offerings from Freeview was BBC Three, launched in February 2003, a younger channel focused on new comedy and drama that nonetheless produced arts-related programmes, including co-commissioning an installation and film with the Baltic Arts Centre with the mass-participation nude photographs of Spencer Tunick, the smart-looking contemporary architecture and design series *Dreamspaces* (2003) and the first screening of Tracey Emin's feature film *Top Spot* (2004). BBC Three also transmitted two highly imaginative live-music performances: *Flashmob: The Opera* (2004) and *Manchester Passion* (2006), the latter a contemporary retelling of events leading to the Crucifixion staged in the streets of the city with music from local bands and appearances from members of The Stone Roses and Happy Mondays. *Flashmob: The Opera* was a love triangle broadcast from Paddington station with arias from Mozart, Verdi, Bizet and others, and it drew on the contemporary game of bringing together instant crowds of people to a place they are informed of only minutes before by mobiles and texting.

'It lasted under an hour', wrote an anonymous blogger on *Rogue Semiotics*,

> and only really involved the mob for the very end of the climactic number. But it did work … In the second half the atmosphere grew with the flash-mob, who had evidently been asked to arrive for about two-thirds of the way through the performance. It all moved swiftly towards a conclusion with Sally being persuaded to catch the train to sin and Swindon, while Mike failed to grab her attention with a rendition of 'Nessun dorma'. Cue the flashmob, circling Mike, blasting out a quick chorus, and sending Sally scurrying back towards her one true love.[7]

BBC Four's offerings in particular constituted a heady cultural diet, especially after the comparative dearth of serious programming on the main BBC channels. Not all of it was successful, and the attempt to make cheap and cheerful recordings of theatre productions with multiple cameras in auditoria was soon abandoned. But the channel extended the television coverage of the Proms and other classical music offerings and many of the documentaries, both those commissioned and those acquired from abroad, were challenging and distinctive. Early carping about the channel, however, included an attack by the novelist John Lanchester describing the service as 'not so much television as radio with pictures; the closest thing the BBC has to what used to be the Third Programme' (2002: 3). More serious was the widely-held concern that, welcome as BBC Four's output was, the BBC was now going to exile its arts programming to a specialist channel that could only be viewed by a comparatively small proportion of the population. Among the voices cautioning against this strategy was the Channel 4 journalist (and National Gallery Trustee) Jon Snow: 'As a public-service broadcaster, the BBC has let the side down. This is obviously the shape of things to come. You are going to get more and more specialist programmes. We will all end up as specialist people who don't talk to anyone else' (in Thorpe 2002: 7).

John Hambley, the chief executive of Artsworld, a commercial competitor threatened by the new service, was more outspoken: 'We are extremely sorry the BBC has been given this enormous amount of public money for something so unnecessary', he was quoted in an *Observer* article just before BBC Four's launch. 'It is a waste, because it is only ghettoising the arts ... If the BBC was putting more arts programmes on to BBC1 or BBC2, rather than just trying to out-soap and out-dumb the commercial opposition, then that would be another thing entirely. That would mean it was taking the arts seriously' (in Thorpe 2002: 7).

Five years after the launch of BBC Four, as this book was being written, the debate about its ghettoising of the arts rumbled on, but the realities – and the advantages – of a multi-channel world were more widely accepted. Sixty per cent of households had access to digital television by 2006 and it was unquestionable that BBC Four had significantly extended and enriched arts programming. Dozens of the Promenade concerts were screened each season rather than the handful that had made it to the main channels. *Jazz Britannia* (2005), *Folk Britannia* (2006) and *Soul Britannia* (2007) were smart, enjoyable ways into the history of popular music in Britain, while art historian Joseph Leo Koerner explored the *Northern Renaissance* (2006) and Andrew Graham-Dixon considered early Christian and Byzantine art in *The Art of Eternity* (2007). Even if under channel controller Janice Hadlow, who took up the post in 2004, BBC Four refocused to be brighter and more appealing, and British social history became a dominant concern, the channel still produced a strong range of solid, thoughtful (if rarely truly adventurous or innovative) arts programming.

Along with the growing audiences, especially among the young, for Internet-based media, television's shift to something closer to a radio model, with particular interest groups or demographics served by niche channels, exercised fewer critics. There were still some who believed that television had once startled and converted mainstream audiences by a chance meeting with a modernist masterpiece, and it was recognised that those encounters with the unexpected in the burgeoning schedules had become rare indeed. Even so, BBC Director General Mark Thompson claimed that the opportunity for such still existed: 'One of the BBC's greatest strengths in culture has been the power of serendipity', he said in a 2005 speech; 'I do think BBC Four plays an important role … but it must always be accompanied by a significant presence for the arts on mass audience channels' (2006: 11).

So as Channel 4 approached its 25th anniversary in November 2007, what was the state of the arts on those mainstream channels? Some personal reactions are included in Chapter 4, but it was noticeable that no longer, as had been the case a decade or so before, was there a general chorus of disapproval. Critics concerned about the medium's values had other preoccupations, including the extremes of reality television. The arts had their place – marginal perhaps but present nonetheless – on BBC One and ITV, as well as more significantly on BBC Two and Channel 4. However, what was coming into focus was the mutation of arts television into other genres of 'arts-lite' programming. In 2005 BBC One screened an arts series, *A Picture of Britain*, that was really a travel show. In the same year BBC Two made two major dramas about composers, *The Genius of Beethoven* and *Riot at the Rite* (about the first night performance of Stravinsky's 'Rite of Spring'), in which the music at times seemed incidental. Channel 4 constructed documentary talent series in the worlds of opera, *Operatunity* (2003) and ballet, *Ballet Hoo!* (2006). Involving human dramas, these series achieved a successful hybrid of the arts with a familiar and popular television format from another context. But the films in *A Picture of Britain* were polite heritage travelogues in which the visual arts of the English regions were treated by presenter David Dimbleby as secondary to the landscapes through which he travelled. In 2006 Channel 4, working closely with the Tate, transformed its *Turner Prize* programme into an attempt to discover a new television arts presenter. And Controller of BBC Two Roly Keating indicated something of the new thinking when he spoke about his channel's approach in 2006 to the Royal Academy of Arts Summer Exhibition. 'In terms of TV', he said 'we've found a way on BBC Two to televise major events such as Crufts or the Chelsea Flower Show, but so far we've been slow to do this with the arts, especially the visual arts' (Keating 2006: 49). The programmes that emerged, hosted by designer Laurence Llewellyn-Bowen, suggested that television still had some way to go to find the ideal form for this.

CHAPTER 3
'THE ODD COUPLE?': THE ARTS COUNCIL AND TELEVISION

In the first five years of its existence, from 1945 to mid-1950, the Arts Council of Great Britain disbursed no monies whatsoever to films or filmmakers. In the last five years of the twentieth century, what had become the Arts Council of England was the conduit between April 1995 and March 2000 for more than £90 million pounds of public funds to film production. As the 1990s wound down, the overwhelming majority of that support, derived from Lottery tickets holding out the hope of an effort-free fortune, was directed into forgettable feature films searching, invariably in vain, for box office success. In contrast to these times of famine and (for a very few commercial producers) feast, in the years between 1951 and 1999, the Arts Council supported and distributed more than 480 modestly-budgeted documentaries and performance films, a significant number of them innovative or experimental in their form and content. This chapter charts the changing production context for those films against both the developing environment of arts funding as a whole and the Council's complex and conflicted relationship with broadcasting.

State patronage creeps in

'God help the Minister that meddles with art', warned the nineteenth-century statesman Lord Melbourne, and through to the start of World War Two almost every administrator in Britain was happy to heed his words. Museums and galleries received some subsidy, councils paid for brass bands to entertain their ratepayers, and after 1933 the British Film Institute enjoyed parsimonious state funding. But as one historian has observed, 'the greatest contribution to national culture by parliament [in the inter-war years] was to export it overseas'; through the energies of the British Council, set up in 1934, 'the British Empire was given more state subsidy for the arts than the mother country' (Sinclair 1995: 20).

During the war, after prompting and pump-priming from the Pilgrim Trust, the Council for the Encouragement of Music and the Arts (CEMA) oversaw the channelling of modest Treasury monies to creative activities. The motives were mixed – providing employment for artists, boosting national morale – and the disparate outcomes included factory concerts, touring repertory companies, travelling exhibitions and the sending of the Sadler's Wells Ballet to Birmingham.[1] From April 1942 onwards the Chairman of CEMA was the economist John Maynard Keynes, who soon recognised that the fledgling funding body offered the opportunity to shape a national culture for all. Thanks to his vision and persistence, it was announced just before the July 1945 election that a successor to CEMA would have a permanent role in post-war Britain, and Keynes, who died just a year later, ensured that it would be forged in his image: London-focused, committed to excellence, with major roles for opera and ballet, his favoured art forms, and no place for film, in which he had no interest. 'I do not believe it is yet realised what an important thing has happened', Keynes confided in a BBC radio broadcast in July 1945; 'state patronage of the arts has crept in. It has happened in a very English, informal, unostentatious way – half-baked if you like. A semi-independent body is provided with modest funds' (1945: 31). But if the beginnings were ever so humble, the aspiration for the new world of post-war Britain was anything but, as the defining purpose of the Arts Council of Great Britain was characterised (in part) in its 1946 Royal Charter: 'developing a greater knowledge, understanding and practice of the fine arts exclusively, and in particular to increase the accessibility of the fine arts to the public throughout Our Realm'.[2]

Among the early tasks for the Council, along with supporting ballet and opera at Covent Garden and encouraging the Edinburgh Festival, was the planning of arts events to accompany the 1951 Festival of Britain. 'Dangers and anxieties continue to beset Great Britain', the retiring Chairman of the Arts Council wrote as he looked back at the Festival, 'yet in this year of so many shadows, there has been more art and music to be seen and heard in this country than ever before' (in Sinclair 1995: 83). The Council also made a central contribution to the nation's next communal celebration, the Coronation of Elizabeth II in 1953. It again organised important musical commissions and mounted exhibitions of paintings by Gainsborough, as well as the works of contemporary artists Graham Sutherland and John Piper (both soon to be profiled in BBC films directed by John Read). During these early years a tension emerged between the sustenance of excellence, which is how Keynes had envisaged the Council's work, and a commitment, recognisable in the early war years of CEMA, to bringing the arts with the highest standards to the widest audiences in the most accessible forms. Throughout the 1950s the Council was preoccupied with resolving the choice of which road to follow. The shorthand version of the dilemma became enshrined in the question 'Raise or spread?' 'Few, but roses', was the pithy version of the path more often chosen.

The fortunate 'roses' were mostly the exponents of an elite, patrician culture. 'What enthralled and bedevilled the Arts Council at this time', the Council's official chronicler Andrew Sinclair has written, 'were the problems of opera' (1995: 118). In a spiky polemic in the journal *Encounter* in 1955, the American sociologist Edward Shils critiqued the manner in which intellectuals in post-war Britain had been reconciled with the political establishment by the creation of the BBC Third Programme, the Arts Council and the British Council. As he saw it, what had happened was 'the vindication of the culture associated with aristocracy and gentry, and its restoration to pre-eminence among the guiding stars of the intellectuals. All English society has undergone this process of submission to the moral and cultural – but not the political or economic – ascendancy of the aristocracy and gentry' (1955: 6). Two decades later the leftist cultural critic Raymond Williams echoed Shils' argument when, drawing on his experience of being a Council member from 1975 to 1978, he wrote: 'The British State has been able to delegate some of its official functions to a whole complex of semi-official or nominally independent bodies because it has been able to rely on an unusually compact and organic ruling class' (in Gable 1989: 44). Certainly this chimed with Rodney Wilson's sense of what the Arts Council was like as an organisation when he joined as Arts Films Officer in 1970. 'You had this kind of upper-class strand of people', recalled Wilson, who was to oversee the Council's art film production for almost thirty years. 'The Head of Art Robin Campbell had a Victoria Cross and a wooden leg. But there were also people like Alan Bowness as the propagandist for modern art and with an incredibly broad range of interests in the visual arts ... So there was this odd relationship between the administration of the Arts Council, which was very much the establishment, and the arts.'[3]

In large part because of a confidence in shared values and attitudes, a formal distance from the Council's paymasters could be enshrined in what became known, in a phrase coined by the civil servant Lord Redcliffe-Maud, as 'the arm's length principle'. It was accepted that the government provided a framework, budget and reporting structure for the Council's operation but detailed decisions on funding and strategy were delegated to the Council and its constituent elements. Yet a critical assessment in 1982 by a former employee of the Council, Robert Hutchison, has held broadly true throughout the Council's history: 'The independence of the Arts Council is heavily qualified by ... ties and understandings with Government departments. More generally the Arts Council has to, and does, work within the grain of Government policy' (1982: 19).

'An emphatic success': the art film tours

Just before the Festival of Britain, in the Korean War winter of 1950–51, the Arts Council's Art Panel[4] decided that alongside exhibitions of original artworks, shows featuring photographic reproductions of old masters and the provision of lecturers, it would offer presentations of documentaries about the arts. This new initiative, developed in co-operation with the British Film Institute, meant that, as the 1950–51 *Annual Report* enthused, 'any society or club willing to pay a modest hiring fee' (1950–51: 30) could now rent 16mm film prints from the Council, along with a projector and operator. The titles included films by the Italian film-maker Luciano Emmer, as well as other documentaries from Italy and France including the 1949 documentary *Images Médiévales*, written and directed by William Novik with colour cinematography by Guy Delecluse. Expenditure on the service in this first season was £443, 4 shillings and 10 pence, and the project was officially celebrated in the *Annual Report* as 'an emphatic success' (ibid.).

The following year the offerings took in John Read's BBC film with Henry Moore as well as a title on Le Douanier Rousseau and William Chapman's colour documentary *Lascaux, Cradle of Man's Art* (1950). As the 1951–52 *Annual Report* noted, the screenings in 110 locations 'have stimulated an appetite which is going to be difficult to satisfy and cultivate' (1951–52: 32). Under consideration as a solution to this problem was 'a joint plan of operation' between BBC Television, the Council and the BFI. For the third winter when the service was active the Council and the BFI produced a printed catalogue with detailed descriptions of the 29 available films (Arts Council of Great Britain 1953). The list now featured additional British titles, including three from the series *Painter and Poet*, produced by John Halas for the Festival of Britain,[5] as well as *Looking at Sculpture*, an 11-minute title 'intended to suggest the best way of looking at a work of art'. The complexities of funding documentaries in these years of austerity can be traced in the credit line 'Produced by the Realist Film Unit (GB) for the Central Office of Information on behalf of the Ministry of Education with the co-operation of the Victoria and Albert Museum'. By 1953–54, when the showings in 101 places between October and April 'brought forth a vivid response', the Art Department was working directly with the Documentary Films Division of the BBC and contributing funding to new productions by John Read. *Artists Must Live* (1953) and *Graham Sutherland* (1954), both of which had been 'aided and abetted by the Arts Council' (Arts Council of Great Britain 1953–54: 35), were ready for inclusion in the repertory, and underway were films on the life of Walter Sickert and the history of British cartoonists and caricaturists, subsequently titled *Black on White* (1954).

ARTISTS MUST LIVE

directed by John Read; produced by John Elliott
a BBC Television Film made in association with the Arts Council
of Great Britain
28 mins, 1953

Artists Must Live, the first film to receive Arts Council funding, is a rarely-seen document that is as fascinating as it is frustrating. Essentially a corporate film praising and promoting the activities of the Council, it declares itself to be 'about the artist's place in Britain today'.

Introduced and narrated by the art critic and historian Basil Taylor (who hosted studio presentations of artists' works for BBC Television, as well as contributing art reviews to *Panorama*), the film offers a vivid visual sense of the circumscribed art world of the early 1950s. A host of visual artists of the time are featured, but mostly the shots or sequences are only tantalisingly brief. Keith Vaughan and John Piper are shown, and Reg Butler contributes a statement in his studio about how hard it is to make a living as an artist. Patrick Heron and Rodrigo Moynihan appear, Ivon Hitchens is shown working on a mural, and there are glimpses of both William Scott and Kenneth Armitage.

How, the film asks, are these and other artists meant to make a living? What opportunities are there for John Jones, an art student at the Slade, who is seen in the studios there and taking his work around to the London dealers, including the Beaux Arts Gallery. In the second half of the twentieth century the tradition of aristocratic patronage is long dead and private galleries can bring only a few figures to a small market of buyers. Enlightened advertisers are employing artists for posters and if all else fails painters and sculptors can always teach their skills to others. But how can artists be best supported to do what they are there for, their art?

Arts Council bureaucrats ponder the complexities of funding in *Artists Must Live*

This question was a significant pre-occupation at the time. In 1946, the newly appointed Director of the National Gallery, Philip Hendy, lamented that only a few middle-aged artists could expect to charge £100 or more for a picture and so live off their work. The problem remained an urgent one seven years later, but fortunately, at least according to the film, the Arts Council had (some of) the answers.

The camera of A. A. Englander (who later shot *Civilisation*) captures some striking scenes – filmed mute on 35mm monochrome stock – of the Council's activities, including the major show of Mexican culture at the Tate Gallery, as Basil Taylor considers how commissions and competitions (supported by the Council) can contribute to the economy of the arts. There are, he finds, also new institutional patrons in post-war Britain, including the Anglican Church with its support of Graham Sutherland and Henry Moore at Northampton.

Other featured examples include a commission for Edward Bawden on the cruise liner 'Oransay', Moore's sculptures for the Time-Life building in central London, and imaginative schemes for artworks to brighten up the schools of the post-war world. Directly or indirectly, the film suggests, it is the Arts Council which has created these new possibilities – and on the evidence the viewer is left in little doubt that the Council is essential for the future health of Britain's visual arts. In return for a very modest investment, the BBC and John Read presented the eight-year-old Council with a strong statement of its legitimacy.

In addition to its support of BBC titles, the Arts Council was taking the first steps towards co-producing other films for inclusion in what were now being described as the Art Films Tours. The 1952–53 *Annual Report* recorded that 'a colour film directed by Basil Wright and Adrian de Potier and based on the magnificent exhibition of drawings by Leonardo da Vinci held at Burlington House in the spring of 1952, was produced by a number of public and private guarantors, of which the Council was one' (1952–53: 35–6). *The Drawings of Leonardo da Vinci* was a singular success in the 1954–55 season, the total audience for which was estimated at 18,000, and the Council's investment of £500 in the £2,447 budget[6] was finally repaid when the film went into profit in 1960.

As the *Annual Reports* record, viewers were becoming more demanding or at least 'increasingly alive to the technical quality of art films' (1954–55: 37). The Council's regional offices received complaints about some of the 'musical backgrounds' and about untranslated commentaries in foreign languages. More colour films were demanded too, and 'there is, on occasion, some reluctance to include ... films which have already been seen on television' (ibid.). That year a representative of the Council made the journey to a meeting of the Fédération Internationale du Film d'Art in Amsterdam, where it became clear that Britain was the only western European country organising significant tours of art films. With an expenditure in 1954–55 of £1,914, 18 shillings and 2 pence, of which £999 was returned in income, the Council clearly felt that this was a highly appropriate use of public monies. The annual tours were organised for a further 25 years with, from the early 1960s onwards, artists' films and early computer animations shown alongside documentaries. But by the end of the 1970s costs for the art film tours had escalated without a proportionate rise in revenue. In 1979–80 expenditure was £25,906 against a return of £8,121, and the following year, as a new film distribution system was set up by the Arts Films Department at the Arts Council with Concord Films, the tours were discontinued. Yet the idea lived on with the 'Film-makers on Tour' scheme, launched in 1976, which subsidised personal presentations and performances by artists working with film and video.

First films from the Arts Council and the BFI

Early in 1955 the Council decided that it would no longer contribute funding to BBC films. Instead, it wished to use its limited resources for projects that it could control more directly. As the 1955–56 *Annual Report* also noted about the market in general, 'it is becoming increasingly difficult to obtain films of sufficiently high quality and with the proportion of colour work now demanded' (1955–56: 40). BBC films were produced, as they would be for a decade more, in glorious monochrome. The Council's first production, made in association with the BFI's Experimental Film Fund (see below), was *The Stained Glass at Fairford*, directed by Basil Wright and with a commentary by John Betjeman. In large part because of investment in this title (£3,000 in this year and a further £2,000 in the next), the Council's gross expenditure on art films during 1955–56 jumped from just under £2,000 to £4,591. The glowing new production was ready for screening at the Venice and Edinburgh film festivals of 1956 and was available for hire in both 16mm and 35mm. Ninety of the 137 performances of the art film tour included the film, although attendances that year were smaller than usual because, the Council believed, of petrol rationing. *The Stained Glass at Fairford* was also shown at London's Academy Cinema at 138 morning performances between November 1957 and February 1958 and then in the feature programme for a further three months.

THE STAINED GLASS AT FAIRFORD
script and commentary by John Betjeman
produced and directed by Basil Wright
an Arts Council Film made by Realist Film Unit
26 mins, 1956

We begin deep in rural England, with idyllic images of the Cotswold village of Fairford. The images radiate rich greens and reds; cameraman Adrian Jenkins is working with a glowing colour process. 'The glory of the town is the church', John Betjeman says on the soundtrack, 'and the glory of the church is its famous stained-glass windows.' The camera then picks out details of the exterior of St Mary's church before moving inside.

In a letter to the Director of Art at the Arts Council, Basil Wright argued passionately for a total budget of £5,000: 'I believe that it is possible to make a film of extraordinary importance and impact about the Fairford Glass... The story of Our Lord's ministration, passion and resurrection is here told in terms so aesthetically satisfying, so humanly understandable, and with such a richly satisfying picture of medieval life in Britain, that its effect on audiences in many parts of the world and not least in North America, could be more than striking.'[7]

Working for the Empire Tea Marketing Board, Wright visited what today is Sri Lanka in 1933 and the following year produced *The Song of Ceylon*, a sophisticated poetic collage of images and sounds. Nothing in the rest of his career as a director matches the originality of this, although *Waters of Time* (1951), made for his own company the Realist Film Unit about the Port of London, discovers a comparable poetry much closer to home. As noted, he worked with Adrian de Potier on *The Drawings of Leonardo da Vinci* (1953), for which he secured a funding guarantee from the Arts Council, and then with the eloquence evident in the above quote he persuaded the Council to start producing their own films.

The film also secured support from the BFI's Experimental Film Fund, though no acknowledgement of this appears in the credits of the copy held in the National Film and Television Archive. Wright was a stalwart of the Experimental Film Fund's committee from 1952 to 1965, and he continued to contribute to funding decisions when it became the BFI Production Board in 1966.

In *The Stained Glass at Fairford*, once the camera has moved into the church it concentrates solely on close-up images of the great windows. Initially it picks out details, snap-shots of medieval life, from the profusion of pictures. But as Betjeman reminds us: 'The whole purpose of the Fairford windows is that they are a complete scheme for teaching the Christian faith.' The 28 windows comprise England's only complete set of ecclesiastical stained glass to escape destruction by the iconoclasts of the Reformation and the Commonwealth. They were made around 1480 and were probably designed by the Antwerp painter and engraver Dirk Vellert. But the film has no interest in conventional art history; much like the films of Italian frescoes by Luciano Emmer, its concern is to draw out of these medieval images stories from the Bible.

Technically, the film is remarkable. In initial tests Wright and Jenkins realised how little light came through the dense colours of the windows. Because of this, their colour film stock required comparatively long exposures and so it became clear that the film needed to be shot in stop-motion, frame by frame. But it was impossible to employ a conventional rostrum camera, and so George Cooper – 'Realist's technical expert' – devised a kind of moveable, horizontal animation camera that could be installed on scaffolding platforms close to each section of the windows that were filmed. Apparently, 'the area covered in the shots so taken varied from some 20 feet by 15 feet to something as small as a packet of cigarettes' (Ellis 1977: 25).

Highlights of the Bible story are presented through details from the windows, although after an introduction with Adam and Eve we jump quickly to the Nativity and then the story of the Passion. Betjeman's descriptive commentary is complemented by a strong score from the young composer Julian Leigh and by Robert Donat's readings from the Authorised Version of the Bible. As the film takes us through the Crucifixion, the Ascension and then the spectacular images of the Last Judgement, a remarkable sense is developed of getting close to these images. Here is the camera offering access – in a way that the naked eye never can – to a supreme cycle of images from more than five centuries ago.

The Vision of William Blake, written and directed by Guy Brenton with advice from, among others, Sir Anthony Blunt, aimed to repeat the success of *The Stained Glass at Fairford*. Conceived to mark the 1957 bi-centenary of the radical poet's birth (but not actually appearing until the following year), the colour film was made by a special trust set up with funding from the EFF and the British Council and with a guarantee of £400 from the Arts Council. 'Numerous difficulties arose over the production', the 1957–58 *Annual Report* noted, and viewed today the film's relentless montage of images, poems, quotations from Blake's writings and narration is a tough watch.

Enthusiasm for initiating new productions waned after *The Vision of William Blake*, although in 1959 the Council's Art Department contributed £450 to *The*

Reclining Figure, a short about Henry Moore's commission for the UNESCO headquarters in Paris, with the British Council offering more than four times as much. Two years later the Council gave £100 to *La Cathédrale Engloutie*, with the balance coming from the Art Committee of the Welsh Arts Council (£400, half grant and half guarantee) and from Marlborough Fine Art, the gallery of the featured artist Ceri Richards. Marlborough Fine Art also invested £1,522 in *Francis Bacon: Paintings 1944–62*, produced by Samaritan Films in 1963, to which the Art Department gave £300 and for which it secured a loan from the National Film Finance Corporation of £2,000. Cannily, as the Council was increasingly seeking to do, it ensured that its contribution, even though less than one-tenth of the £3,822 budget, secured the copyright to the film. Judging by the remarks in the official review of each year contributed to the *Annual Reports*, the Art Department in these years no longer had the same focus on either the art film tours or new productions. After warmly positive reports across the decade, in 1959–60 the tours warranted only an acknowledgement that they had been maintained in collaboration with the British Film Institute, and in 1960–61, the *Report* noted simply: 'The Art Department ... supplies a service of art films to art galleries, schools and societies' (1960–61: 42). In 1963–64 and again the following year there is no mention at all in the *Report* of any art film activities outside the requisite lines in the formal accounts.

From the 1950s to the 1990s, apart from the Arts Council (and the broadcasters), the British Film Institute was the only significant source of public funding for documentary and experimental filmmaking. Initially, the BFI's very modest monies were distributed through the Experimental Film Fund, which in the mid-1960s expanded and mutated into the Production Board. Before and during the war the documentary movement of John Grierson, Paul Rotha and Basil Wright had produced films like *The Song of Ceylon* (1934), *Housing Problems* (1935) and *Night Mail* (1936) with a mix of state sponsorship and corporate support. But in the years after 1945 these filmmakers found it difficult to adapt, as the then Director of the BFI Denis Forman later reflected: 'The war had used their talents and they found it difficult to change gear' (in Sinclair 1995: 73). At the start of the 1950s the government withdrew its funding from the last state-sponsored documentary group, the Crown Film Unit, and the BFI had no funds to sustain ambitious productions.[8] New documentaries came only from a clutch of industrial film units, such as British Transport Films which produced shorts extolling the modern joys of railway travel. Just occasionally, as with John Piper's hosting of *An Artist Looks at Churches* (1959), such films could touch on the arts, invariably in conjunction with some uncontroversial aspect of Britain's heritage.

The Experimental Film Fund, established in 1952, was neither conceived nor operated as any kind of replacement for the Crown Film Unit and its like. Instead, it developed from a committee set up to identify experimental films for the BFI's Telekinema at the Festival of Britain. To maintain its activities after the Festival, this committee secured a modest grant of £12,500 from the Eady fund, the industry's tax on domestic box office receipts. In October 1953 the committee adopted a brief that stressed the envisaged focus on experiment.

According to this the EFF was 'to explore proposals to give the creative artist, such as the painter or the composer, much closer control over the design and production stages of a film' (in Ellis 1977: 21), as well as specifically to consider new uses for colour and different screen dimensions in filmmaking. Shortage of funds meant that the EFF would only invest in projects which had secured other sources of funding.

Experimental projects under all three headings were undertaken, but from the late 1950s the EFF increasingly contributed to low-budget 16mm documentaries and dramas. The shift was partly in response to the success of the documentary screenings between 1956 and 1959 organised by Lindsay Anderson, Karel Reisz and others under the banner of 'Free Cinema'. 'These films are free in the sense that their statements are personal', the group proclaimed, and six of the eleven Free Cinema films made in Britain had support from the EFF. As Stanley Reed, Director of the BFI, later explained of the fund, 'the revitalisation of the British film industry by the introduction of new talent and ideas was always the central concern' (1977: 130). Ken Russell's first film *Amelia and the Angel* (1958) was made with EFF funding, as were early productions by Jack Gold, Peter Watkins, Stephen Frears and Ridley Scott. Closer to the spirit of the Fund's founders was the early co-production with the Arts Council, noted above, on *The Drawings of Leonardo da Vinci*. 'Filmmakers in Britain have, in general, been slow to tackle the problems of art films', the authoritative *Sight and Sound* reported, 'and this film is one of the first major productions to be undertaken here … it is also interesting as showing the possibility of the forthright tradition of British documentary entering on a new phase – the documentary of aesthetics and ideas' (Hutchins 1954: 200).

As discussed earlier, the EFF subsequently collaborated with the Arts Council on *The Stained Glass at Fairford* and *The Vision of William Blake*, but the Fund also contributed to films about art in which the Council was not involved. These included, in addition to the Technicolor *Rowlandson's England* (1955) and *Coventry Cathedral* (1958), Dudley Shaw Ashton's *Figures in a Landscape* (1954), which places the sculptures of Barbara Hepworth against the Cornish settings that inspired them. 'We have here the work of an artist and a poet', the great Dutch documentarist Henri Storck enthused, 'a master of the most sensitive means of expression in the cinema … The film itself becomes a work of art' (in Ellis 1977: 24).[9] The Fund continued to operate with an additional £10,000 grant from the Gulbenkian Foundation and from revenue from the sale of films. Its administrative effectiveness, however, was constrained by the absence of a full-time staff member at the BFI, even if the hand-to-mouth operation may have had its benefits. The catalogue of EFF productions notes, for example, 'a record of five rolls of Kodrachrome (worth about £11) being given to Kenneth Anger to film the 1955 Francis Bacon exhibition at the Institute of Contemporary Arts' (in Ellis 1977: 22). Sadly, the resulting images remain elusive. Effectively dormant by 1960, the Fund was reinstated in 1966, thanks to the offices of Labour's Minister for the Arts Jennie Lee. Henceforth under the new name of the BFI Production Board it would have its own equipment and a full-time

Head of Production, Bruce Beresford. At the close of the 1960s the Production Board undertook the filming of a number of Arts Council films, including *Barbara Hepworth at the Tate* (1968) and *Lichtenstein in London* (1968), both of which were photographed and directed by Beresford, and *Picasso the Sculptor* (1968) and *Henry Moore at the Tate Gallery* (1970), which was shot by the feature film cinematographer Walter Lassally.

An area of the artist's retrospective from
Henry Moore at the Tate Gallery

A guardian angel for the arts

After a decade and more of struggle to secure adequate funds, in 1963 the Conservative government awarded the Arts Council an uplift of nearly half a million pounds, its largest increase to date. While the principle of subsidy to the arts was now established the terms of the debate were beginning to change. Tony Field, assistant finance director at the time, recalled much later that the rationale to justify government support which was to become dominant in later years was put in place at this point. Field remembered ruefully:

> In our discussions with [Treasury] officials, they wanted public accountability for money spent. We were vulnerable because [former Secretary-General Sir William Emrys] Williams based his claim for funds on the Quality of Life argument. I said that we must change the argument to get more funds. We must say that money spent on the Arts was not subsidy but investment ... I led the Arts Council into its sad future decline of quantifying the arts in material terms. (In Sinclair 1995: 129)

Harold Wilson's Labour Government, elected in 1964, quickly brought out its White Paper, *A Policy for the Arts*. The Council's grant-in-aid was significantly increased, with an unprecedented rise of 45 per cent for 1966–67 up to £5,700,000, and with a further 26 per cent rise for 1967–68. *A Policy for the Arts* also recognised a definition of culture more appropriate to the times: 'Diffusion of culture is now so much a part of life that there is no point at which it stops. Advertisements, buildings, books, motor-cars, radio and television, magazines, records, all can carry a cultural aspect and affect our lives for good or ill.'

Responsibility for the Council was shifted from the Treasury to the Department of Education and Science and Lord Goodman was appointed as Chairman. Goodman enjoyed an excellent working relationship with Jennie Lee, the first Minister for the Arts, who came to be seen as the new guardian angel for culture. 'My function is merely a permissive one', she told a journalist, outlining views remarkable for a politician then or now; 'I keep repeating that like a gramophone record ... permissive, permissive, permissive. I want simply to make living room for artists to work in' (in Hewison 1995: 141).

The historian Robert Hewison has explored how thinking on the left through the preceding decade, and particularly in the circles identified as the New Left after the Russian invasion of Hungary and Britain's failed Suez incursion in 1956, had focused the government's mind on arts policy. '*A Policy for the Arts*', he wrote, 'ushered in a new and expansive period for official support for the arts, coming as it did at a time of renewed cultural confidence (built on the radicalism of 1956) and apparent economic improvement' (1995: 122). In this expansive environment, the 1966 Arts Council film *Turner*, co-produced with the British Council, prompted internal changes to the financing of art films. As Tony Field, by then the Council's Accountant, noted in an internal minute in 1971:

[Finance Director James McRobert] and I became concerned [after *Turner*] that the Council's financial involvement in these films varied considerably; some involved investment in the production costs, another was made with a loan from the NFFC and all meant complicated production contracts and distribution agreements ... We agreed therefore that all further films should be made by the Arts Council meeting the production costs in full and the BFI should be responsible for the distribution of them.[10]

As a consequence the allocation for expenditure on art films jumped from £4,000 in 1966–67 to £19,735 in 1967–68. This in turn facilitated an increase in new productions: three films were completed in 1967, four in 1968, and three more in 1969. Reflecting the increase in the Department's activities in sponsoring art films, at the suggestion of Alan Bowness, in January 1967 the Art Panel set up a sub-committee for art films. Later that year it was decided 'in order to facili- tate the financial procedure for the production of art films'[11] that this committee should in fact be a sub-committee of the full Council, although funds continued to be allocated by the Art Department. The difference was perhaps mostly sig- nificant for the bureaucrats, but in Rodney Wilson's view the committee being responsible directly to the Council gave to art film production an enhanced place in the Council's thinking over the next two decades. Since a Council member was chairing the committee, it was perhaps more difficult for the Council to discontinue the activity. Kept in order by Sir William Coldstream, who was also Chairman of the BFI between 1964 and 1971, and supported by an Art Film Of- ficer, Hugh Evans (appointed after the Council approved the creation of the post in October 1967), the new committee decided that their task 'should be directed towards producing art films that were informative and educationally useful and which might not otherwise be made'.[12]

In something approaching a manifesto, the new committee used the 1968– 69 *Annual Report* to discuss both its intentions as well as its feelings about recent films supported by the Council. The Committee noted:

In the belief that better quality is achieved by filming directly from the original, we are taking the opportunity where appropriate of making films based on major exhibitions ... They are conceived more as aids to the teaching of art history and are based on the premise that it would be valuable now to have film records of such major events as the 1910 Post-Impressionist exhibition in London or the 1914 Armoury show in New York. (Arts Council of Great Britain 1968–69: 28)

The influential critic David Sylvester played a significant role here: he was a member of the Panel, he curated the Henry Moore show which was among the shows to be documented and he was directly involved in the filming of the Moore film and of *Lichtenstein in London*. The Lichtenstein film, *Barbara Hepworth at the Tate*, *Henry Moore at the Tate Gallery* and *Kinetics* (1970) do not, nearly forty years on, have perhaps quite the historical significance that Sylvester and the committee envisaged, but their different strategies towards documenting significant Arts Council exhibitions (discussed in Chapter 4) remain instructive. Intriguingly, Anthony Caro was approached about a film based on his exhibition at the Hayward Gallery, but according to the minutes of the sixth meeting of the Art Film Committee, 'after careful deliberation, Mr Caro had reluctantly decided that he did not want such a film to be made as he felt that his sculpture could not be adequately portrayed on film'.[13]

Distribution for these films was just beginning to be a concern, and responsibility was now exclusively contracted with the BFI. *The Pre-Raphaelite Revolt* (1967) enjoyed a run of 19 weeks at London's Curzon Cinema, although this was perhaps mostly to do with the feature which it was supporting, Luis Buñuel's suburban brothel fantasy *Belle du Jour* with Catherine Deneuve. 'Television', it was noted in the 1968–69 *Annual Report* more in hope than expectation, 'is another potential outlet of which fuller use could be made' (1968–69: 29). Yet even with all of this activity, the commitment to producing art films was at this point, as it remained, marginal in financial terms to the Arts Council's operations as a whole. In 1969–70 production expenditure totalled £17,898, which represented just 0.2 per cent of the Council's total budget of £8.2 million.

The traditional art form boundaries were challenged in the late 1960s as artists increasingly explored installation-based practice, unconventional performances and happenings, and participatory forms. The imprint of these ideas can be seen in two remarkable productions by James Scott: *Richard Hamilton* (1969) and the two-screen *The Great Ice-Cream Robbery* (1971). Both were made alongside Arts Council-organised exhibitions of Pop Art, the first to complement 'Pop Art Redefined' at the Council's new Hayward Gallery and the latter Claes Oldenberg's retrospective at the Tate Gallery. Their complex free-form approach and their culturally confrontational attitude brilliantly encapsulate much of the excitement and openness of this moment.

RICHARD HAMILTON

directed by James Scott in collaboration with Richard Hamilton
produced by Maya Film Production for Arts Council of Great Britain
25 mins, 1969

'I don't like art films…' says the artist's voice as the viewer is confronted in the first frames with a film leader and intercut fragments of newsreel. Starting from the very beginning, it is clear that nothing is going to be conventional about this film.

'We resist that kind of activity which is primarily concerned with the creation of style … What is needed is not a definition of meaningful imagery but the development of our perceptive potentialities to accept and utilise the continual enrichment of visual material.' Hamilton wrote this for the catalogue of 'This is Tomorrow', an exhibition at the Whitechapel Art Gallery held in the autumn of 1956. Hamilton's contribution to that show juxtaposed commercial imagery from consumer advertising with demonstrations of the ambiguities of perception. Much of his work since has brought together these concerns – and this exhilarating film collaboration with James Scott extends those interests.

Fragments of Hamilton's works are integrated with newsreel images and (non-synchronous) sounds, with magazine details, with movie trailers (includ-

Advertising imagery included in the dense visual mix of *Richard Hamilton*

ing in an 'Intermission' commercials for Coca-Cola, Marilyn Monroe in *The River of No Return* (1954) and the full-length, uninterrupted cinema advertisement for *The Desert Hawk* (1950)), with hand-drawn marks over photographs, and with self-referential elements of media, such as the artist's mouth filmed in close-up on a television screen. Hamilton offers a commentary on his works in an audio track, but this too is interrupted by 'found' sound that is layered, disrupted and concentrated. From this dense, disorienting and often very funny patchwork emerges something that is both an evocation on film of Hamilton's paintings and a perceptual analysis that avoids conventional explanation yet which reveals (some of) the ideas that shaped his art.

'The object was to involve the artist as much as possible in the process of making the film', James Scott said in an interview in 1973. 'I didn't want to stand outside an artist and show him as I saw him, but I wanted to use the film to appropriate what he did through painting. And I think the Hamilton film is the closest I came to that. Where I feel the film falls down is that I never really put Hamilton into perspective, he's treated so subjectively' (in Hodgson 1973).

The film was made in the year that Hamilton showed his 'Swingeing London 67' prints, along with beach scene paintings, at the Robert Fraser Gallery. One scene of the film replays and re-works newsreel coverage of the trial of Fraser and Mick Jagger for unlawful possession of drugs. A press photo of Jagger and Fraser handcuffed together in a police van was the source for the 'Swingeing London' series, and the cutting-up, colourising and layering of the newsreel precisely parallels Hamilton's working methods whilst at the same time rendering absurd the earnest words of the commentators.

Scott had been an art student at the Slade, after which made the film *Love's Presentation* (1966) with David Hockney working on etchings to illustrate poems by Constantine Cavafy, and then an Arts Council-backed film with R. B. Kitaj. Scott's father, the painter William Scott, then suggested a film about Hamilton. 'The need for a figurative element and the way people were looking at media of all kinds in a new way led me towards the so-called "pop" artists', he has said. 'And as a filmmaker, I could see that film could not only express these interests, but also complement them and add to them. Whereas, painting itself, especially that of a pure and abstract kind, could never be mediated through a film. That would have been a contradiction in terms.'[14]

Hamilton's fascination with Hollywood is revealed in the documentary through the visual analysis of a scene from the Douglas Sirk film *Shockproof* (1949), the source for his works 'Interiors I + II'; at the same time, with the inclusion of low-rent impersonations of Mr Universe and Miss World, the artist's aspiration to make a big-budget movie is parodied. Scott has recalled that his filmic influences at the time took in American 'B' movies and 'underground' cinema, including the works of Stan Brakhage and John Cassavetes' *Shadows* (1959) as well as a wide range of French, Italian and Japanese art-house film. With these cinematic references laid across Hamilton's artwork, treated with wit and yet at the same time demonstrating an appropriate respect for the artist's ideas, *Richard Hamilton* is an exemplary collaboration between artist and filmmaker, as much an extension of Hamilton's work as a critique of it, and one that remains delightful nearly forty years after its production.

It was an art film tour screening of *Richard Hamilton* that prompted Rodney Wilson to apply for the job of Art Film Officer in 1970. At the time Wilson was Assistant Lecturer in Drawing and Painting at Loughborough Polytechnic, where he had also established a film studies course. 'Here was this film about an artist which seemed to be using the language coming out of the European art cinema and underground film', Wilson recalled. 'When I got [to the Arts Council] I found that I'd inherited mostly some very, very traditional art history lectures made on 35mm film.' Starting with a position paper 'Concerning a Policy for Art Films' in March 1970,[15] he began to push the committee, and the Council's executive, towards new forms of production practice, increasingly working with cheaper, more flexible 16mm cameras and encouraging more assertive ideas of documentary authorship.

At its first meeting in January 1968 the Art Film Committee decided that as well as documentaries 'some money was to be set aside for films which might be considered an actual extension of the artists' work as a painter or sculptor'.[16] David Hall's *Vertical* (1970) and *The Link* (1970) by Derek Boshier were the first films supported in this context. In contrast to the arrangements for traditional documentaries, where the Council invested funds and held the copyright in the commissions, a principle was established early on that for artists' work the copyright in the works would remain with them. The 1968–69 *Annual Report* acknowledged that there might be trouble ahead from the BFI's response to this extension of the Council's territory: 'It should ... be pointed out that the Council in no way intends to duplicate or encroach on the facilities which the British Film Institute Production Board already provides' (1968–69: 29).

The Attenborough Enquiry

At the February 1971 meeting of the full Arts Council, Professor Lawrence Gowing, who also served as Chair of the Art Film Committee, raised for discussion the question of the Council's commitment to film. He prompted a searching debate carried on through a Committee of Enquiry chaired by the film director Richard Attenborough and a subsequent territorial spat with the British Film Institute. The ruminations of the Enquiry and the confidential report that it produced provide a historical snapshot of debates about film, funding and the technological future.

The Enquiry was established on 31 March 1971 and after five meetings and much discussion produced its report in July 1973. The members of the committee included Humphrey Burton, at that time an LWT executive, the director Karel Reisz and Colin Young, director of the recently established National Film School. Among those who made presentations to it was Mamoun Hassan, Head of the BFI Production Board. The committee's directive was

> ...to consider the extent to which film-making and video-recording should fall within the area of the Arts Council's responsibility, taking into account the funds likely to be available for the purpose and the present commercial and other existing organisations in this field (for example, the British Film Institute and National Film School)...[17]

Early drafts of the final report indicate that the committee felt that the central question which they were addressing was 'Should the Arts Council be making films?', although by the final report the main issue had become whether the basis for grants to filmmakers should be changed. The agreed draft was very positive about the Art Department's work to date with film, and in particular it praised the funding of films and videos made by artists as a direct extension of their work.

As far as the committee could see, the experimental and non-narrative artists' films, which explored 'the manipulation and use of film as a fine art medium',[18] were not supported by the BFI's Production Board, and this in itself was one important reason why the Council should 'embrace and encourage filmmaking as a fine art activity'.[19] An initial sum of £25,000 was proposed to support such work. The Council should also purchase video equipment to use for documenting artists' work and with which artists could experiment. Separately, it had become clear to the committee during its discussions that it was an anomaly that funding should be restricted to films about the visual arts only. This, it was recognised, had come about because of the historical location of the production initiative in the Art Department; the Enquiry recommended that films should be made across the range of the subject areas with which the Council dealt.

Keith Lucas, Director of the British Film Institute, was one of those to whom an early copy of the Report was sent. 'The main problem', he responded grumpily in a letter to Secretary-General Hugh Willatt, 'is that the Report seeks to define the Arts Council's recommended area of activity as that which is thought to be excluded by us ... we feel that this has led to assumptions about the kind of films that we support which are both too narrow and too rigid.'[20] The BFI did not want to be seen to be handing over responsibility for any area of filmmaking activity in Britain, but by this point the Production Board under Hassan had clearly begun to shift its priorities towards low-budget narrative feature films that were not being developed within the mainstream industry. Bill Douglas's *My Childhood* (1972) and *Winstanley* (1972), directed by Kevin Brownlow and Andrew Mollo, had been completed, and comparable 'art cinema' features were underway from, among others, Peter K. Smith and David Gladwell.

Seeking to head off a confrontation with the BFI, the Council directed that further consultations should be held, and revised recommendations were finally agreed. The main one was that the Council should 'expand film activities *as a recording medium* to all departments of the Council instead of restricting them to the Art Department'.[21] The italicised (and largely meaningless) phrase was not part of the Report's original wording. Similarly, a new drafting of the Report's second recommendation now encouraged the Council 'to assist artists wishing to use film as an extension or development of their work and others doing similar work where there is no conflict with the BFI's role as the institution grant-aided by the Government to support film as art'.[22] No prizes for spotting what might have been added here. Despite the changes, the institutional sparring in this recondite turf war continued to afflict relations between the Arts Council and the BFI for at least a further decade. Amalgamation of the department and the Production Board was considered by the respective officers in 1979, but it was determined that no savings would be made and centralisation of funding was undesirable. An uneasy truce was put in place.

The best of times

The Attenborough Report, together with the enhanced funding that came in its wake, imparted a new impetus to the Art Department's film activities. Responsibility for artists' films was given, in September 1972, to a sub-committee of the Art Film Committee. Over the next 25 years small but essential grants stimulated a major body of artists' film and video work, much of it nurtured to the screen by the department's officer David Curtis. The outline of the parallel history of the funding of artists' films has been admirably chronicled by Curtis elsewhere (2007), and the enhanced output supported by the main committee is in any case sufficiently extensive and diverse to occupy our attention.

In the early 1970s, with the Conservative Edward Heath as Prime Minister, Britain's economy spiralled slowly into crisis. Inflation and oil price rises were accompanied by increasing political unrest, including the miners' strikes of 1973 and 1974. Early in the decade the Arts Council's consensual relationship with the government was disrupted by the unsympathetic Conservative Arts Minister Lord Eccles, and by 1976 expansion in funding activities had been curbed by grant increases below the rate of inflation. The first effective moves were made towards a greater proportion of monies going to the regions, and the Regional Arts Associations were strengthened. Devolutionary policies were also boosted by the conclusions of a report funded by the Calouste Gulbenkian Foundation in 1976, 'Support for the arts in England and Wales'. Produced by Lord Redcliffe-Maud, this contained the startling assertion that 'large areas of Britain constitute a Third World of under-development and deprivation in all the arts and crafts'.

Yet despite the wider economic difficulties, the small corner of the Arts Council's operations responsible for art films enjoyed a productive period in the mid-1970s. A project started in 1973 involving the Tate Gallery and the BBC to create straightforward filmed interviews with elderly living artists got no further than a planned and then cancelled ('owing to extreme illness') shoot with David Jones. But in the same year ten films were completed, the highest production target attained to date, and not to be exceeded until the 15 titles made during 1978. The visual arts brief, which had been interpreted through an exclusive focus on painting and sculpture, was now widened to take in films on architecture, the first of which, co-funded by the BBC, was the robust portrait *Jim Stirling's Architecture* (1973) directed by Ron Parks. This was followed by an argumentative essay, based on Theo Crosby's analysis, about the failures of urban planning, *Playing the Environment Game* (1973), and by Mick Gold's *Building the Industrial Revolution* (1975). Design and the decorative arts also featured for the first time, in *Odeon Cavalcade* (1973) and Christopher Mason's elegant *England Home and Beauty* (1975), about domestic modernism in the 1930s, as well as in Michael Whyte's human study of two fairground sign-writers *Our Business is Fun*.

The Attenborough-endorsed extension of art form focus, which permitted and indeed encouraged Arts Council-funded films to explore subjects beyond the visual arts, led to dance being first featured in the frankly dreadful *Imprint* (1974), while very disparate forms of performance took centre-stage in *Outside In* (1973), *Performance Art* (1975) and *Love is Like a Violin* (1977). Music appeared in the output a little later, with poet Linton Kwesi Johnson in *Dread Beat and Blood* (1979) – which can also be seen as a key early film in the department's engagement with black culture – and *Music in Progress* (1978) with Mike Westbrook. Animation too was an important additional element in the mix, with *Lautrec* (1974), designed and directed by Geoff Dunbar, and Tony White's *Hokusai: An Animated Sketchbook* (1978). Funding was also made available for a group of oddball productions that with hindsight suggest that the Art Film Committee passed through a mercifully brief 'hippie' phase. *How Does it Feel?* (1976), directed by Mick Csaky, is an earnest R. D. Laing-influenced 'celebration of sensory experience and enhanced awareness' (Arts Council of Great Britain 1977: 76). Jeremy Marre's *Tao: The Way and its Power* (1976) takes in the then-fashionable oracle book *I Ching*, while *Reflection* (1977) explores artist Keith

Critchlow's nutty numerology. Each of these productions carries traces of mysticism and more, as does *A Trilogy on Tibet* (1978) for which the committee provided finishing funds.

In the wake of increased production through the decade came enhanced expectations about distribution. When he arrived in 1970, according to Rodney Wilson, 'there was a sense that exposing people to the arts through film was a good thing, but there was no sense of quantification, and it was not really a problem if only a few people saw it either. You could make things where there was no obvious way of reaching an audience. It was an activity worth doing for its own sake was more the reasoning than anything else.' This attitude changed fundamentally in the 1970s. The Arts Council took back responsibility for distribution from the BFI and the 1973–74 *Annual Report* noted approvingly that *Mantegna: The Triumph of Caesar* had run for 16 weeks at London's Academy Cinema, and that the BBC had transmitted four Arts Council films during the year. Iranian television – this was just before the fall of the Shah – purchased 27 Arts Council films. The following year, the *Annual Report* recorded that support for sales had been stepped up with increased staff. *Lautrec* was a particularly popular title, and in retrospect Rodney Wilson singles it out as probably the most commercially successful of all Arts Council productions. It won the coveted short film Grand Prix at Cannes and was widely broadcast internationally.

The department appointed a Sales Executive in 1976 ('a production system without a distribution system to match it was a futile exercise', the Art Film Committee minuted at its meeting on 5 March 1976) and the following year, now acknowledging the plural of arts in its title, it produced its first printed catalogue. The introduction included a statement of purpose:

> The Arts Films Committee does not commission films to be made on specific subjects in accordance with a determined set of criteria: it selects from ideas submitted to it. Far from attempting to create a house style the committee deliberately chooses projects that show originality in the filmic approach to their subjects … With greater emphasis on the way the film was to be made, the role of the director has become more important. (Arts Council of Great Britain 1977: 5)

The films supported by the Arts Film Committee through the 1970s and later, including a number discussed in detail in Chapter 4, benefited from, and significantly contributed to, a disparate but vital and energetic independent film culture that was emerging in Britain. Shaped in part by the 'underground' culture of the late 1960s, the new understandings of film's potential were also catalysed by the political events of 1968, including the anti-Vietnam War protests and student radicalism at the Hornsey College of Art and elsewhere. Also important was Marxist theory commingled with developing ideas of cultural studies, and these ideas filtered into filmmaking via magazines including *New Left Review* and, from 1975 onwards, the influential film journal *Screen*. Different models were conceived for the production of 16mm films, and these were often linked with new conceptions of distribution and exhibition. The modernist avant-garde coalesced around the London Film-makers' Co-operative, but elsewhere collectives were formed with understandings of film grounded in social practice, in which distribution and exhibition, the development of audiences and the discussion of new ways to understand and use film, were all important. The Other Cinema distributed the films of Jean-Luc Godard, American independents and cinema from Latin America. Cinema Action, formed in 1968, toured film screenings to pubs and factories, while Amber Films began their decades-long project of working closely with communities on Tyneside.

The politics of much of this work involved not only engaging with topics such as the Republican struggle in Ireland or, soon, the emerging feminist movement, but also, and crucially, with developing new film languages. To collapse into near-caricature many complex arguments, the dominant languages of mainstream drama and documentary were seen to express in their very structures the hegemonic politics of class oppression, patriarchy and colonialism. The expression of alternative, oppositional ideas demanded the development of new film forms, new ideas of narrative and new ways of addressing audiences. Film form was as politically charged as the content of films, and a number of collectives, including Film Work Group with *Justine* (1976) and Berwick Street Collective in *Nightcleaners* (1976), explored how to create alternative film languages. The Director of the BFI Production Board, Peter Sainsbury, attempted to summarise the concerns of those engaged with this new 'independent cinema':

> Independent cinema … came to include a variety of aesthetic practices defined against, or as subversive of narrative form, as developments within film of the tenets, preoccupations and innovations of other arts media under a rubric of modernism, as engagements with a number of differently conceived political programmes, as involvement with developing theories of film aesthetics and permutations of all of these as well as the pre-existent forms of documentary representation and narrative fiction. (In Ellis 1977: 12)

Work funded by the Arts Council did not embrace with strands of this new film culture as wholeheartedly as did that created by the BFI Production Board. Rather than work with the new collectives, the Art Film Committee backed ideas from a new generation of directors who were now coming out of film courses set up around 1970. In particular, graduates from the film course at the Royal College of Art were central to Arts Council-supported films through the decade, including the filmmakers Ed Bennett, Mick Csaky, Mick Gold, Keith Griffiths, Lawrence Moore, Phil Mulloy, Thaddeus O'Sullivan and Michael Whyte. The director Jana Bokova and producer Michael Radford, who worked together on *Love is Like a Violin*, were among the first graduates from the National Film School.

Documentaries from these filmmakers also began to tackle more directly questions of representation, as in Ed Bennett's *Hogarth* (1976), with its central concern for the circulation and consumption of the artist's engravings, and Peter Wyeth's *The Third Front* (1978; discussed more fully in Chapter 4), which sought to create a contemporary film form to express the ideas of the radical Weimar Republic theatre director Erwin Piscator. Leftist politics too were written through films that chose to develop conventional forms, such as Alister Hallum's drama about William Morris, *News from Nowhere* (1978); Phil Mulloy's *Give Us This Day*, about Robert Tressell, author of the classic study of trade unionism *The Ragged Trousered Philanthropist*; and *Käthe Kollwitz* (1981), a film by Ron Orders, Norbert Bunge and Arpad Bondy. During the 1970s Ron Orders was part of the collective Liberation Films, which had developed from the Camden branch of the Vietnam Solidarity Campaign. The group organised screenings and discussions and moved into production, making among other films *Fly a Flag for Poplar* (1975), a political portrait of the East End borough, to which the Production Board contributed finishing monies, and, for the Arts Council, *Morgan's Wall* (1978). *Morgan's Wall* documented the work of community-based mural painters in London, but as publicity materials for the production underlined, the film 'avoids any attempt to reproduce the works as completed "art" – inviting the viewer instead to discover the murals for themselves, in the open, in their proper context'. As Rodney Wilson recalled, '*Morgan's Wall* documented the kind of art which people from the establishment on the Committee dismissed as propaganda. But hang on a minute, if we're doing things that won't get made otherwise, this is absolutely legitimate. That was actually an argument that went on until I had a couple of very bruising encounters with [Chairman of the Arts Council] William Rees-Mogg'.

'Politics are inextricably woven into the fabric of the arts', declared 'The Arts and the People', a 1977 policy document produced by the Labour government in power between 1974 and 1979. But Labour's politics had little time for cultural theory and questions of representation. Hugh Jenkins, the Arts Minister under Harold Wilson, was a former official of the actors' trade union Equity, and he pushed to have the Arts Council opened up to greater democratic control. After two years he admitted defeat, worn down by what he called the 'snobocracy', the still-powerful combination of establishment figures and 'high art' advocates at the core of the Council. Things could only get worse. 'With the arrival of the 1979 Conservative Government', Robert Hewison has recorded, 'a demoralised Arts Council was confronted by the values of the new enterprise culture … The Arts Council began the Thatcher years at a low ebb … An internal investigation by a former Council vice-chairman, Jeremy Hutchinson QC, reported in 1979 that there was a widespread feeling of malaise, and uncertainty about the Arts Council's function' (1995: 245). Margaret Thatcher's new administration held the grant-in-aid below the rate of inflation, and in an agenda-setting speech at a conference of the Regional Arts Association in November 1979, the Arts Minister Norman St John-Stevas gave the arts community a sense of its future: 'We must look to the private sector for new sources of money. That's where the possibilities for the future lie.' In December 1980 the Council responded by withdrawing funding entirely, and without warning, from 41 companies.

Monies for Arts Films activities see-sawed during this period, with the 1979–80 *Annual Report* recording that, 'Notwithstanding the immense strides made in the Council's support for arts films from the most modest beginnings at the end of the 1960s, 1979/80 was an exceptionally difficult year in this area, primarily because the rate of inflation in film far outstripped both general inflation and the increase in the Arts Council's total grant-in-aid' (1979–80: 27). However, the following year the allocation was increased to £500,000 and twelve arts documentaries were put into production. This was the point at which the art film tours were finally wound up, to be replaced in part by a 16mm film rental distribution library of 200 titles (including non-Arts Council films[23]) organised with Concord Films. But a new dawn, for distribution and much else, was visible on the horizon: along with the cuts and the enterprise culture the Thatcher government, in the autumn of 1980, received Royal Assent for the Broadcasting Act that brought into being the fourth television channel.

DREAD BEAT AND BLOOD
directed and produced by Franco Rosso
50 mins, 1979

Dread Beat and Blood is a portrait of the poet Linton Kwesi Johnson and – three decades on from its making – a still-powerful document about politics in Britain during the 1970s. Far more than most arts documentaries of the time (or indeed since) the film has the sense of a close-up experience of (parts of) its subject's life. Expertly shot in *vérité* style by cameraman Ivan Strasberg and edited by David Hope with an edgy immediacy and without narration, it follows Johnson in the streets of Brixton, going to a poetry reading and talking with school kids in Tulse Hill. Throughout there are substantial extracts of poetry in performance, often backed by a strong reggae beat.

'Poetry isn't only what you read in books', Johnson says, acknowledging the strong influence on his work of reggae artists and of the culture of soundsystems. The film's title comes from Johnson's first album, credited to Poet and the Roots. His innovative fusing of poetry and music found a wide audience.

The film's conceit of having its subject interviewed by a middle-class, white radio presenter facilitates the sketching of basic background information about Johnson. He speaks of his closeness to Jamaica and of his need to write in Jamaican Creole because standard English is too dead, too sterile to record the experiences of blacks in Britain. He talks too of the political struggles against the Far Right, and against Thatcher's government. The 'sus' laws (under which people could be stopped and searched on suspicion of being involved in a crime) are a particular focus for resistance, seen by Johnson and by many blacks as racist in intent and application.

Director Franco Rosso came to London from Italy when he was nine, and the experience of meeting hostility and distrust as an immigrant made him empathise with Johnson and with black experience at the time. Working on this documentary led to his feature film *Babylon* (1980), funded by the National Film Finance Corporation, which features Aswad guitarist Brinsley Forde and chronicles a group of black kids following a reggae soundsystem. His later documentaries included a profile of singer Ian Dury and films with the New York artists Tim Rollins and Kids of Survival and the Greek-Cypriot painter John Kiki.

Linton Kwesi Johnson in the recording booth
in *Dread Beat and Blood*

The later part of *Dread Beat and Blood* brings the political struggle of the time into sharp focus with scenes of street fighting. Police action is shown as intemperate, violent – and the disturbances as a response to this. These sequences make a vivid, direct impact, especially when accompanied by Johnson's music. This is not the measured 'objective' view of Britain familiar from BBC news broadcasts, and there is little doubt whose side the film is on. At the close of the sequence, an elderly English woman picks her way through the debris-strewn streets after the clashes. The shot has an iconic quality, a crystallisation of one aspect of England in the late 1970s.

Towards the end of the film, Johnson participates in a protest march in Bradford. With its characteristic raw immediacy, the film takes up and extends the poet's rallying call for urgent political change.

Channel 4 changes the rules

During the 1970s, in addition to sales to broadcasters abroad, a handful of the Arts Council-funded films were sold to the BBC. A number of these productions were directed by filmmakers who worked for the BBC in other contexts at other times, including Peter K. Smith's *Edward Burra* (1973) and Barrie Gavin's *One Foot in Eden* (1978). In 1979 *Dread Beat and Blood*, the profile of Linton Kwesi Johnson containing forthright criticism of police treatment of young blacks, became a minor *cause célèbre* when its planned screening in the *Omnibus* strand fell foul of the regulations governing broadcasting in the run-up to the hastily-called May election. Press coverage of the film's 'banning' ensured that when the film was finally shown after Margaret Thatcher's victory it secured one of the highest ratings for the series. But while the BBC was prepared to purchase films, it refused to enter into co-productions with the Arts Council[24] and Rodney Wilson found it impossible to build a consistent relationship with the BBC.[25]

Jeremy Isaacs started work as Channel 4's Chief Executive in January 1981, and among the stream of hopeful visitors to his temporary offices at the Independent Broadcasting Authority near Harrods was Rodney Wilson. Like many others, he was hoping to work with the new structures (outlined in Chapter 2) for the support of independent productions. 'I went to see Jeremy looking for co-production', Wilson remembered; 'I took Steve Dwoskin's Brandt film (which became *Shadows from Light*), Nick May's John Cooper Clarke (*Ten Years in an Open-necked Shirt*), and a third, and he just said I'll give you so much, I want seven years, it's a deal. And after all the problems with the BBC, it was just wonderful.' It was particularly welcome given that this coincided with cuts within the Arts Council which reduced the annual Arts Films Allocation for 1982–83 by more than fifty per cent to just £150,000. As the Director of Art Joanna Drew explained to the 55th meeting of the Arts Films Committee, 'faced with inadequate grant, the Council had decided to cut its own activities and directly controlled expenditure as opposed to the strategy the previous year when a number of clients had been cut off'.[26] From this point on, as Wilson later acknowledged in remarks to the seventh meeting of the Film, Video and Broadcasting Advisory Panel on 4 November 1987, 'the priorities of the Arts Films Production Committee were television broadcast and increased co-funding arrangements with TV'.

This initial arrangement with Channel 4 developed into annual support for the Council's documentaries at a level of around £150,000. Commissioning editors could bid internally for these monies to enhance their budgets if they committed to projects from independent producers that would be co-funded by the Arts Council. The key relationship was with the channel's arts' commissioner Michael Kustow, but projects were also made with Rod Stoneman of the channel's Independent Film and Video department. The channel's education editor. Naomi Sargant also collaborated, including on a charming oral history of the Staffordshire pottery painters, *Pottery Ladies* (1985). The Arts Council *Annual Report* for 1982–83 celebrated the new relationship: 'The advent of Channel 4 has opened a new outlet for the showing of films to a large audience. The Arts Council films *The Pantomime Dame* and *Give Us This Day* were screened shortly after the new channel opened' (1982–83: 21). Other successful projects included a quartet of films about experimental filmmakers, profiles of Jeff Keen, Margaret Tait and Malcolm Le Grice and a collective portrait of women working with film associated with the distributor Circles; in his memoir of his time at Channel 4, Jeremy Isaacs wrote of these, 'all were unlike the normal run of television: austere, abstruse, complex, combative these films gave us, as art should, to pause and consider [sic]' (1989: 173).

As Channel 4 and its satellite independent producers flourished, the Arts Council was increasingly embattled, assailed by doubts in Whitehall about its effectiveness and organisation, and curtailed by static funding levels. 'As Culture Minister it is, I am afraid, also my duty to administer something of a culture shock', opined Lord Gowrie in 1985, clearly relishing his words; 'The party is not over, but the limits of hospitality have been reached. From now on, central government funding will remain broadly level in real terms.'[27] The Council's response was the document *The Glory of the Garden*, which acknowledged, 'for some years the Council has been stuck in a groove' and carried further the decentralising moves already underway (Arts Council of Great Britain 1985: 1). In his introduction to this document, Chairman Rees-Mogg seemed unenthusiastic about the potential of television and related audio-visual technology: 'The arts, human, creative, inspiring, individual, warm, alive, provide a natural healing to

[the] sense of depersonalisation, and the appreciation of beauty can transcend the moon-like chill of an electronic world' (1985: 5).

The enterprise values of Thatcherism began to percolate throughout an often-resistant and suspicious arts world, while the Council did its best to promote sponsorship, marketing and business efficiency. Like all other public bodies, the Arts Council now had to prove that it was providing 'value for money' and performance indicators began to assume crucial importance. 'The Economic Importance of the Arts in Britain', a 1988 report from the Gulbenkian Foundation and the Office of Arts and Libraries, underlined the new focus: 'It is an important conclusion of this report that the arts sector is capable of great expansion which will benefit the economy. It is an even more significant fact that this will increase the artistic experience of the British people for present and future generations' (Myerscough 1988: 164). One fall-out of this new focus was the production of a tape for arts organisations explaining why marketing is really a very good thing: *Marketing the Arts* (1988), which is now most interesting as an earnest trace of the concerns of its time, carries the singular credit, 'Initiated and funded by the Minister for the Arts, Richard Luce MP'.

In 1986, as part of a drive to increase effectiveness, and along with new departments for Marketing and Planning, the Arts Council brought into being the new Film, Video and Broadcasting department (FVB).[28] Responsibilities for arts films and artists' film and video that had been sustained for thirty years within the Art Department were transferred to the entity which for the first time had direct control of its budget. An advisory panel for the department was put in place, together with a committee charged with the selection of projects to fund (with a sub-committee continuing to focus on artists' films), although in the new structure as in the old, Rodney Wilson exercised significant influence over what was funded. 'There were things that interested me and I could advance those', he remembered; 'But it was never that straightforward; there were things that I wanted to do that I just could not get past the committee. On the other hand, the committee gave me cover if there was a political row over a film'. Throughout the 1970s, the Arts Films Committee was composed of eight to ten members, and then slightly fewer after the mid-1980s when the Production Committee was set up as part of the FVB. At times, they were joined by representatives such as the director of the British Council films department or a member of the Arts Council's finance department. Among the members were curators and art historians including Alan Bowness, Lawrence Gowing, Norbert Lynton, Eric Rowan, Dawn Ades and Lisa Tickner. Filmmakers and film educators were also well-represented with Colin Young, Edgar Anstey, Ian Christie, Barry Gavin, Stuart Hood and Elizabeth Wood among those contributing to decisions, as well as Mark Kidel, John Akomfrah, Yugesh Walia, Laura Mulvey, Judy Marle and Jane Thorburn. The chair of the Art Film Committee was initially drawn from the membership of the Council, with the role being taken by Anthony Quinton, David Astor, Lady Vaisey and Brian Young, but again once the department had been established it was mostly independent producers who presided, including Mike Dibb, Margaret Williams and Ed Bennett.

Once the FVB was a full department, it acquired a Panel to oversee its operations and review strategy. This had a wider catchment including Clare Mulholland, who was a particularly effective chair, the radio critic Gillian Reynolds, broadcasters Cresta Norris and Paul Corley, director Mick Csaky and for some years also, me. Selection, both for the Committee and for the Panel, was something of an *ad hoc* process, with people being invited to serve for two years with the possibility of a further two. 'Wisely, many people I would have loved to be involved didn't want anything to do with committees', Rodney Wilson recalled; 'Finding good people was difficult and names for possibles came from a variety of sources: the existing committee membership, the other departments of the Arts Council, from the BFI, FVB staff and so on.'

In the mid-1980s it was acknowledged within the Council that opportunities for the new department were constrained by the funding environment but television seemed to offer great potential. 'In particular', the 1985–86 *Annual Report* noted, 'the focus on co-productions with broadcasters that had developed since the arrival of Channel 4 seemed to address the Council's new business priorities' (1985–86: 18). From the committee minutes and production output in the mid-1980s it is clear that television co-production became a determining factor in decisions about which projects received funding. It is not too fanciful to see those 'new business priorities' driving the choice of an unremarkable albeit lavish film like *Jessye Norman – Singer* (1986), made by Malachite Productions as a co-production with the BBC strand *Omnibus*. The subject is starry but the filmic treatment is penny-plain standard; this is an admiring profile of the kind that had often been made before by the BBC from its own funds. The principle that the Council's money should support 'difference' was here elbowed aside by the allure of a mainstream BBC1 slot and the expectation of revenues from international sales (it was eventually sold to more than 15 countries). From the same time, *Jacob Epstein* (1987) is a conventional biography of the sculptor presumably interesting to FVB because it was the first co-production with an ITV company, in this case Central.

'Everywhere the accountants were taking over', Robert Hewison wrote in a pertinent analysis of the cultural community throughout the land, 'and the values of the market had penetrated so deeply that it seemed impossible, or futile, to discuss the merits of the arts in anything but economic terms' (1995: 285).

PICTURING DERRY
directed by Dave Fox and Sylvia Stevens; produced by David Glyn
a Faction Films production for the Arts Council in association
with Channel 4
50 mins, 1985

The camera sits high above a table, looking straight down. Spread across the surface are photographs of the war in Ireland. An anonymous female voice establishes the premise of the film: 'There is a war of pictures and it's about the way places are seen and remembered through those pictures.'

Picturing Derry is a combative analysis of photographs from the frontline in Derry. Its sympathies are Republican, but its approach has a measured intelligence and questioning attitude that makes its final declaration all the more effective. The filmmakers want to understand how the meanings of a photograph are constructed, how images circulate and are used, and how they can be weapons as well as ways of resisting aggression, consolations for loss as well as ways for the marginal to speak, the invisible to be shown.

The film talks with a range of those who have made images in Derry since the start of the Troubles in 1969. Among those who discuss their practice are local photojournalist Willie Carson, Fleet Street photographer Clive Limpkin and photojournalist Terry Fincher. Derry photographer Eamonn Melaugh vividly recalls the events of Bloody Sunday in 1972 while artist Willie Doherty speaks thoughtfully about his juxtapositions of words across his images: 'I think of these works as my first act of resistance.' Both the London-based picture editor Bryn Campbell and the photojournalist Ian Berry discuss the limits of what photographers can do in war – and also how newspapers can inflect and distort the meaning of an image.

Contrasted with the professionals are young people who took part in a community photography project organised with Camerawork. Their concern is to create positive alternatives to the dominant media images. More chillingly, an anonymous photographer working for the RUC speaks about the images he takes as evidence of incidents. 'We're not in the business of dramatising things. What we want is a photograph which shows the individual persons actually engaged in, say, street disorder situations or whatever.'

The film's final testimony comes from Eileen Robson who leafs through the kind of album in which everyone (at least in a pre-digital time) kept their family snaps. But hers includes a photograph of the shirt worn by her 15-year-old son when he was shot dead on Bloody Sunday; successive snapshots of a board counting the days of Bobby Sands' hunger strike; and alongside images of

Long-shot of the city from *Picturing Derry*

weddings and birthdays there is a letter from prison, written by a hunger striker on toilet paper and smuggled out to her. She is unequivocal about her admiration for those she sees as martyrs to the Republican cause. 'It takes a special kind of man to die like that', she says of the hunger strikers.

The film has a human dimension and, even when the makers clearly disagree with the views being expressed, people are listened to and respected. At the same time, the images have an intellectual, self-referential quality that accepts and makes explicit the directors' awareness of their own roles in a process that continues.

A concluding dialogue about photography poses the questions that have been implicit in the film to that point. 'Can you get away from a photography that is based on spying or based on the laws of the market?'; 'But don't you think in places like Derry it's possible to see the beginnings of a new photography, where people who started with family photographs found themselves forced to go beyond this to record what was happening outside?' The questions are asked at a time long before the profound changes prompted by ubiquitous digital cameras and mobiles, and by Flickr and YouTube. Yet they are questions that remain relevant and resonant.

Collaborations with Channel 4, including those showcased in a seven-film season of Arts Council films that started in June 1986 with the distinctive *Wall of Light* (1986), can be seen in retrospect to be more distinguished than the first BBC and ITV films and closer to the department's declared aims. *Picturing Derry* (1985) is an intelligent hard-edged film about photography in Northern Ireland and *Vita Futurista* (1987) is a stimulating and richly illustrated study of the early twentieth-century art movement. The FVB also began to draw other Arts Council departments into working with television, as in the poetry series made with Border Television, *Word of Mouth* (1990), which – in a first for the organisation – was jointly financed with the Literature department.

The success of the relationship with Channel 4, as well as the new opportunities with the BBC and ITV opened up by the 25 per cent quota of production from independents, was encouraging the FVB department to envisage a rosy future. The 1986–87 *Annual Report* suggested that the Council 'intends to develop a truly international role in the field of broadcasting. The Panel is taking the first, inevitably tentative steps towards defining that role' (1986–87: 18). *Steve Reich – A New Musical Language* (1987), directed by Margaret Williams, for example, was co-financed with WNET Thirteen in New York, and European monies were attracted to other productions. In a separate initiative, an 'investment funding' allocation of £50,000 per annum was set aside for the department's sales office to contribute 'top up' funding to projects (such as *Barcelona with Robert Hughes* (1992), made as an independent production for BBC1, and *The Soul of Stax* (1995)) in return for distribution rights, but in retrospect it is hard to divine what artistic vision drove these financing decisions.

As FVB was looking hopefully abroad, its public support for film and video culture in Britain was complemented by not only the BFI and its Production Board (by now fully launched on a policy of supporting 'culturally significant' feature films like Peter Greenaway's *A Draughtsman's Contract* (1982) and Sally Potter's *The Gold Diggers* (1983)) but also by the Regional Arts Associations (RAA). In line with the devolutionary forces that would gather momentum in the next decade the twelve RAAs, with budgets from the Arts Council, BFI and others including even regional television companies, were beginning to develop facilities and training centres across the country. Yet the achievements here were mixed, as an internal memo from the Film Officers Group of the RAAs acknowledged in 1985–86: 'the quality, success and level of commitment in RAA work has been uneven'.

Film accounted for only a small part of the RAA's total budgets, just as at the centre expenditure on Film, Video and Broadcasting remained modest, especially when compared to the Council's global budget. In 1988 FVB consumed just 0.55 per cent of the overall Arts Council budget, and in 1990–91 the funds allocated for arts film production totalled £409,000. By way of context to give a sense of broadcast budgets in the 1980s, five years before this the budget for a single six-part Channel 4 series about the visual arts, shot in the United States, Europe and Australia, was £630,000. A Council discussion document produced in March 1991 highlighted another problem for the FVB:

> There is a strong and almost inevitable tendency for the maintenance of an internal funding status quo at a time of limited real increases in arts funding. In spite of the setting up of the Film, Video and Broadcasting department, it remains marginal to the Council's other departments. (Arts Council of Great Britain 1991b: 25)

Identity and diversity

At the start of the 1980s a public cultural policy was offered by the Greater London Council (GLC) as an articulate alternative to the expressed consensual attitudes of the Arts Council. The GLC, together with six metropolitan county councils, had been created by the Heath government in 1972, and as alternative centres of political power they were deeply resented by the Conservatives under Margaret Thatcher. She eventually succeeded in abolishing them in 1986, leaving among other legacies a significant shortfall in arts funding in London, Manchester, Liverpool and elsewhere, which the Treasury was coerced to make good. With a left-wing Labour group controlling the GLC from 1981 onwards, the council's Arts and Recreation Committee chaired by Tony Banks developed a broad vision of the arts (encompassing photography, video and community radio) with a radical agenda. 'We could', Banks said, 'use the arts as a medium for a political message' (in Bianchini 1987: 105). At the heart of the GLC's politics was a strong agenda for social inclusion, working with and promoting the concerns and interests of groups emerging from the fragmenting social unity of post-war Britain: blacks and Asians, feminists, those who identified themselves as gay or lesbian. The GLC's budget for 'ethnic arts', for example, grew from £400,000 in 1982–83 to £2 million pounds in 1985–86.

Campaigns for racial equality, feminism and gay rights began to develop during the 1960s, but it was only in the following decade that they came to occupy a central place in politics, social debate and indeed culture. In the tiny circle with which this chapter is primarily concerned – the arts films funded by the Arts Council – it is striking that more than fifty films had been directed by men before one was entrusted to a woman: Jana Bokova's reflective and subtle study of a theatre group working with the elderly in Hammersmith, *Love is Like a Vio-*

lin. The work of Barbara Hepworth was featured in the 1968 documentation of her Tate Gallery retrospective and the eccentric film *Rolanda Polonsky Sculptor* (1971) also had a female focus. But it was really only with *Bridget Riley* (1979), made by director David Thompson, and then *Käthe Kollwitz*, that women artists take centre stage in Arts Council films.

In the 1980s the Council supported a range of films that centrally engaged questions of feminism and feminist practice. *Frida Kahlo & Tina Modotti* (1983) is a deceptively simple, schematic study of two feminist art history icons. *Margaret Tait* (1983) and *Seeing for Ourselves* (1983) explore contrasted aspects of feminist film production, while Judith Williamson's *A Sign is a Fine Investment* (1983) is a rich analysis of the language of advertising and the absence from its world of images of work. More conventional and less explicitly engaged projects were then developed with Channel 4, including Margaret Williams' sympathetic and moving profile *Elizabeth Maconchy* (1985), the quiet oral history of the women who worked in the Midlands ceramics industry, *Pottery Ladies* and then *Five Women Painters* (1989), with profiles of Winifred Nicholson, Dora Carrington, Laura Knight, Nina Hamnett and – the only artist of the quintet who was still alive at the time – Eileen Agar. With the BBC's *Bookmark* strand, forty years after the publication of *The Second Sex, Daughters of de Beauvoir* (1989) wove the life of Simone de Beauvoir together with the testimonies of women who had been profoundly influenced by her work, including the professional writers Kate Millett, Eva Figes and Marge Piercy.

Feminism and race, and their distinct but related re-thinkings of representation, were fundamental to developing independent film practices in Britain throughout the 1980s. As this outline of the Arts Council's initially cautious but far from negligible engagement with women's film suggests, there was an overlap with, but hardly an enthusiastic embrace of, these cultural forces by the funding body. The BFI Production Board proved to be more explicitly engaged, supporting work as diverse as *Riddles of the Sphinx* (1976) by Laura Mulvey and Peter Wollen, Jane Jackson's *Angel in the House* (1979) and Sue Clayton and Jonathan Curling's *Song of the Shirt* (1979), as well as the influential explorations of racial identity, Horace Ové's *Pressure* (1974) and Menelik Shabazz's *Burning an Illusion* (1981). 'At that time there were some pretty reactionary attitudes about', Rodney Wilson recalled; 'I don't think it is a misrepresentation to say that arts films suffered because within the Arts Council we were seen as too radical. Look at *Grove Music* [1981; a film about black music and the Notting Hill Carnival]. There was talk about banning the film but we said it would cause a bigger fuss. The film provoked a nasty row and a real onslaught – how dare these people criticise the education system, how dare we facilitate this subversion? In the end – and it was the only time this happened – a disclaimer had to be put on the front of the film saying something about these aren't the Arts Council's views.'

Questions of race and identity were central to many films made in the context of black independent film in the 1980s, including Black Audio Film Collective's *Handsworth Songs* (1986) and Sankofa's *The Passion of Remembrance* (1986). Production practice during this decade was often organised through filmmaking collectives, including Sankofa, Ceddo and Black Audio Film Collective, and much of this generation of work was made without Arts Council support. But as issues associated with the arts of ethnic minorities became more important to the cultural community, arts film funding assumed an important place in developing new black and Asian talent and in producing films by, among others, Isaac Julien, who with FVB support made *The Darker Side of Black* (1994), an analysis of homophobia and the traces of the violence of slavery in reggae, raga, hip-hop and dance hall music in Jamaica and worldwide, and *Frantz Fanon: Black Skin, White Mask* (1995).

Black arts had struggled to achieve mainstream recognition even into the 1970s. 'Although the 1976 report "The Arts Britain Ignores", on the arts of ethnic minorities in Britain, has had some influence on attitudes', Robert Hutchison wrote, 'such arts activities are still, all too readily, dismissed as amateur, even when part-timers and full-timers, amateurs and professionals, are working together' (1982: 55). But in the following decade, in part because of the profile and demonstrable achievements made possible by GLC funding, the issue became more urgent; in 1988–89 the Council, under William Rees-Mogg, agreed to make an additional allocation of half a million pounds specifically for black arts. Around the same time the Arts Council instituted a cultural diversity project which committed a minimum of four per cent of funding from each department to work by non-white practitioners.

By this point films like *Dread Beat and Blood* and *Grove Music* had explored aspects of black culture, but relatively few FVB productions had been made by black or Asian filmmakers. The financing each year of a small number of comparatively high-budget films made it difficult for the department to develop new non-white talent. As a response, the Black Arts Video Project was established with an annual budget of £100,000 committed to non-broadcast videos on black arts subjects and issues. The initiative was focused on encouraging new talent and on 'training through doing'. The first productions, chosen from an open submission process, were completed in 1989 and the scheme ran until 1996. Comparable concerns motivated the three years of the co-funded *Synchro* (1993–95), a collaboration with the ITV company Carlton. This gave black directors the opportunity to make their first short arts documentaries for television, which were transmitted in the Midlands region in compilation programmes.

The Black Arts Video Project, initially overseen by Juliet McKoen and then by James van der Pool, provided small grants of £5,000 for first-time directors as well as more significant contributions of £12,500 to a handful of more ambitious projects. Directors with an articulate and expressive vision were encouraged, and the scheme produced a broad diversity of short films, made without either the expectations or the inevitable constraints of a broadcast transmission. Among the significant filmmakers supported by the scheme were Pratibha Parmar (*Memory Pictures* (1989), about the photographer Sunil Gupta), Kwesi Owusu (a drama about an African musician and his girlfriend, *Love in a Cold Climate* (1990)) and Alnoor Dewshi (*Latifah and Himli's Nomadic Uncle* (1992), with wry musings about modern nomads). By 1995, both the filmmakers and those responsible for the scheme aspired to make more ambitious films, and Channel 4 agreed to co-finance a series of culturally diverse films about music, *Black Tracks* (1996). The channel, however, scattered the films around the schedule and they made only a modest impact, as did one further iteration of the idea, three films about black arts under the title *Moving Image* (1997), again produced with Channel 4. These programmes, and the Black Arts Video Project, are strands in a British film culture in the 1990s that increasingly saw black and Asian filmmakers enter the industry, but in contexts where the political imperatives of the 1980s had to a degree dissipated.

One further FVB response to questions of diversity in the 1990s was the modest Disability Arts Project, which provided production funds to films put forward through the Regional Arts Boards. FVB also supported a number of other works that confronted questions of disability, including two compelling dance films, *The Fall* (1990) and *Outside In* (1994) as well as *Behind the Eye* (1991), a documentary co-financed with Channel 4 about three visually-impaired painters.

Television times

By the mid-1980s, building on the success of the Channel 4 collaborations, the Arts Council's moving image work, as already chronicled, was primarily focused on partnerships with broadcasters. Television offered the potential of co-funding but, most importantly, it delivered access to substantial and quantifiable audiences. Yet the broadcasters, then as well as both before and since, were more than a touch disdainful of the Arts Council. Channel 4's Director of Programmes Liz Forgan betrayed something of the broadcasters' attitudes in a dismissive contribution to the *Guardian* in 1992: '...if we run arts coverage on TV as a branch of the Arts Council we shall get lousy TV and do no good to the arts' (1992: 23).

Even from reading the run of Arts Council *Annual Reports*, it is clear that throughout the Council's history television has been a perennial problem. Perhaps the Council made a mis-step right at the start when in the early 1950s, as noted above, it contributed funding to a number of BBC documentaries. After two years, however, it withdrew from the arrangement to use its film funds for the Council's own production of *The Stained Glass at Fairford*. Writing in March 1955 to the film's director Basil Wright, the Director of Art felt that no great damage had been done: 'We have thrashed things out with the BBC and all is peace and friendliness: all they are anxious about is that we shall allow them to show the film when it is made!'[29] Across the following fifty years there was to be no truly effective, large-scale arts media partnership involving the Council and any of the broadcasters, and in particular no strategic partnership with the BBC. Channel 4 supported productions in the 1980s and in the 1990s the co-financed performance strands worked well with the BBC. But these remained modest, localised achievements, falling somewhat short of what the Chairman envisaged in 1970: 'We have, perhaps for the first time, made really effective progress in our liaison with other great media of communication', Lord Goodman enthused in his 'Introduction' to the 1969–70 *Annual Report*;

Our relationship with the BBC – always friendly – has become much closer ...
We have now established a permanent Committee, in part designed to investigate the possibilities of using the material that we assemble for presentation to the massive audiences that they command. (1969–70: 6)

Permanent the new committee might have been, but no further mention of this initiative is made in the *Annual Reports* that follow.

The Council started fretting publicly about television as early as the mid-1950s. 'Whatever the consequences of TV may prove to be', speculated the anonymous writer of the 'Introduction' to the 1954–55 *Annual Report*, 'those who care about the arts, both the optimists and the pessimists, have every reason to make common cause in the face of these momentous transformations of social habit' (1954–55: 8). At that point, however, she or he felt the need to stress that television would not replace direct experience of the arts. Even if the treasures of the National Gallery could be brought into people's homes, on bigger screens and in full colour, then in the writer's view that would hardly be an argument for closing the gallery and keeping the pictures in stacks in a TV studio.

From the earliest years the Council wanted broadcasting both to recognise its responsibility towards supporting the arts and also to act as a potent means of dissemination. 'If TV is to be accepted ... as the major mode of diffusion in the future', the 1959–60 *Annual Report* reflected, 'those who command its resources must be aware of their duty to replenish the arts they consume on the screen' (1959–60: 11). Remarkably (at least from the perspective of a more parsimonious moment in the early twenty-first century) the new ITV companies, perhaps aware that their first years' operations would soon be judged in the Pilkington Report, in 1958 and subsequent years collectively donated £100,000 to the arts and sciences. Two advisers from the Arts Council helped them distribute the monies; grants included £1,000 each from ATV to the Friends of the Tate and Whitechapel Art Gallery, while Granada gave £200 each to eight regional theatres. The money was welcome, of course, but what the Council and its clients really wanted, and indeed still crave, was television's attention. The 1976–77 *Annual Report*, for example, celebrated the positive impact that an *Omnibus* programme about Terry Frost had had on the size of the audience for an exhibition of the artist's work at the Serpentine Gallery in London. Frustratingly, however, others seemed to the writer not entirely to welcome, on the rare occasions when it was extended, television's embrace: 'A number of artists see themselves in conflict with the purposes and aims of our society and this perhaps contributes to their lack of rapport with a large section of the public' (1976–77: 32).

In 1972 the Council contributed to a working party to investigate the possibility of more broadcasts of performances by Arts Council-supported companies on Independent Television and more reflection of the arts in programmes. Five years later the *Report of the Committee on the Future of Broadcasting* chaired by Lord Annan was categorical about what should happen:

We recommend that the broadcasting organisations approach the Arts Council with a view to sharing the cost of recording for broadcasting, particularly on the fourth channel, and for other showings, some of the work of the major opera, ballet and subsidised music and drama companies. (Annan 1977: 327)

But even when Lord Rees-Mogg was both Chairman of the Arts Council and Vice-Chairman of the BBC in the mid-1980s, he found it impossible to bring the two bodies together in any meaningful way. As Andrew Sinclair noted: 'He found that the officers of the Corporation did not want to go "out of house". They had their own pride and practices and problems' (1995: 301). The broadcasters, although they would never state their position quite so baldly, felt that they alone would decide which productions and activities to record or discuss, and that they were sufficiently well-funded not to need the comparatively small funds (and consequent obligations) that might be on offer from the Council. 'More than any other art form department', FVB recognised in the 1988–89 *Annual Report*, 'we function within a context over which we have little direct control – the broadcasting system. In the world of broadcasting we are small players...' (1988–89: 14).

The shadow minister for the arts, Mark Fisher, noted the disjunction between the broadcasters and the Council in 1992. 'In view of [their] mutual interests', he wrote in the *Guardian*, 'it is surprising that there is almost no formal liaison between the Arts Council and the BBC and ITV companies ... Separate stances present no difficulties when broadcasting's commissions, or coverage, of the arts are increasing.' But Fisher saw the problems ahead: '...the growing challenge from satellite TV and the recession together threaten a period of instability which could drive the main terrestrial channels away from a diversity of quality programmes, including the arts' (1992: 23).

The most focused attempt, at least prior to the fundamental changes at the Arts Council in the mid-2000s, to develop a strategic approach to the Council working with television developed in the run-up to the 1990 Broadcasting White Paper. The Council issued a three-year plan for 1989–91 in the 'Introduction' to which it stated,

> ...in the past the main benefits of public subsidy of the arts have gone to the many thousands who attend theatre, dance, music and opera performances and art exhibitions or who read literature. The Arts Council aims to extend these benefits to the millions who watch television and video by encouraging broadcasters to record and transmit the best of British arts. (Arts Council of Great Britain 1989: 2)

Plans for this were developed from 1987 onwards, with Rodney Wilson reporting to the eighth meeting of the Arts Films Production Committee on 22 January 1988 that a feasibility study for an 'off shore' company was being developed. This company, he said, 'would televise performances of major Arts Council clients, was expected to have an annual turnover of at least £1 million a year and would be profit-making within 5 years.'

In line with these aspirations, in February 1989 the Council issued the document 'Bringing the Best to the Most' as its response to the consultation process towards the planned White Paper. The Council proposed establishing an independent agency, Arts Council Television (ACTV), 'to produce high quality programming derived from the work of the Arts Council and the Regional Arts Authority clients' (1989: 5). Consultants Coopers & Lybrand were engaged to explore the idea's feasibility, but it was acknowledged that

> this development can only work within a sympathetic and encouraging environment. We have therefore evolved a twin-track argument; that the Government should ensure encouragement for arts programming throughout the system, while also contributing to our new agency as a means of increasing competition, choice and quality. (1989)

The Coopers & Lybrand Report presented in September 1989 offered a rosy vision of the possibilities, suggesting that ACTV would generate and marshal programme ideas; provide funding but also attract sponsorship; sell programmes and videos; and promote events and raise the profile of arts programmes. 'The company will, in the long run, have a major role as a deal maker', the report suggested. 'However, in the first few years it will be necessary to invest in programmes originated by broadcasting companies to gain profile and to generate revenues'. It was recognised that 'access to airtime and appropriate scheduling will be difficult', but otherwise nothing in the report addressed the fundamental problems in collaborating with broadcasters that the Council and FVB had faced elsewhere.

More in hope than expectation, the Council suggested that the Government might consider taking a small percentage of the levy on revenue of commercial television to contribute to the financing of ACTV, the costs of which were estimated at £1.5 million annually. This agency's funds would be available to all broadcasters for arts programming. In retrospect, the proposal as a whole can be seen to echo those of the Public Service Broadcasting Council, put forward in the July 1986 *Report of the committee on financing the BBC*, chaired by Professor Alan Peacock, to the discussions about 'top-slicing' in the discussions around the BBC licence fee in the mid-2000s, and Ofcom's suggested Public Service Publisher idea floated at the same time (these propositions are discussed further in Chapter 5).

Successive sets of circumstances conspired against ACTV and ensured that it progressed no further than the reports of consultants. The first was political. Rodney Wilson recalled discussions in the run-up to the 1990 Broadcasting Act with the political adviser to the then Home Secretary Douglas Hurd. It eventually became clear that the idea could not be supported by the Government. The perception was that this could be 'the stray thread' that would unravel the Home Office's arguments for a quality threshold that the new ITV franchisees would have to meet. If the central fund was in place, it could be seen as an admission that the new system, proposed in the White Paper, would not on its own sustain arts programming, and therefore quality television of all kinds. Such an implication was not acceptable to the Government.

A re-thought ACTV was kept alive within the Arts Council (and would resurface in the mid-1990s), but the FVB discussion document prepared in March 1991 for the Council's 'National Arts and Media Strategy' related why the idea was not realised subsequently. Funding had been provisionally allocated by the Office of Arts and Libraries as part of an initiative to support arts partnerships with private monies called the Incentive Funding Scheme:

> The sudden termination of the Scheme and the transfer of funds into Enhancement Funding [for existing revenue-funded companies] presents an interesting case-study of the marginalisation of arts broadcasting at a time of financial stringency. The Arts Council's principal revenue clients, suffering from growing accumulated deficits succeeded in putting enough pressure on their political masters to arrange a diversion of funds. The Incentive Funding Scheme was the victim. New developments such as ACTV, which gain only limited support from an arts lobby consumed by its immediate concern for the revenue-funded performing arts, are ultimately easier contenders for sacrificial lambs than established clients. (Arts Council of Great Britain 1991b: 25)

Like so many internal papers this had no credited author, but clearly for the person who drafted this document the wider arts world reaped what was sown by a few self-interested lobbyists short-sightedly protecting their theatres or dance companies. Little wonder that arts broadcasting, on terrestrial channels at least, faced a bleak future.

SOUND ON FILM
a BBC/Arts Council co-production, with certain films also co-produced with NPS
various producers and lengths, 1995–97

Films with modern and contemporary composers is one of the strengths of the work funded by the Arts Council Arts Films Committee, and they also supported occasional productions about classical music such as *Like as the Lute* (1979), a film with Anthony Rooley and Emma Kirkby about the Renaissance instrument and its precursor, the Arabic oud. In the 1980s support was given to measured (and in archival terms invaluable) profiles of modernist composers, including Anna Ambrose's *Alan Bush: A Life* (1983), an absorbing study of Bush's left-wing politics and his compositions. Margaret Williams made a thoughtful, admiring tribute to *Elizabeth Maconchy* (1985) as well as *Steve Reich – A New Musical Language*, while Philippe Regniez's *Cornelius Cardew 1936–1981* (1986) seeks to understand the meeting points of Cardew's radical politics and truly experimental music. Each of these films includes generous sections of performance.

Contemporary music is also explored in the Arts Council collection in *Lol Coxhill's Frog Dance* (1985); *Clocks of the Midnight Hours* (1988) with immaculate filming of the work of sculptor and performer Max Eastley; *Gavin Bryars* (1988) directed by David Rowan; and *Great Noises that Fill the Air* (1989), with the Bow Gamelan Ensemble. Then there is the oddball *Pastorale* (1982), a study of a music theatre piece by Trevor Wishart that too often has the air of self-parody.

After the success of *Dance for the Camera*, the BBC and the Arts Council collaborated again on three series of films, *Sound on Film*, that this time paired a creative director with a contemporary composer. Early films backed by the Arts Films Committee had commissioned contemporary composers to complement montages of paintings with bold scores, as Elizabeth Lutyens had for *Francis Bacon: Paintings 1944–62*. Also, the BBC had made an earlier (and unconnected) *Sound on Film* series in 1988 with imaginative film and video shorts involving music by Steve Martland, Michael Finnissy, Mark Anthony-Turnage and Judith Weir. The films in the first quartet of the new run were produced as half-hours, but none of them justified this length, and the second and third series were commissioned at 15 minutes.

The first batch of *Sound on Film* produced in 1995 includes an absurdity: *Passover* directed by Jamil Dehlavi with music by Paco Peña. This elaborate Spanish tale features (of course) flamenco and bull fighting but also circumcision, goat sacrifice, a severed ear, naked lovers, a crucifixion and a lot more besides. More measured is Mike Grigsby's documentary collaboration with composer Paul Englishby, *Pictures on the Piano*, about the importance of music in the lives of a Blackpool entertainer, a piano teacher and others. Grigsby and Englishby also worked together for the third *Sound on Film* series on *The Score* (1998) about the rituals of a Saturday afternoon football game.

The majority of the second and third season (1999) films aspire to be short chamber operas, often with narratives involving strong elements of fantasy. In *1 in a Million* director Terry Braun and composer Django Bates create a tale about the recently-introduced National Lottery while *Hello Dolly Goodbye Mummy* is a contemporary fairytale about a wicked grandmother to a score by Judith Weir. *Market of the Dead*, like *Hello Dolly Goodbye Mummy* directed by Margaret Williams (who later made the film operas *Powder Her Face* (1999), *Owen Wingrave* (2001) and *Armida* (2004) for Channel 4), is a fantastical drama about two orphans from the Caribbean. Similarly dotty is *SOS Songs of Seduction*, music by Jenni Roditi and direction by Jane Thorburn, which is set in a capsized boat with a trapped yachtswoman communing with finmen. The land of make-believe is also the setting for *Something to Make You Sing*, written and directed by Tim Rolt with music by John Woolrich and a clutch of sinister Heath Robinson-like contraptions.

The two stand-out successes of the series share certain characteristics. Neither uses conventional narrative and both draw on documentary traditions rather than drama or opera. *Gift* is set to music by Ulf Langheinrich that is derived from the sounds of industry in the Wolfen Bitterfeld in the former GDR.

This is a blasted landscape with monstrous cranes and mining machines, and director Mike Stubbs discovers a succession of extraordinary images. He focuses on the industry and the scars that it has left on the land, but he also brings in the local agriculture and, crucially, the workers of the area.

Blight, directed and edited by John Smith with a score by Jocelyn Pook, is located closer to home, on the demolition and building sites of the M11

Link Road in East London. Smith and Pook focus on the houses being knocked down in the name of progress, and on the fragmented memories of those who lived there. The noises of the workers, of creaking timbers and crashing walls, are woven together with evocative spoken phrases suggesting a sense of community and rootedness. One particularly effective moment has (unseen) people speaking their ages and birthdates over a shot of tree rings exposed after a tree has been cut down.

The noises of demolition contribute to *Sound on Film: Blight*

After the closure of the Arts Council Film, Video and Broadcasting department in 1999, the BBC made one further *Sound on Film* series, co-producing with Dutch broadcaster NPS. Feature film directors Werner Herzog, Hal Hartley, the Brothers Quay and Nicolas Roeg were paired with, respectively, music by composers John Tavener, Louis Andriessen, Karlheinz Stockhausen and Adrian Utley of Portishead. The Quay Brothers/Stockhausen collaboration is particularly powerful and original.

A new era

Presenting the keynote speech, 'The Odd Couple?', to the Arts Council's conference about the arts and broadcasting at Brighton in October 1992, the director Richard Eyre said that 'in spite of the coy question mark tagged on at the end' the title struck him as 'diffident, defensive and defeatist'. He ended his address with a rallying call ('If things are to change, we must force the changes ourselves') but by the end of the decade all of those involved with arts and mainstream television were, if not diffident, unquestionably defensive and defeatist. One thread of what was to come was that by 2000 the Arts Council had shut down it arts films production activities and the Film, Video and Broadcasting department had transmuted into Broadcasting and New Media.

As outlined in Chapter 2, by 1990 it was recognised that broadcasting was facing profound change, although in a world still largely ignorant of the Internet no one knew how fast and fundamental the transformations would be. Although it had been providing a range of channels since 1984, Sky was launched fully in 1989, and the following year it was permitted to take over its rival in the provision of satellite channels, British Satellite Broadcasting. A fifth terrestrial service was envisaged in the 1990 Broadcasting Act, but a multi-channel world of satellite and cable was now imminent, and the challenge that the new channels would pose to the old was to be the defining force in television well into the next century.

A further aspect of increasing consumer choice was the growth of home video which was explored by FVB as a possible extension of its activities. The Art Film Committee first considered what was then called 'cassette television' in 1970, when 'members expressed the view that the Arts Council should wait until the market exists before committing itself to a major financial initiative.'[30] In the early 1980s, Video Access Libraries were established with Arts Council support in arts centres and libraries, including the ICA in London, the Midland Group in Nottingham, Sheffield Central Library and elsewhere. Users could access tapes from the Arts Council and from other sources on site, but the scheme proved too expensive to sustain. In 1990, a second attempt at video access was piloted by FVB, this time centred on loans from public libraries; 24 titles were initially released, followed by a further twelve, but pressures on funding for libraries (which were expected to purchase the loan copies) meant that returns were modest.[31] An additional problem was that rights in the paintings, performances, music and more included in many of the films had been cleared only for broadcast and non-theatrical screenings. Additional clearances for home video demanded greater resources than could be made available.

For the Arts Council in general, the first years of the 1990s were focused on responding to a hostile report delivered in September 1989 to the Office of Arts and Libraries by Richard Wilding. Wilding was especially critical of the costly and inefficient duplication of effort between the Arts Council and the Regional Arts Associations, and he proposed a radical new devolutionary structure. Delegated responsibilities would now be administered by ten Regional Arts Boards (RABs) which began operating in October 1991. By April 1994 the Arts Council itself had direct oversight of only the four main national opera and theatre companies and 125 annual revenue clients. A sympathetic Chief Secretary to the Treasury, David Mellor, was successful in winning significant extra funding for the arts, but in return the Council had to respond to the Wilding Report's criticism of its 'lack of any longer-term vision' for the arts.[32] With the RABs, the BFI and the Crafts Council, the Council co-ordinated the extensive (and, at a cost of around £500,000, expensive) consultation process 'Towards a National Strategy for the Arts and the Media' and, in 1993, published the glossy policy document *A Creative Future: The way forward for the arts, crafts and media in England*. It was, as Robert Hewison commented, 'long on good intentions, but lacked any proposals as to how they might be achieved structurally, and any estimate of what they might cost ... [The report] was ignored by the Department of National Heritage' (1995: 263).

'In the view of many of the broadcasters consulted', *A Creative Future* discovered, 'the arts still have too low a priority on radio and television' (Arts Council of Great Britain 1993: 141). Certainly that now appeared to be the case at Channel 4 where the new Chief Executive, Michael Grade – who had arrived in early 1990 – marginalised a number of productions (including, in mid-run, my second series, organised in collaboration with the Arts Council, of the artists' video series *Ghosts in the Machine*) and summarily cancelled the funding partnership with the Arts Council that had been established by Jeremy Isaacs. With the RABs increasingly seeking their own partnerships with the regional television companies, the focus for the Arts Council's arts films productions quickly switched from Channel 4 and the regional companies to the BBC. Following on from the provisions of the 1990 Broadcasting Act directing it to take 25 per cent of its output from independent producers, the BBC was now actively looking for partners. A number of individual documentaries from independents were co-funded with the BBC, including *Joseph Cornell: Worlds in a Box* (1991), *Sickert's London* (1992) and *Vanishing Rembrandts* (1992) with Simon Schama, but by mid-decade the opportunities for such productions were diminishing rapidly. 'Television scheduling has changed completely', Wilson pointed out in 'Working with Television', a presentation to a May 1996 conference at the Royal Institution in London, 'and one of the real difficulties is finding a home for an independently-generated one-off idea ... Projects simply get lost and don't happen because there is no home.'

At the same time there was a sense of a loss of confidence in projects being submitted for Arts Council co-funding. 'How can the quality of ideas and projects submitted ... be improved?' the Arts Films Production Committee debated at its 23rd meeting on 18 March 1992. Joint commissioning schemes with broadcasters seemed to be one answer, for what could still squeeze into the schedule were short films, which were valued for filling the gaps in a BBC2 schedule that increasingly needed to establish common starting times for programmes, say at 10pm, with BBC1. So what quickly clicked for both the BBC and the Arts Council were collaborations on series of creative shorts. *Dance for the Camera* (1993–2003) was the most successful of these series (and is discussed in a Chapter 2 sidebar), and it became the model for the later initiatives *Sound on Film* (1995–97) and *Picture House* (1995) (the former discussed above; the latter also the subject of a Chapter 2 sidebar). Each film therefore occupied only a short time in the television schedule and so the possibility of experiment and risk-taking, both in form and talent, was greater. At the time, the BBC schedules welcomed short films to enliven the mix – two other examples are films by first-time directors, *10 x 10* (1989–2000) and the elegant architectural essays *Building Sights* (1988–96) – although by the end of the decade the increasing demands of keeping viewers hooked to a particular channel squeezed out such slots.

'Channel 4 hadn't actually commissioned a dance film for two or three years and didn't look set to be doing so', Rodney Wilson remembered about the moment at which *Dance for the Camera* started. 'Dance as it was commonly thought of in television terms was fairly shaky as an element of BBC Music and Arts and we were really looking for a framework that would ensure that there was any dance at all, at least in addition to ballet, on television.' So support from FVB was also justified by the sense that without the Arts Council's support both dance and film with a strong sense of 'difference' from mainstream programming would not reach the television screen.

By the mid-1990s developing digital technologies were being explored by artists in FVB co-commissioning schemes like *Experimenta* (1995) and the Hi-Tech Fund, both with Channel 4 and the latter with a number of Soho-based facilities companies. But the continuation of broadcast support for these, like the performance strands and imaginative commissioning schemes for artists such as *One Minute TV* with BBC2's *The Late Show*, was always subject to changes in commissioners, who were replaced rather more frequently within television than at FVB. A notable new project begun in 1995–96 was the commissioning of the first *Expanding Pictures* (1997) series, a collaboration with BBC2 and the Combined Arts Department (discussed in a Chapter 4 sidebar). Nine films were produced with performance artists or groups working closely with filmmakers. Less successful, however, was the series *Oil on Canvas* (1997), a well-funded but dull BBC Continuing Education series entered into by FVB when the BBC cancelled plans for the third *Sound on Film* series.

In all of this work the Arts Council was – rightly – a demanding partner, stipulating practices that were standard in the arts community but alien to the closed practices of broadcasters. 'We are very interested in the transparency of process', Wilson told the 'Working With Television' meeting in 1996; 'We like to involve advisers in the selection process, we want to bring artists closer to the filmmaking process, and we want to encourage diversity in the origination and expression of ideas. We want to be able to deliver Arts Council corporate policies in crucial areas like cultural diversity and disability and we are keen to promote opportunities for new talents. We are very interested in innovation, pushing the form, and we want all this to happen in the shape of an extremely good television programme.'

TWO MELONS AND A STINKING FISH
produced, directed and filmed by Vanessa Engle
an Illuminations production for BBC and the Arts Council of England
48 mins, 1996

One of the things you notice is that the artist Damien Hirst and other inter-viewees, as well as the film's subject Sarah Lucas, sometimes have the film-ing microphone casually, carelessly pinned to the front of their T-shirts. But by that point such a detail only underlines how informal and, at least for its time, unconventional is this profile made by Vanessa Engle. (The film was made for the BBC series I was editing, *Tx.*)

Shot by the director on a lightweight camcorder, and edited by Sabrina Burnard, the film has the light touch, the humour, the apparent carelessness and the casual craft that distinguishes Lucas's art. The raw camerawork is done without lights and is mostly hand-held, and the sound quality is, at best, variable. (As the film's executive producer, I was accused at an internal BBC Programme Review meeting of sloppiness and the programme of being sim-ply amateurish.) There is no narration, no developing narrative, no participants apart from artists and friends, and no music apart from fragments accompanying a couple of animations. These quirky loops are by the artist and then boyfriend of Sarah Lucas, Angus Fairhurst, and like the other elements they are thrown without explanation into the mix.

What we are offered is a sequence of scenes: Sarah making sculptures like 'Two Fried Eggs and a Kebab' (1992) and 'Au Naturel' (1994) that now, a decade later, are recognised as central to British art of the time; Sarah at a White Cube opening of a show by her friend Cerith Wyn Evans; Sarah and Angus Fairhurst, in a brief throwaway shot, enacting a *pièta* on a park bench. Then there are the posed portrait shots of Sarah, each without commentary, which show her in backstreet urban locations: the artist clasping a large, glistening fish; the artist standing beneath the panty-clad crotch of a pair of legs advertising a Frankfurt sex shop; the artist standing outside a locked men's toilet.

The cast list alone indicates that, in its unconcerned way, the film is a central document in the history of the group that was, for a time, successfully marketed as the yBas (Young British Artists). Gary Hume (credited as 'Ex-boyfriend and artist') is here, as well as Hirst, artists Jake and Dinos Chapman (they smirk silently, standing by one of their disfigured mannequins), art dealer Jay Jopling, New York gallerist Barbara Gladstone and Sarah's friend Tracey Emin. Some of them attempt to say why they like Sarah's art, but just as constitutive of the film's meanings are Hume's parodies of Sarah's art, like two tomatoes and a small carrot in his crotch, or two paint tins and a wilting paint brush.

The film also visits key locations of the yBas' 1990s world: the original White Cube, but also the Atlantic Bar and Grill and the fish restaurant Whitebait. Sarah's character, together with the texture of the times, comes through as, fighting a hang-over, she relates a story about drinking all night, going round as day breaks to someone's house (she assumes we will know whose it is) and the drunken crowd – apart from Angus – signing their names in the spots on a Damien Hirst artwork. Throughout, people at parties are asked to provide a question for Sarah ('Are you mad?'; 'Which is your favourite football team?'), only some of which she answers on camera. Arsenal is one (perhaps inevitable) answer.

The film is lewd – Gregor Muir says of a 1991 photowork by Lucas, 'You can smell her minge from here' – and (seemingly) honest about the market: Sarah Lucas tries to remember how much some recent works sold for. 'About £6,000' is her sense of what Charles Saatchi paid for a piece. Remarkably few films about artists are anywhere near as salacious, or as straightforward about money.

Throughout the early 1990s BBC2's *The Late Show* documented the rise of the yBas, and for the opening of BBC Four Vanessa Engle revisited this story in *Britart* (2002), a gossipy three-part series about the lives, loves and financial success of many of those featured here. That *Two Melons and a Stinking Fish*, along with its rushes, was such a central source for that retrospective project underlines that this is a document made from inside the scene as it was unfolding. Its authenticity (as well as its contrived knowingness) is comparable to Ken Russell's portrait of the art scene of 1962, *Pop Goes the Easel*.

To see the force of the comparison, take a look at the finely-crafted films in the BBC/Arts Council series *Date with an Artist* (1998). This series is a contrived and often uneasy attempt to bring the yBas into a television format derived, a couple of generations on, from lifestyle programming like *Changing Rooms*. In each 15-minute segment, an artist is paired with someone for whom they must make an artwork to hang in their home or – in Chris Ofili's case – in an inmate's cell in Wormwood Scrubs. The polished filming records encounters, usually accompanied by bouncy 'indie rock' from the time, that feel forced, and the artists are confined in a polite package that only the Chapman brothers, making a mannequin for Justine Frischmann from Britpop band Elastica, manage (hilariously) to subvert. Among the strengths of *Two Melons and a Stinking Fish* are its avoidance of bouncy backing tracks and the fact that it contains not a single polite frame.

Endgame: the Lottery and a legacy

The National Lottery Act of October 1993 presaged and to a large degree prompted the most fundamental changes to arts funding since the start of the Arts Council nearly half a century before. The Council was appointed as one of five distributors to good causes of a percentage of profits from this state casino. Tickets first went on sale in November 1994 and over the next seven years the Arts Councils across the United Kingdom disbursed over 21,000 grants worth nearly £1.8 billion. Initially, this money was restricted by statutory requirements to capital funding, a provision introduced to protect existing revenue funding for the arts. As a consequence of the commitment to capital projects, numerous new venues were opened and run-down facilities refurbished. One accounting anomaly, however, was that feature films could be legally defined as capital projects – and the Arts Council, despite having next-to-no experience in this field, took responsibility for investing in movie production.

At the same time as it was beginning to deal with lottery monies the Council had to adjust to two decisions of John Major's new government. One was the creation of a mega-ministry responsible for the arts and much more, the Department of National Heritage (DNH); the other was the ruling that, from April 1994, the Arts Councils of Scotland and Wales should be granted their independence. The smaller Arts Council of England would also have to be leaner, as Michael Portillo, Chief Secretary at the Treasury, set the increases in grant-in-aid for 1993–94 and 1994–95 at below the rate of inflation. Within the Arts Council, FVB was caught between a separate and increasingly assertive Lottery Film department bidding for exclusive control of the Council's media production funding and discussions at the level of Council about the need, driven by the tightening of the grant-in-aid, to make significant cuts in the organisation's activities. A proposed way forward, which brought back into play the ideas behind Arts Council Television six or seven years before, was that FVB should become an agency, separate from but with links to the Arts Council, and established and capitalised with Lottery funding. In a climate that had been developing for two decades of increasingly devolved project and client funding, this plan would also meet the criticism directed at FVB's centralised 'hands-on' approach to production.

Reporting on a detailed consultation process (which included the May 1996 'Working with Television' meeting), the vision for the new agency was set out in the 1996–97 *Annual Review*:

> Debate focused on whether [the Arts Council] should externalise its arts broadcasting activities and set up a new, independent body to channel Lottery production funding into arts programmes for television. At the heart of this debate lay the argument that the art form had never received adequate funding. Lottery funds would enable more practical support to be offered to independent producers and broadcast partners; expansion into new, relatively high-cost areas, such as full-length operas for TV; and development on new collaborations with regional broadcasters. (1996–97: 18)

Preparations for establishing the agency were well developed before the Council received clear government advice that the provisions of the Lottery Act did not permit funds to be utilised in this way. But by this point, in April 1997, it had been assumed internally that the agency would receive the go-ahead and FVB's budget for the coming year from grant-in-aid monies had already been reallocated to other departments. The organisation as a whole was then further disrupted by the controversial resignation of its Secretary-General, Mary Allen, who left to run (albeit for less than a year) the Royal Opera House, which had only recently received a Lottery grant of £78.5 million. In the fall-out from this, as it was dealing with what a participant described as 'a lot of sweeping up',[33] the Council was unwilling to reverse its earlier decision not to allocate a budget to FVB.

The department was relocated to temporary offices away from the main building and given a year to wind up its operations. Certain of its activities, including artists' films, were transferred to Visual Arts, and the funding of broadcast co-productions was discontinued. In 1996–97 FVB had been a partner in 17 terrestrial television programmes, including the intimate profile of artist Sarah Lucas, *Two Melons and a Stinking Fish*, three sharp films by young black directors for the *Moving Image* initiative with Channel 4, and new series with BBC2 of *Sound on Film* and *Dance for the Camera*. Projects in production, like the heavily formatted BBC series *Date with an Artist*, were played out and three further series of *Dance for the Camera* were made with Rodney Wilson, now working on a freelance contract, as the Arts Council England executive producer. The seventh series of *Dance for the Camera* was selected in May 2002 and delivered in April 2003, but at the conclusion of this, responding to its new cultural priorities, the BBC decided that it no longer had any interest in continuing the scheme.

Fall-out from the Lottery continued. The Arts for Everyone (A4E) scheme, which offered small grants to the widest range of organisations and individuals, took the Council back to its roots supporting amateur activities under the auspices of CEMA. In 2000, responsibilities for Lottery funding of feature films was given to a new strategic body, the Film Council, which created problems of definition and even survival for the BFI. Nearly a decade after its founding, the new body has shown few signs of support for a policy of cultural film. In the November 1999 restructuring of the Arts Council, the department of Broadcasting and New Media was created (with a very modest 1999–2000 budget of £231,000) to develop new strategic relationships with television and to support emerging digital arts, but the Council also directed that each artform department should engage in their own way with broadcasting. The Council as a whole continued a seemingly endless process of restructuring. In 2002 the Arts Council of England and the ten RABs merged, as the Council's online history recorded, 'to create a simpler, more transparent funding system for artists and arts organisations, and make savings on administration' (2004). In February 2003 this new organisation unveiled its name: Arts Council England.

All of this activity took place during a period when, largely thanks to Lottery funding, spending on the arts saw significant increases. According to a summary of the achievements and failures of 'the Blair years' published in April 2007, 'spending on the arts has more than doubled since 1997 from £186 million [each year] to £412 million. Attendance at museums and galleries has risen by 83 per cent. Extra money was invested in regional theatre, with audiences up 8 per cent' (Thorpe 2007: 47). 'From the iconic Tate Modern to the Lowry in Manchester', a 2004 Arts Council England press release enthused, 'the National Lottery has transformed the cultural landscape of this country for artists and audiences alike.' In a March 2007 speech at Tate Modern, Prime Minister Tony Blair claimed that London was now 'the creative capital of the world'. Even so, Britain was still spending less than half the amount of public money per head on culture than were France, Germany, Italy or Sweden. The Department of Culture, Media and Sport and Arts Council England had a public spat in 2004 about whether or not the impact of a budget announcement amounted to a £30 million cut in arts funding for the following three years. In addition, the costs of the Olympic Games, to be staged in London in 2012, were beginning, in 2007, to draw monies away from the arts. Critics also attacked what John Tusa, managing director of the Barbican Centre, described as 'blind instrumentalism' in the Labour government's attitudes to the arts. 'What [the Government] have insisted is that the arts must fulfil a social, political, environmental, educational or economic purpose', Tusa wrote, 'in other words they must be an "instrument" for "delivering" other government policies' (2007). The relationship between the political world and the arts communities remained – predictably and healthily – spikey, but during the sixty years of the Arts Council, Britain had seen profound changes and enormous advances in the creation, provision, understanding of and access to culture; changes to which television had made a central contribution.

'When the Arts Council [in 1986] finally came round to setting up [the Film, Video and Broadcasting Department]', Andrew Sinclair wrote, 'it was forty years too late' (1995: 301). Certainly the absence of an initial commitment (and the turf-war protectionism of the BFI) hampered any possibility of the Council making a central contribution to the development of film art and, later, arts broadcasting. Even as the Council stumbled into these areas, the relatively low cultural status of television and, to a degree, film, reinforced the marginality of these media in its deliberations and ensured that the funding made available was a consistently tiny proportion of the Council's overall budgets. The television companies too, apart from Channel 4 in its first years, were in general arrogantly resistant to working on any basis with the Council apart from that of taking its public funds to resource the individual programmes in which they, the broadcasters, were interested. Nonetheless, the legacy of the involvement by first the Art Department and then FVB in producing, funding and collaborating on arts films is a valuable one. Individual productions, including *Richard Hamilton*, *Shadows from Light* and *Franz Fanon*, are among the most distinguished and challenging documentaries to be made in Britain in the second half of the twentieth century. The full catalogue of productions is, as the remainder of this book aims to demonstrate, a rich resource for the documentation of artists, for original approaches to performance and for bold filmmaking strategies.

My final reflection here concerns the absence across forty years of any overall strategy towards production. Funding decisions were essentially reactive, responding to individual applications and to the perceived opportunities in partnerships with broadcasting and others. For a time, especially during the 1970s, there was a strong commitment to 'difference', to supporting work that would not and could not be funded elsewhere, although this was diluted as the relationship with television became increasingly important. But there was never a sense that, say, an attempt would be made to document each of the significant visual artists working at a particular time or that overarching themes would be applied as the basis of making choices about which performances to bring to the screen. The opportunistic approach can be recognised as a weakness, since it meant that the films in total lacked definition and so were hard to market not only to audiences but also to those (including members of the Council) on which their continuing existence depended. Yet the openness and plurality should also be recognised as strengths. Without the consistent application of these principles, there would be far fewer quirky delights and provocative challenges waiting for discovery in the Arts Council films collection.

CHAPTER 4
MAINSTREAM APPROACHES AND ALTERNATIVE FORMS

Typology appears to be a particular preoccupation for a number of the happy few who write about the arts in film and television. Perhaps because television arts programming can be seen to possess a clear core but increasingly fuzzy boundaries, critics seem to feel compelled to develop a classification system for *kinds* of arts programmes. John A. Walker's book *Arts TV: A History of Arts Television in Britain* noted that the critic John Dugdale proposed in 1985 a three-category system (reportage, subjective filmmaking, polemical 'essays') and that in an earlier article I had offered five kinds of programme. Walker himself put forward a 12-format approach, encompassing among other types event relays, 'how to' programmes and 'pundit series' (1993b: 15–16).

In this chapter I first discuss a group of Arts Council films to consider the ideas of telling and showing in documentary. The main argument proposes that the recognition of three fundamental forms helps to define and understand the mainstream traditions of arts films and television programmes. These forms predated television, and indeed the cinema, but they were refined for the small screen in the 1950s and early 1960s. They have also proved to be remarkably stable and, albeit often in hybrid combinations, they remain dominant today. These forms or strategies are the lecture, the encounter and the drama. Although each has many precedents, a founding father for each can be identified within British television in the 1950s and 1960s: respectively Kenneth Clark, John Read and Ken Russell. The study of the works of these figures, and those of their later equivalents, means that this chapter is initially concerned with the mainstream of arts filmmaking; a discussion then follows of a number of oblique, marginal and oppositional responses to the arts. There are inevitably also approaches, perhaps most notably those exemplified by review programmes, that are neither adequately encompassed by my proposed trilogy of forms nor are engaged with in the second half of this chapter. Most such programmes, however, have only an ephemeral interest dependent largely on the protagonists. The writing of their critical history will have to wait for a more dedicated researcher than myself.

Tell and show

Click. A low electronic hum. Light – and a light, an arc lamp, on the screen. This is the start of *The Nativity* (1966), when a filming light is switched on to illuminate Piero della Francesca's fifteenth-century painted panel propped on

Piero della Francesca's masterpiece examined in *The Nativity*

an easel. The jolt of a reminder that a constructed film is mediating this artwork is smoothed over by a narrator's voice. This presentation, the voice explains respectfully, by the Arts Council of Great Britain, carries commentary from Sir Philip Hendy, Director of the National Gallery, London. The camera moves slowly closer to Piero's scene as Hendy, heard but not visible, introduces the work. Deliberate moves by the camera across the painting are complemented by a modest number of cuts and dissolves. An area of damage to the painting is highlighted both visually and by the voice. Hendy offers a predominantly formal and connoisseurial analysis before the camera pulls away from the easel. Throughout the twelve minutes, we see nothing but the painting.

This is a short, straightforward lecture for a general audience about a single work, and in its resolute purity is typical of a small group of films narrated by prominent scholars made in the first two decades of the Arts Council's funding of films. These include three works about the art of old masters Nicolas Poussin, Claude Lorrain and Andrea Mantegna with commentaries written and spoken by Anthony Blunt, who in the 1960s and early 1970s was the Director of the Courtauld Institute. Another is *Rubens and England* (1974), presented by the art historian Gregory Martin. Only in the Rubens film is the lecturer shown on-screen, and then but briefly, standing beneath the ceiling of the Banqueting Hall, Whitehall. Nor does Martin speak to camera, but only on the soundtrack. As the next section explores, these art history lectures have been, and continue to be, paralleled by numerous, often more complex films on television. The comparative simplicity and directness of these early documentaries, however, facilitates the introduction of the contrast in their address to the viewer between 'telling' and 'showing'. The former idea is grounded in communication by words, the latter in what a dictionary defines as 'presenting to view'. While the distinction as introduced here lacks a theoretical grounding, it can be useful for approaching films about the arts, most of which work with a combination of both modes of address. In the lecture form, it is invariably telling that is privileged.

Now consider another group of short documentaries made early in the Arts Council's sponsorship of films about art. There are three films from the same moment as the Hendy, Blunt and Martin lectures which aim primarily to offer a record of a major Tate exhibition. *Lichtenstein in London* offers shots of the installed galleries and of individual works by Roy Lichtenstein along with, as an opening title states, 'commentary by members of the public and the artist'. The painter's contributions on the soundtrack come from media interviews, and these are interspersed with often thoughtful ideas from visitors, including the imagining of narratives for characters from the paintings. The next major show at the Tate in 1968 was also filmed by the Arts Council. *Barbara Hepworth at the Tate* pans round and tracks through the artist's extensive retrospective, accompanying images of the works with elements from an audio interview with the artist. Hepworth speaks about carving and materials, light and form, before the film's final extended sequence shifts from the galleries during the day, with visitors walking around, to the deserted museum at night, with only a lush musical score as accompaniment. The influential critic and curator David Sylvester devised and scripted the Lichtenstein film, and he is credited as co-director (along with cinematographer Walter Lassally) of a film record of the 70th birthday exhibition of Henry Moore's work. The camera of *Henry Moore at the Tate Gallery* moves as before through the show (which Sylvester curated) but this time there is only ambient sound; neither artist nor visitors, and certainly not the critic, tells the viewer anything. The curator simply shows.

Francis Bacon: Paintings 1944–62 shares some characteristics with these films, and was made alongside the Tate Gallery's retrospective in 1962. It abstracts images of Bacon's paintings from the gallery and presents them in an elaborate visual montage alongside photographic sources that the artist acknowledged: a reproduction of Velasquez's portrait 'Pope Innocent X', images of animal and human movement by photographer Eadweard Muybridge, the frame still of a bloodied and screaming face from *Bronenosets Potyomkin* (*Battleship Potemkin*, 1925). The harsh, intense film aims to impart, using camera movement and montage, a strictly visual experience of Bacon's work, which is enhanced by Elizabeth Lutyens' atonal score. Mamoun Hassan, who was editor Kevin Brownlow's assistant on the film, recalled that Bacon came several times to the cutting room to watch progress on the film and seems to have approved of what was being done with his work.[1]

Kinetics (1970) is another significant 'showing' of an exhibition. This was produced by Lutz Becker and the Film Department of the Slade School of Fine Art, an influential department established in the early 1960s under Thorold Dickinson, from which numerous key figures in British film culture emerged, including Becker, Charles Barr, Peter Whitehead, Raymond Durgnat and Simon Field. 'You are watching a film…' says the introductory narration of *Kinetics*, explaining that it is a record of the 1970 exhibition of kinetic art at the Hayward Gallery. One shot features a reflection of the camera crew. Although the narration at times offers thoughts about the art and its popularity ('Kinetic art tames technology'), for the most part the film simply presents moving, flickering, projecting artworks, accompanying them with a harsh, technological score.

These films *show*, as of course to some extent do all films about the arts, but television has rarely been comfortable with permitting showing to be the dominant form. Television is a telling medium, and has become ever more so in recent years. Documentaries now tell the viewer in the opening moments what the film to come will be about and then at the close tells again what the viewer has just seen. Television in the main aims to achieve singular meanings, to dislodge ambiguity and to bring clarity to what might otherwise be obscure or puzzling or challenging. But of course the arts are frequently obscure and puzzling and challenging, and their power feeds on these qualities. The arts ask mostly to be shown, even if television wants always to tell.

The lecture: a television (and radio) tradition

The early development of the television lecture about the arts is outlined in Chapter 1. Brief discourses about paintings and sculptures, along with many other subjects, were broadcast from the Alexandra Palace studios pre-war, and singular presentations of aspects of the visual arts continued on the BBC throughout the 1950s. For *Monitor* the painter Michael Ayrton spoke in 'The Last Michelangelo' about the work the artist left unfinished 'because it was impossible to finish', and John Berger contributed a presentation on 'Four Bellini Madonnas'. All of these extended, with the obvious additional attraction of images, the tradition of radio 'talks' that dates back to the late 1920s. Hilda Matheson, Head of Talks from 1927 to 1932, is generally credited with locating and refining the tone with which speakers could most effectively engage the nation. Matheson, as she later recorded, felt that it 'was useless to address the microphone as if it were a public meeting, or even to read it essays or leading articles. The person sitting at the other end expected the speaker to address him personally, simply, almost familiarly, as man to man' (1933: 75–6). This, of course, is the tone that radio and television has adopted as natural for the last seventy years and more, whatever the speaker on the screen is presenting. Assessing Matheson's legacy, Paddy Scannell and David Cardiff state:

> Broadcasting could not treat its audience as a crowd. It had to learn to speak to them as individuals. Its task was the domestication of public utterance. Available models of public talk – the sermon, lecture or political speech – were all unsatisfactory ... Since it was received by family groups [radio talk] should be conversational in tone rather than declamatory, intimate rather than intimidating. (1991: 161–2)

Yet even if the tone of the art history lecture was inappropriate, the influence of this form in other ways (as the next section considers) remained strong.

Kenneth Clark found his tone during the 48 programmes that he recorded for ATV in the late 1950s and early 1960s:

> I will not weary the reader by describing the stages by which I gradually came to terms with the medium. The first stage was to learn that every word must be scripted; the second was that what viewers want from a programme on art is not ideas, but information; and the third that things must be said clearly, energetically and economically. (1977: 207)

The programmes migrated from a discussion format with other contributors to a classic studio lecture with projected slides, such as *Five Revolutionary Painters* (1959) and the three-part *Rembrandt* (1962). The lecture then came out into the world with *Picasso at the Tate*, a half-hour talk broadcast as the artist was walking round the gallery's major retrospective, and subsequently with location-based films *Great Temples of the World* (1964–66), of which Chartres, St Mark's in Venice and Luxor were completed. Here, and in a subsequent joint BBC/ITA film *The Royal Palaces of Britain* (1966), was the creation of the format of *Civilisation*, the combination of an art history lecture with an elaborate travelogue taking the surrogate viewer around the cultural wonders of the world.

By the time *Civilisation* reached the screen, the lecture form was also being used by others for more modest ends, most especially in the BBC2 series *Canvas* (1966–70) in which a critic, artist or historian was filmed speaking in front of a single work. David Hockney eulogises Domenichino's frescoes in London's National Gallery and Jonathan Miller considers Joseph Wright's pictures 'The Orrery' and 'The Experiment with an Air Pump'. Later variations on the format have included *One Hundred Great Paintings* (1980–82) and *The Secret Life of Paintings* (1986) with Lady Wedgwood. *Building Sights* is a livelier architectural version, in which an informal and lively lecture about a building is presented by an enthusiast from the location. One of the most provocative contributions to *Canvas* was a short lecture about Leonardo's 'Mona Lisa' by the Australian art historian Robert Hughes, in which he showed more interest in the cult of the painting than its aesthetic qualities. Hughes became, after Clark, the next notable lecturer for television about the visual arts, making an ambitious history of modernism, *The Shock of the New* as well as *American Visions*, eight films about the art of the United States from the Pilgrim Fathers to Jeff Koons, and individual films about, among others, *Caravaggio* (1976), *Rubens* (1977) and *Goya* (2002). About *The Shock of the New* when it was first shown, I wrote:

> Hughes features as a presenter elaborating one particular interpretation of art history ... paintings, archive footage, interviews and contemporary film are edited around him to support his interpretation ... The technique isn't bad, but it is limiting, offering single meanings for works which are by their nature ambiguous or resonant. (1980: 18–19)

Among those who have followed in the footsteps of Clark and Hughes are

Andrew Graham-Dixon, who has presented *A History of British Art* and *Renaissance*; Matthew Collings with *This is Modern Art* and *Hello Culture*; and Brian Sewell, who has made *The Naked Pilgrim: The Road to Santiago* (2003) and *Brian Sewell's Grand Tour* (2005–6) for Five. The address to the audience develops over the years, with Collings introducing strident strains of the demotic and Sewell relishing language at the borderline of parody, but the form – lecture plus travelogue – is essentially unchanged. In the early twenty-first century, the lecture form, like much other television, became increasingly hybridised, so that in 2006 Simon Schama's *Power of Art* relies heavily on dramatised scenes (without dialogue) to conjure up the Rome of Caravaggio and Bernini, with the artists fancifully impersonated by Italian actors. Two films screened early in 2007, *Tchaikovsky*, in which Charles Hazelwood lectured with orchestral illustrations about the composer's music, also featured short dramatic scenes. Staged with neither the budget nor the committed energy that Ken Russell brought to his feature film *The Music Lovers*, these elements too often appeared simply risible.

As the Tchaikovsky example shows, the lecture format has by no means been confined to the visual arts on television. Margot Fonteyn presented *The Magic of Dance*, Richard Eyre offered a personal view of the story of theatre in *Changing Stages*, and Howard Goodall has made a number of series about music for Channel 4, including *Big Bangs* and *20th Century Greats*. Yet it is striking that television's most notable large-scale projects have been concerned with the visual arts. This may perhaps have to do with the continuing influence of a framework of art history lectures established at least a century ago.

BEAUBOURG: FOUR FILMS BY DENIS POSTLE

written, produced and directed by Denis Postle
a Tattooist International Ltd production
50 minutes, 1980

The documentary opens with the filmmaker outside the recently-completed Pompidou Centre in Paris. In lecture mode, Postle says direct to camera, 'Because Beaubourg is such a big, complicated phenomenon what we've done is to make several self-contained films about it, each of which presents the centre from a different point of view.' The films that follow not only take differing viewpoints in their narration, they also – to a degree – adopt different filmic conventions to make their points. Meaning is created between the arguments, and rather than being directed by a lecturer's voice the viewer is actively encouraged to find their own place.

The first is an official view, the Beaubourg's corporate self-presentation from an accredited guide. The second, with a different narrator, listens respectfully to the architects Renzo Piano and Richard Rogers, together with Peter Rice from Arup who gives a technical explanation of the building's structure.

Perhaps the most intriguing of the films is the third in which the architectural critic Reyner Banham suggests that Beaubourg was strongly influenced by the ideas developed in Britain during the 1960s by the Archigram Group. Key figures from Archigram, among them Cedric Price, Peter Cook and Ron Herron, are bundled into a minibus and taken to Paris to confront the building for the first time. Their response is uncertain and ambivalent, and they are particularly critical of the unchanging, inflexible nature of the edifice; Archigram envisioned an urban world in constant flux.

Before the fourth film, Postle takes up another idea that documentaries rarely explore: he shows the film as it is at that stage to some of the participants and elicits their feedback. Renzo Piano agrees with Cedric Price's comments about the building being too fixed, but explains that that is the nature of a large, institutional structure.

At this point, Postle brings in his personal responses to the building. 'So if you like, this [the fourth offering] is my film.' He acknowledges the drama of the building, but confides his sense of unease about the way it is working. Using military images from a Bastille Day parade, he shifts from an architectural focus to develop a critique of Beaubourg grounded in its use. 'So many of the exhibits seemed to be celebrating bland politeness', he says, suggesting that it is most of all a temple to bureaucratic arts. Rogers tacitly supports Postle's critical position when he reveals that the architects had intended the facades to feature screens for projecting photographs and films but that political concerns had prevented this. Ultimately, for Postle, there is no sense of risk about the activities, no surprise; culture is embraced by Beaubourg primarily as a marketable commodity.

'Certainly for me', the director confesses, 'Beaubourg has been a very sharp reminder of the difference between culture and art. Culture, like steak, can be very nourishing. But unlike steak, art – if it is art – is alive, it's full of mischief and surprise. Art opens us up, culture shuts us down. Art seduces, culture bullies.'

Postle then discovers in the crowd mingling in the Beaubourg's public piazza an eccentric, entirely personal resistance to what he characterises as the Beaubourg's bullying. A couple, schoolteachers from a Paris suburb, wander through the crowd in strange masks. 'I couldn't take my eyes off them', Postle admits, as the camera tracks them. 'They said nothing, they did nothing. But somehow they were managing to be part of the solution rather than part of the problem.'

Lanternists, lecturers and connoisseurs

When Sir Joshua Reynolds and J. M. W. Turner delivered their lectures at London's Royal Academy of Arts in, respectively, the late eighteenth century and early nineteenth century, they had no access to photographic visual aids. As Robert S. Nelson wrote in an important essay chronicling the art history lecture, Reynolds 'might assume ... that the audience would have seen the paintings mentioned on prior Grand Tours' (2000: 423). Turner handed around prints and his own drawings, and sometimes the works discussed were available on site. In the 1840s the architect and professor C. R. Cockerell accompanied his Royal Academy presentations with 'two large sheets, or rather assemblages of sheets ... showing in comparative juxtaposition most of the famous structures of antiquity, the one in elevation, the other in section' (in Watkin 1974: 106–7).

Photographic images on glass which could be used for projections in magic lanterns were presented in London at the 1851 Great Exhibition and as the cost of producing them dropped they began to be used by lecturers recounting distant travels. Dissolves and other optical effects could be achieved by projectors with two or three lenses. Photographic slides of paintings and sculptures, Nelson recorded,

> were discussed at the First International Congress of Art History in Vienna in 1873 and gradually introduced into university classes in Germany during the following decades. The widespread use of the slide projector depended upon not only the invention of the photographic slide but also the electric light, which afforded a strong, steady light source, developments that came together by the end of the 1880s. (2000: 429)

Herman Grimm, a professor of art history at the University of Berlin, recounted in an 1897 article how lantern slides permitted the projection of artworks at fullsize, and Grimm's successor at Berlin, Heinrich Wolfflin, was equally an enthusiast for the technology's potential in teaching art history. The use of two slide projectors side-by-side is acknowledged as Wolfflin's innovation, allowing him to show details of an artwork alongside a reproduction of the whole. Hand-colour lantern slides were gradually replaced by manufactured ones after Agfa invented a mechanical method in 1916, and the invention of the Kodachrome colour process in 1936 facilitated the production of the familiar format of 35mm slides.[2] By the early twentieth century, Wolfflin and others were using two-screen slide shows to construct arguments that were as much visual as verbal, showing as well as telling. Narration accompanying and commenting on a succession of images was also a dominant form for early cinema, when a speaker offered explanations for what was being shown, developed narratives from and for the short, fragmentary films, and made topical and local references to enhance the entertainment. Standing unseen next to Kenneth Clark throughout *Civilisation* are the lanternists and early cinema pioneers of a century before as well as Grimm, Wolfflin and other masters of the slide lecture.

Clark begins *Civilisation* with a quote from *il miglior fabbro*, the greater master. 'Ruskin said', Clark muses in voice-over as he strolls through the grounds of the Louvre, '"Great nations write their autobiographies in three manuscripts: the book of their deeds, the book of their words, and the book of their art ... of the three the only trustworthy one is the last." On the whole, I think this is true.'

Referencing the tradition in which Clark understands his position, he also quickly brings in the first-person mode of speech that is fundamental to the lecture form. Not only does he use the singular pronoun 'I' but he prefaces his main statement with the confidingly cautious qualifier 'on the whole...'. In the shift from objective quotation to personal reflection, he moves from the distanced academic referring to Ruskin to a colloquial aside addressed directly to the viewer – such changes in conversational footing are characteristic of both lectures in the classroom and of the television lecture format.

'Italy. 1610. Michelangelo Marisi da Caravaggio is on the run – again.' Simon Schama, opening his *Power of Art* almost thirty years after Clark, plunges us *in media res*. Accompanying his voice-over are jump-cut images of an actor in costume stumbling along a seashore – we are to assume that this is the artist. When he first appears on-screen, Schama stands next to Caravaggio's canvas 'David with the Head of Goliath' and speculates on how it was shaped by events in the artist's life. Immediately, he too is drawing us in with a reiterated inclusive 'we'. 'We like to think, don't we', he says, 'that the genius is the hero.' By now we should be seated comfortably in a story's circle of listeners hearing him tell of the dirty deeds in an artist's life.

Similar strategies are employed even when there is no physical narrator. In films like *The Pre-Raphaelite Revolt*, *Picasso the Sculptor*, *Matisse: A Sort of Paradise* (1969) and *Art in Revolution* (1972) – chosen almost at random from the early Arts Council films (numerous later examples could also be cited from television) – the lecturer is the filmmaker. He or she is developing the argument, selecting the slides (and film extracts for *Art in Revolution*), and constructing the narrative (even if it is delivered in the voice of a professional narrator). Referring to Picasso's three-dimensional works, the actress Jill Balcon may give voice to the words 'Throughout, we find in his sculpture the shape of *life*', but the meaning comes from the critic (and friend of Picasso) Roland Penrose, credited as writer and director of *Picasso the Sculptor*.

Yet whether or not the lecturer appears on-screen, the television lecture form is hung on the personality of the storyteller. Clark may name-check John Ruskin, but opinions and interpretations, narratives and information are apparently derived only from the knowledge and sensitivity of the speaker. He (for it has been invariably 'he') has been to the places he is showing us, he has looked at the artworks on display, and now he can impart the knowledge so gained. He rarely needs to refer to another, whether they be a historical source or a living witness. He almost never admits to uncertainty or doubt, to ambivalence or to the existence of competing theories. Any kind of self-reflective alignment with, or opposition to, a body of knowledge, an ideology, a way of understanding the world, is unnecessary. Sources and pre-existing scholarship (and this is a central difference between the lecture hall and television) have no place and require no acknowledgement. Assertion of the individual's ideas is all-important, combined with the coaxing along of an audience that, unseen and unfelt, may be losing interest. The ideas too are complete in themselves, formed into a singular satisfying narrative, whether of a man's life or of the development of civilisation, and admitting no gaps or problems, no alternatives and no sense of difference.

In travelling the world and imparting their subjective sense of what they have learned, Clark, Schama and many other television lecturers act as connoisseurs. 'One who knows' is among the older definitions of the word, but the Italian art historian Lionello Venturi, writing in 1934, explored the idea more fully:

> The practice of the connoisseur is one which derives from the habit of looking and re-looking at the works of art of a certain period. By intuition those works of art are distinguished as belonging to individual groups … and from the quality of a group is deduced if a work of art to be classified is worthy to enter it, or should be excluded; whether it be an original, and how preserved, or a copy, and of what time, or, finally, a forgery. (In de Koster 1998)

Clark and almost all of his successors as television lecturers on the arts have perpetuated this sense of connoisseurship, and with it a profoundly traditional, Western, male and – for many critics – individualist and bourgeois idea of art history. Clark acknowledged this in his autobiography.

> My approach to art history was unself-consciously different from that now in favour in universities, which sees all historical change as the result of economic and social processes. I believe in the importance of individuals, and am a natural hero worshipper. Each programme had its hero … The majority of people share my taste for heroes. (1977: 226)

The words could have been written by Simon Schama about *Power of Art*, and apply also to the overwhelming majority of television lecture series made between these two landmarks. Yet art history in the three decades at the end of the twentieth century underwent profound change, assimilating – unevenly and sometimes uncomfortably – theoretical frameworks from Marxism, semiotics, structuralism, feminism and psychoanalysis, and engaging centrally with ideas of class, identity and sexuality. Films written by Andrew Graham-Dixon and a handful of others nod towards this work on occasions, or make use of its insights, but for the most part (and with John Berger's work excepted) little of this has made any impact on either the content or the form of the television art history lecture.

One further aspect of the interest of Clark's series is that it was made at the foundational moment for this 'new art history' (and for so much more): *les evenements* in Paris and elsewhere in May 1968. In a survey of recent developments in art history Jonathan Harris wrote:

> The creative, interrogative and critical scrutiny that, for instance, Marxist and feminist art history has shown over the three decades emerged out of … the social and political disturbances of May 1968 that occurred in numerous countries throughout the world. (2001: 3)

The Paris filming dates for *Civilisation* coincided with this moment. 'Rioting was going on all around us', producer Michael Gill recalled in the documentary biography of Clark, *K: Kenneth Clark 1903–83*; 'Riot police were standing just off camera, fifty-strong, I was gassed...'. One of the scenes shot then is of Clark standing beside Rodin's tortured statue of Balzac. Celebrating the writer's 'prodigious understanding of human motives', in episode twelve of *Civilisation*, Clark launches into a peroration containing an eccentric but clearly deeply-felt catalogue of current ills. The writer, he says, 'should inspire us to defy all those forces that threaten to impair our humanity: lies, tanks, tear-gas, ideologies, opinion polls, mechanisation, planners, computers, the whole lot.'

John Berger strikes back: *Ways of Seeing*

In the opening sequence of the first film of *Ways of Seeing*, made three years after *Civilisation* was first shown and conceived in part as a riposte to it, John Berger walks up to Botticelli's 'Venus and Mars' and wielding a sharp knife expertly cuts out Venus's head. We are not in the television world of *Civilisation* any more – even if we will return there, in the company of Robert Hughes, Andrew Graham-Dixon and others, on numerous occasions in later years. No other programme or film since *Ways of Seeing* has offered as radical a critique of and engagement with the television lecture form as the four half-hour films made by Berger with his collaborators Sven Blomberg, Chris Fox, Michael Dibb and Richard Hollis. The attention-grabbing opening, and the 'reveal' that Berger is in a television studio with a reproduction Botticelli, is typical of one aspect of its distinctiveness. For throughout, Berger and the production team are constantly exposing how the films are constructed. The script speaks of a cut about to be made or music that is going to be added, and with extracts from Dziga Vertov's *Chelovek s kino-apparatom* (*Man With a Movie Camera*, 1929), the process of editing is foregrounded. John A. Walker wrote:

> The first programme set out to demystify the mechanics of film and television. Berger did not do this for aesthetic or formalist reasons but to lend authority to his critique of orthodox art history and to legitimise his alternative strategy revealed at the end of the first programme. (1993b: 93)

Located almost exclusively within the television studio, and with Berger taking on the persona of the lecturer speaking directly to camera, he is explicit about his position and intentions in a way that no other presenter has taken on. (Although it could be argued that Matthew Collings' jokey asides in *This is Modern Art* and other series are the ironic or postmodern equivalents of Berger's Brechtianism.) 'I am controlling and using for my own purposes', Berger states towards the end of the first film, 'the means of reproduction needed for these programmes. I hope you will consider what I arrange – but be sceptical of it.' He also acknowledges, at least to a degree, sources for his ideas, most especially in the use he makes in film one of the ideas of Walter Benjamin's essay 'The

Work of Art in the Age of Mechanical Reproduction'. Following Benjamin, Berger asserts that mass reproduction of images has diminished the 'aura' attached to what were formerly sacred artworks; this loss means that such images can now be used in new ways, whether for commercial ends in advertising or, potentially, for progressive purposes.

The subsequent films consider images of women and patriarchy in the mainstream of European art, ideas of possession and power in oil painting and the seductive glamour of advertising. Throughout, the films play with images, and with conjunctions of sound and picture, in original and still startling ways. Accepted masterpieces are juxtaposed with advertising, and both are interrogated about their conditions of production, their implied audiences and the uses to which they are put. Resistance to these uses within capitalism is preached, and many viewers have been seduced by the arguments and become disciples, even if – as we are encouraged – we have not taken on this role uncritically. As the critic Geoff Dyer wrote in a detailed analysis of *Ways of Seeing*,

> The influence of the series and the book that Berger wrote ... was enormous. Throughout the 1970s it was the key text in art colleges in Britain and in the USA; for many students and teachers alike it represented a turning point in their thinking about art. It opened up for general attention areas of cultural study that are now commonplace – decoding advertisements, for example – but which in 1972 were either virtually unknown or existed only in embryonic stage within the academy. (1987: 96)

Yet the influence of *Ways of Seeing* has been far stronger in that academy than within television itself. Just over a decade after the series was first shown, Nick Levinson, a producer with the Open University (who produced the films for their important 'Modern Art and Modernism' course), characterised how the arts on television continued to resist the ideas that underpinned Berger's polemic. Levinson wrote:

> On television the history of how and why art exists, as well as why we have certain attitudes towards it, has not been prised apart from the values art has been given by the dominant classes. Although the broadcasting world has largely ignored such questions, they have become central to much art criticism, history and teaching in this country for more than two decades. (1984)

Isolated responses to Levinson's critique can be identified in broadcasting's output. In 1991 BBC2 broadcast *Relative Values* which examined the idea of the artist as genius, the art market and the formation of the museum. The Channel 4 film from 1988, *England's Henry Moore*, sought to understand the history of how and why the sculptor had attained such an exalted and popular position at the centre of twentieth-century modernism. For the most part, however, his words are as pertinent in the early twenty-first century as when he wrote them in 1984.

A SIGN IS A FINE INVESTMENT
written and directed by Judith Williamson
45 minutes, 1983

There is a group of films in the Arts Council collection that attempt to combine the ways of *Ways of Seeing* with the semiotics and structuralism of continental film theory as it was filtered, via Roland Barthes, Christian Metz and others, into English in the later 1970s. The most successful of these is *A Sign is a Fine Investment*, Judith Williamson's study of advertising images and their relation to work. *Machines for the Suppression of Time* (1980) is perhaps the most eccentric.

Advertising and spectator in
A Sign is a Fine Investment

Machines for the Suppression of Time, written and directed by Lizbeth McCulloch and Douglas Lowndes, attempts to make a poetic, creative film from a structuralist critique of language. Its form combines didactic captions ('What do these images refer to?'), staged tableaux of famous paintings by Courbet, Ford Madox Ford and others, analysis of photographs and citations from books with a lengthy extract from a Futurist performance called 'Moon Hotel'. Viewing it more than 25 years after its production, I admired its intentions, but even with a glancing knowledge of its concerns I found it entirely opaque.

Photomontage Today (1982) also tips its cap at Berger in its explicitly pedagogic investigation of political photomontage. An early production made on videotape, this too features strident titles: 'Images are nothing – it's the relationship between images that matter.' Artist Peter Kennard's photomontages are contextualised by comparison with the work of John Heartfield, who appears in a brief archive extract. Eisenstein, Brecht and Fernando Solanas are among the other influences cited, standard references for leftist filmmakers of the time struggling with the politics of representation .

The languages and effects of advertising are targets for *Photomontage Today*, but *A Sign is a Fine Investment*, drawn in part from Williamson's influential book *Decoding Advertisements: Ideology and Meaning in Advertising* (1993), offers a far more nuanced and engaging analysis. Part of its pleasure comes from the wide range of archive extracts included, ranging from the 1916 'Shine Sir' advertisement made for the Kiwi Polish Company, through an extract of Basil Wright's *The Song of Ceylon*, financed by the Ceylon Tea Propaganda Bureau, to a Lever Bros.-funded film commercial *Close-ups of the Stars* from 1947, with Valerie Hobson extolling the glories of Lux toilet soap.

In her analysis of these and other films, Williamson investigates how depictions of work have over the years disappeared from advertising images. She is concerned to move beyond the conventional ways – simply as marketing or perhaps as 'art' – of seeing commercials. To this end she considers when work can or could be shown: when there is a clear separation between the worlds of the workers and that of the expected consumers, when it imparts worth to a nation and not to a class, or – as with housework – when the work depicted involves the consumption of products.

A Sign is a Fine Investment makes extensive use of titles, and with 'When is work not shown in advertising?' Williamson here focuses on the family, and a consistent setting that features throughout the film is a working-class home with a woman preparing dinner. Into this studio-constructed environment (the camera can move from one room to the adjoining one) advertising images and soundtracks are projected, pointing up the distance between dreams and reality. Towards the close, a modern worker comes home from his factory to a housing estate and then to this room. On the soundtrack are fragments from a 1946 commercial for Horlicks called 'An Englishman's Home'.

'Advertisements try to capture change', explains the narrator, 'and fix the image of our way of life as if it couldn't be any different.' The sophistication of the analysis reinforces the political position. 'Advertising itself cannot be changed until change becomes more than a question of changing one image with another.'

Encountering the real thing

Obvious as the point may be, the translation of the arts to film and television often entails the camera being in the same space as the artwork. This is not always the case: a television lecture can use only transparencies; a drama like *Surrealismo* (2002), produced for BBC Four, can be a story of Salvador Dalí without including any of his paintings. There is, however, a fundamental quality to filming a painting, a building, even a performance. The work is caught, captured, collected within the frame, although to impart to others the experience of being with the work entails, at least conventionally, the editing together of separate shots, the creation of a narrative, perhaps the addition of music to suggest a mood, and frequently the imposition of words on the soundtrack to pin down meanings and intentions. Perhaps the camera too meets with the artist, observing her or listening to him. More rarely the camera confronts the creative process, in a rehearsal room perhaps, or a sculptor's studio. Again, methods of mediation shape and shrink the meeting, converting it to a form and a length thought to be acceptable – and hopefully, compelling – for viewers.

I want to suggest that these meetings between camera and artwork, artist, performance and process, together with their mediated versions on-screen, are a fundamental form for arts films and television. The encounter form encompasses relays of performance from opera houses as well as documentaries that purport to visualise the moments of creation in an artist's output. The encounter embraces a single shot of a sculpture and the elaborated construction of a documentary profile of a living artist. Perhaps bringing such different film types together risks rendering meaningless the identification of the form, yet all of these types share showing – as opposed to telling – as their strategy. All too rest on an empirical attitude to film's potential and an acceptance of its limitations.

The real, in this understanding, is 'out there', available to be observed, recorded and reproduced (although not necessarily naively) with film. These ideas were challenged fundamentally by, among others, independent filmmakers working in the 1970s. A statement of the opposing position can be found in a key text from this time – a catalogue edited by John Ellis of the British Film Institute productions from 1951–76. The uncredited writer explains:

> Anti-empiricism rests on the idea that 'reality' is not something simply accessible to the observer. Reality (in so far as the word can be used) is the product of a complex interaction of forces ... In order to understand reality, it is not enough to look out of the window, to observe people closely etc. It is a matter of understanding the organisation of society, its economy, its political forms, its self-definitions and ideologies, which underlie and produce the specific situations that can be witnessed. This attitude also stresses that film is itself a part of the process, and has a definite social role (providing a society's self-images) and that the process of filming cannot be 'outside' the events it is filming, but is always very deeply implicated in them. (In Ellis 1977: 109)

Untroubled by these concerns, John Read shows us Henry Moore at work, Murray Grigor presents the architecture of *Carlo Scarpa* (1996), and a simple dance film like *Harmonica Breakdown* (1995) records Jane Dudley's choreography and its performance by a young dancer (as elsewhere in this argument, the examples are chosen almost entirely at random). Almost all art documentaries and performance films are grounded in empiricism and the encounter, even if the additional expression of the lecture form often determines and limits the meanings available. The encounter requires only that the camera – and therefore the viewer – observes the artwork, the artist or the process. This, the encounter suggests, is sufficient for knowledge to be imparted, values recognised, qualities experienced. The camera offers access to the real, yet only in a distanced or debased manifestation. From this understanding comes the concern so often expressed by filmmakers about the technical inadequacy of the reproductive forms available to them, and the inherently secondary nature of their medium. 'Art itself on television', the filmmaker Nigel Finch wrote, 'is at best ... a tease, an introduction not a substitute for the real thing and the producer's function is to find a way of compensating on television for what has been lost' (1984).

Mediation understood like this is always a problem, and the opportunities and possibilities that it might offer are rarely recognised as such. Television demands colour to reproduce paintings properly, and then stereo for music to be properly transmitted, and then 5.1 sound. High Definition imaging is seen as enhancing arts programming in particular, and several channels – including Sky Arts in the UK and Gallery HD in the United States – build their marketing proposition around this. Even so, despite the limitations, the encounter suggests that it alone is sufficient for knowledge to be imparted, values recognised, qualities experienced. Which has been, and remains, the case.

TOM PHILLIPS
directed by David Rowan, produced by Margaret Williams
an Arbor Films production for the Arts Council of Great Britain
50 minutes, 1977

Tom Phillips works with many of the conventional elements of the encounter profile. The artist speaks about his work, which is illustrated, as are elements of his process. Phillips is charming, the paintings and drawings are intelligently shot, and the film is clearly made with great care and sympathy. The film's formal invention is minimal and the filmmakers bring to the project no explicit critical framework. So perhaps it neither deserves nor requires to be highlighted ahead of other encounters in the Arts Council collection.

Among the earlier Arts Council films there is, for example, one directed by Michael Gill, *Giacometti* (1967), which captures the furious intensity of the sculptor as he works with clay to model a figure. Peter and Carole Smith conduct a fascinating car crash of an interview with the artist in *Edward Burra* (1973) towards the end of his life. Pottering around his suburban bungalow, with straggly hair and crabbed hands covered with rings, he resists the filmmakers' questions with a mumbled reply:

> It's a pretty bother answering them. It seems to be beside the point. I mean, why don't you just show the pictures? I don't know what all this personality has to do with it really. But I suppose you must have that. You must have personality.

Phillips has neither the passion of Giacometti nor the eccentricity of Burra. So the film concentrates to great effect on his works. First there is 'A Humument', a treated book in which the artist obscures elements of pages from a Victorian novel. Then Phillips speaks about 'Benches', a painting based on a found postcard. The importance of music is discussed – 'My interest in music is in the look of it' – and Phillips' opera 'Irma' is seen being recorded. Themes woven through these sections include the importance of chance, a fascination with systems, a concern with techniques of reproduction.

There are numerous other encounters with artists in the Arts Council collection, including a tightly controlled brush with the artist in *Bridget Riley* (1979), who reads a text about her work rather than be interviewed; *Woodman* (1978), an informal meeting with David Nash in the Welsh village where he works; and *Painting Chicago* (1982), a claustrophobic encounter by Judy Marle with Craigie Aitchison as he paints David Smith, who in his youth was a boxer known as the Chicago Kid. *Messages from Bhupen Khakhar* (1983) is another elegant film by Marle, this time echoing the characters in Khakhar's paintings with scenes of daily life in India. The film also neatly incorporates some of the artist's statements as full-screen captions: 'An artist should not preach, talk philosophy, try to reform society, because he constantly revels in illogicality, sensuality and vulgarity.'

This is not the terrain of *Tom Phillips* or of its subject. The painter's 'Art on the Road' focuses on his 'rich looking' at one small part of the world: the overlooked elements such as manhole covers that he encounters on his walk from his house to his studio. Finally, filmmaker and artist collaborate on a unique hybrid drawing-come-film. A large sheet of paper on which Phillips works is photographed every day for three months. He makes marks and then, from about the mid-stage, he begins to erase them, and at the end the paper is used as a screen onto which the film is projected.

In its way, *Tom Phillips* is a quiet film of 'rich looking' at one artist's work. As an involving experience for the viewer, and as an archival record, this is enough.

The idea of 'capturing' the moment of creation is at the heart of this argument. Canonical encounters, like Hans Namuth and Paul Falkenberg's 1950 footage of Jackson Pollock dripping paint across a canvas, are believed to provide access to the creative process. In Henri-Georges Clouzot's *Le Mystère Picasso* (1956) the artist draws directly for the camera, transforming the image again and again in a virtuoso display. In a British context, we have considered how Read strives to suggest creative inspiration in his study of Graham Sutherland (see the sidebar in Chapter 2) and the idea that the encounter could reveal a creative moment is recognised in Patrick Hayman's response to Read's 1957 film with L. S. Lowry. 'The magic of this mysterious occupation comes across in a splendidly satisfying way', Hayman celebrated in *Sight and Sound*, 'as the painting itself grows and changes under the joyful brush of the artist' (1957: 217). Most arts documentaries, and not just those concerned with the visual arts, are driven by the aspiration to show creation, even if they invariably fall back on having participants (and outsiders) tell us about it. Philip Hayward has pointed out the difficulties entailed by this focus.

> This 'extreme fetishisation' of the actual moment of creation has resulted in the production of a number of film texts which, in attempting to record this moment in as direct a manner as possible, have merely served to highlight the shortcomings and contradictions of both their specific projects and the broad approach in general. (1988: 7)

Hayward discusses both the component of the Pollock footage in which he simulates his painting on glass with the camera mounted beneath and a film by Jan Vrijsman about Karel Appel. In this, Appel flicks paint at a glass screen 'in a frenzy of apparent creativity'; 'Both films principally emphasise the inevitability of attempts to simulate the process and technique of painting (etc), being necessarily only representations of that simulation' (ibid.).

An exemplary encounter – and one that could not be further removed from frenzy – takes place in a film directecd in 1979 by Geoffrey Haydon for the BBC series *Seven Artists*. Other artists featured in the series include Roy Lichtenstein and Duane Hanson, but Haydon's low-key film is made with Los Angeles painter Ed Ruscha. 'This is me', Ruscha tells us in voice-over, 'aged 41, 5 foot 10 and a half inches, 160 pounds.' He is in the desert with a friend and together they locate and effortlessly lift up a large rock. In fact, the rock is a papier-maché artwork by Ruscha, and the narrative of the half-hour is the transport of the artwork to the artist's studio, restoration work on it and then its placing back in the wilderness.

The creative process itself is just as prosaic as a couple of guys putting a fibre-glass bottom on their dinghy, but all of this is grounded in images of Los Angeles which echo Ruscha's work, including a carwash and the freeways. Throughout, Ruscha reads in his deadpan voice the texts and titles of many of his drawings and paintings, and includes also their date and dimensions (I can think of no other film that includes the dimensions of every work of art featured). This reiterated litany of works echoes and comments on the events in the film, and are of a piece with its direct yet ironic approach. We encounter Ruscha and his work in seemingly as straightforward a manner as possible (there is no narration, all of the music is motivated by events within the film) and yet the encounter is carefully (and brilliantly) constructed and staged and achieved.

So perhaps the encounter alone is not enough. Artworks after all acquire their shifting meanings, their complexities, their resonances within systems of knowledge and value, and in dialogues with collective and individual histories. These need to be made present, to be questioned and challenged. The individual shot can do this, as Berger does when he cuts into a 'Botticelli', but more often the interrogation is achieved by juxtaposition. Unexpected sounds can suggest new ways of understanding images, as when Mike Dibb in his film profile of Robert Natkin, *Over the Rainbow*, plays the Judy Garland song against the painter's canvases. Contradictory ideas, the unexpected sequencing of ideas within and between encounters, the allusive use of references and comparisons, a category shift in ideas – these and more can build on the encounter and make the experience richer, deeper, more unsettling or more rewarding for the viewer. Yet there is a danger here also, as John Roberts identified in a detailed assessment of a version of these strategies exemplified by *State of the Art* (discussed further below). Roberts wrote:

> The use of a systematic intertextual aesthetic as the basis for documentary work therefore has both advantages and disadvantages. On the one hand, it clearly offers an advance in the complexity and texture of argument over the profile or the lecture, but given the tendency of anti-narrative structure to weaken causality, it can also reduce ideas to a heterogeneous soup. (1988: 73)

EDWARD HOPPER
written and directed by Ron Peck
a Four Corners film for the Arts Council of Great Britain
50 minutes, 1981

An opening caption explains that the film draws on 'conversations between Ron Peck the filmmaker and Gail Levin, curator of the Edward Hopper Collection, Whitney Museum of American Art, New York'. Immediately a mode of address is established with very different qualities from the conventional lecture. Indeed, it feels rather as if the conversation has been extended to take in the viewer.

Peck contributes a reflective, personal commentary built around a quest to understand the power of the paintings, and most especially the qualities of Hopper's most famous canvas 'Nighthawks'. (Three years before this documentary Peck used this title for his feature made with Paul Hallam about a conflicted gay schoolteacher in London.) He journeys to places depicted in the paintings and he talks with Gail Levin. The camera pans slowly around rooms where Hopper lived, as if searching for a secret that they could divulge. Other voices are heard on the soundtrack, including the artist and his wife in recordings made by Levin.

The director's musings take in the key events of Hopper's life, the political context in which many of the paintings were made, their relationship to movies, the sense that the figures in them seem to inhabit stage sets, the narratives they imply and the understanding of them as self-portraits. The sense of Peck coming slowly to knowledge of the works is effectively achieved.

What further distinguishes the film is its trust in the visual power of the paintings themselves. For lengthy sections of the documentary we look only at sequences of the paintings, often with simply silence accompanying them. As with the commentary, there is a strong sense of a painter's work and life being revealed but with encouragement for the viewer to bring their own responses and ideas. Above all, *Edward Hopper* is an impressively 'open' film.

The drama of artists' lives

The use of drama in arts programming has been almost exclusively reserved for biographies. (One exception is the *Arena* film *The Caravaggio Conspiracy* (1984) which staged Peter Watson's attempt as an undercover art dealer to recover stolen masterpieces.) Dramatised artist biographies have a clear point of origin in British television – Ken Russell's *Elgar*, made for *Monitor* in 1962. They have also had a rich literary and then cinematic tradition on which to draw. In the mid-sixteenth century Vasari penned critical lives of a selection of Renaissance artists, but the biographer Michael Holroyd has located the birth of modern biography with two writers, Samuel Johnson and James Boswell, in the later eighteenth century. Holroyd reflected:

> Britain oozes biography to the incomprehension and amusement of the world. It is a speciality of our art as well as literature. What other country has a National Portrait Gallery and a Dictionary of National Biography? Why? Perhaps it is because we are curiously at ease with our history and equate our island state with a precious individuality, as opposed to the collectivism of the mainland. We like our art to be grounded in fact. (2002)

Film too offered art more or less grounded in fact with colourful biographies of creative figures, including Hollywood's fanciful versions of the life of Van Gogh, brought alive by Kirk Douglas for *Lust for Life* (1956) and Michelangelo, played by Charlton Heston in *The Agony and the Ecstasy* (1965). From its earliest days, the British cinema had depicted fictional artists in short features like *The Artist and the Flower Girl* (1898) and *The Sculptor's Jealous Model* (1904), both made by R. W. Paul. Alexander Korda cast Charles Laughton as a largely fanciful *Rembrandt* (1936) and imaginary painters featured in *The Horse's Mouth* (1958), with canvases supplied by John Bratby, and Tony Hancock's *The Rebel* (1960), which parodies the action painting of artist William Green. Green had been featured on a BBC news programme riding a bicycle across a paint-spattered canvas.

Reflecting on why makers of feature films have been so attracted to the biographies of painters and other artists, John A. Walker dismissed the idea that the subject might be seen as an easy route to profit. He suggested that filmmakers

> wish to acquire prestige by association with a form of culture generally perceived to be 'higher' [and] for many who work in the mass culture industries, the arts appeal because they represent a purer realm in which aesthetic and spiritual values count for more than crass commercialism. Also, movie directors and stars are as likely to be seduced by the romantic image of the artist as misunderstood or tragic genius as anyone else. (1993a: 10)

The drama has not achieved quite as central a place as the lecture and the encounter in television arts programming in Britain (partly because of the high costs involved). Yet its persistence, often in hybrid forms with the lecture or the performance encounter, justifies its place as part of the arts broadcasting mainstream. Two imaginative directors – Russell and Leslie Megahey – have created distinguished fictions working both within and against the conventions of dramatised lives. There are in addition other occasional television films that use the drama as a form for creative filmmaking, even if too often artists' lives are presented in poorly-achieved, under-budgeted and overblown costume drama. Artist dramas were also a productive form for filmmakers working with the Arts Council during the late 1970s and 1980s.

The Divine Michelangelo (2004), produced for BBC Television, opens with a helicopter shot of a figure in costume perched precariously on a knife-edge of rock high in the mountains. As the camera swoops above him and orchestral music swells up, the narrator's voice contributes to the bombast. 'This is the story of a sculptor', she says. 'A sculptor, a painter, an architect who strides the history of art like a colossus.' A fast-cut montage of our figure fighting, loving, painting and carving culminates with the letters of the film's title being carved in stone by a chisel. It is as if the man himself is contributing his signature – and his legitimacy – to the film. What follows is a farrago of costume drama clichés, all colour and movement and spurious mood, and largely indistinguishable from, say, similar scenes of Renaissance Italy, even if supposedly from a century later, in the Caravaggio episode of *Power of Art*. Except that Michelangelo, impersonated by Stephen Noonan, on occasions speaks directly to camera, as well as more often dictating his memoirs to Ascanio Condivi. Art historians pop up to tell us that these memoirs are unreliable, and they are also on hand as the programme – lacking faith in its reconstructed fictional world – attempts to reconstruct how the sculptor might have moved his David through the streets of Florence and how he built the scaffolding from which he painted the ceiling of the Sistine Chapel. *Leonardo* (2003), an earlier production from some of the same team, had tried to build some of that artist's designs, but here these modern-day adventures have next-to-no purpose.

This is the arts film form of the drama at its worst: uncertain of its aims, disconnected from the actual works of its subject, crammed with the clichés of melodrama. How different it was when Ken Russell finally got permission from *Monitor*'s editor Humphrey Burton to have Elgar played by an actor (the context is outlined in Chapter 1). Russell's film is understated, with a quiet elegance and featuring extensive sequences of the music which – with engagingly filmed performers – is simply and plainly shown to us. Humphrey Burton's narration drives the film in much the way that Susannah York's does *The Divine Michelangelo*, but his telling is informative and unostentatious whereas hers is written to bludgeon a viewer into paying attention. *Elgar* ultimately has a commitment to the music, a willingness to trust its power, that is all too clearly lacking from *The Divine Michelangelo*.

Throughout the 1960s, Russell's dramatised biographies of musicians and others developed in complexity, so that *The Debussy Film* (1965) parallels events from the composer's life with a scripted tale of the cast and crew supposedly making the biography. Self-reflexiveness is combined with a concern for the core problems of biographical dramas, which is expressed by the fictional director (played by Vladek Sheybal): 'I don't know how to work it in', he laments. 'Gide, Oscar Wilde, Mallarmé, Rodin, Manet – all interacting, all so complicated … There is so little evidence of what really happened.' Responding to *The Debussy Film*, as well as Russell's biographies of Henri Rousseau, *Always on Sunday* (1965) and Isadora Duncan, *Isadora, The Biggest Dancer in the World* (1966), Joseph Gomez wrote:

> [Russell] weaves together facts, speculations and conjectures into penetrating, visually stunning glimpses of his artist protagonists. These revealing,

complex, frequently ambivalent portraits also derive from the manipulation of a tripartite perspective which incorporates the protagonist's own romantic self-image, a more objective view revealed by the perspective of the time, and finally Russell's personal vision of his subject which is most strikingly presented in the editing, the patterns of aural/visual rhythms, and the structure. (1976: 35)

Forty years separate the production of *The Debussy Film* and *The Divine Michelangelo*, and the production context for the latter is fundamentally different from the place that Russell's film enjoyed. *Monitor* was a protected slot on one of only two channels; there was little pressure to achieve the popular rating expected of *The Divine Michelangelo* early evening on a Sunday night when viewers had a media menu with a thousand other choices. The cost of such drama, including its unconvincing digital renderings of scenes from Renaissance Florence and Rome, is similarly linked with the demands for a healthy viewing share. This may in part account for the drama remaining as the least-developed mainstream form of arts television. Despite recent productions like the lecture-drama and arts-science hybrid *Leonardo* and the unremarkable trilogy *The Impressionists* (2006), there are no multi-part landmark dramas to match against the lecture tradition from *Civilisation* to *Power of Art*. Nor in this genre has the drama ever become a staple, stable form like the encounter. Only once after *Monitor's* cradling of Ken Russell did British television offer a consistent context for a filmmaker to explore the artist drama as a form.

ANIMATED ARTISTS' LIVES

Lautrec
design and direction by Geoff Dunbar
produced at Dragon Productions in association with the Arts Council of Great Britain
5 minutes, 1974,

Hokusai: An Animated Sketchbook
written and directed by Tony White
Arts Council of Great Britain
5 minutes, 1978

The Wind of Changes
animation Phil Mulloy, music by Alex Balanescu
15 minutes, 1996

Although animation was never a specific priority for the Arts Films Committee's funding at the Arts Council, a number of films in the collection use the technique with imagination and sophistication. The work of radical animators the Quay Brothers (whose film *Anamorphosis* (1991) is discussed below) features in two films: an eccentric tribute to a Flemish playwright in *The Eternal Day of Michel de Ghelderode* (1981) and, just before this, in *Punch and Judy* (1980), directed by the Quays (the credit from those days is Brothers Quaij) and their long-time producer Keith Griffiths.

Punch and Judy uses a range of techniques, including conventional documentary and dramatisation to tell the 'tragical comedy or comical tragedy' of the character Mr Punch and those through history who have embodied him. The most powerful scene is an animated realisation by the Quays of extracts from Harrison Birtwistle's *Punch and Judy*, an uncompromising and disturbing music theatre work from 1968.

Another effective combination of animation with contemporary music is *The Wind of Changes*, Phil Mulloy's collaboration with the violinist and composer Alex Balanescu, made for the second series of *Sound on Film* (other films from this strand are discussed in Chapter 3). After his Arts Council-funded dramas *Mark Gertler – Fragments of a Biography* (1981; considered below) and *Give Us This Day* (1982), Mulloy seemingly abandoned live-action filmmaking to develop and refine a highly personal, deliberately naïve style of animation. Crudely-drawn figures populate and die, usually violently, in Mulloy's harsh satires like the *Cowboys* series (1991) and *Intolerance* (2000). (Mulloy's early animations were also supported by Arts Council – and Channel 4 – funding, as were many other animated productions in the 1980s and 1990s.) Figures live and frequently die in *The Wind of Changes* too, but there is a humanity here also, with the film reflecting on events in Balanescu's life.

The composer learns to play the violin in Bucharest under communism in the 1960s. 'I felt completely at the mercy of the authorities', he recalls in voice-over woven within his relentless serial score; 'insecurity and fear permeated the whole society.' Mulloy's visualisation is relentless monochrome apart from splashes of colour, like the red blood on a snowman revealed as a neighbour is taken away for questioning. 'A week later we were invited to his funeral.' Balanescu sees music as a form of escape from this, which Mulloy visualises with comically bizarre images of flight.

Balanescu flees to New York, studying at the Julliard School of Music, but he finds his life there little better than the one he has left behind. 'Insecurity and fear permeated the whole society.' He is disillusioned with the life of the professional musician, but he comes to London where, despite the ignorance of backward-looking audiences and the constraints of capitalism, he begins to build something more meaningful with the music of his own time.

More than two decades before Mulloy's 'home-made' production, the Arts Council commissioned an animation, which is almost certainly its most commercially successful arts film, Geoff Dunbar's *Lautrec* (1974). Dunbar worked with Halas and Batchelor's animation company making commercials in the early 1970s before joining fellow animator Oscar Grillo at Dragon Productions, which co-financed *Lautrec* with the Arts Council. This totally delightful short visualises scenes from the myth-drenched biography of Toulouse Lautrec in

Belle Epoque Paris. There are can-can dancers, circus clowns and the music hall singer Yvette Guilbert brought to life in a fluid style, as well as animations of Lautrec's animals from his 'Histoires Naturelles' series.

Lautrec won a major prize at Cannes and has been seen around the world, and four years later Dunbar produced another animation for the Arts Council, *Ubu* (1978). This incarnated in exquisite drawings Alfred Jarry's grotesque theatrical creation Pére Ubu, who overthrows King Wenceslas in a frenzy of scatological ink splashes and guttural nonsense dialogue.

Hokusai: An Animated Sketchbook (1978) written and directed by Tony White, similarly uses animation to give life to drawings by a nineteenth-century artist. White also worked for a time with Halas and Bachelor and then with animator Richard Williams while he made this personal project. Employing a rich variety of elegant styles, the film pays tribute to the Japanese 'old man mad about drawing' with his animals, archers, mountains and his famous wave.

Artists and filmmakers

'The worst thing in the world', Leslie Megahey once told me, 'is to make a film that would have been better as a book' (Wyver 1986). Working for the BBC through the 1970s and 1980s Megahey produced film biographies which developed into full-scale dramas. For a documentary about Georges Rouault, he brought to life the artist's symbols of the clown and the circus. His Gauguin profile entailed the construction of a South Seas paradise in the studios at Ealing; reproducing for the camera the images of Gauguin's canvases, he punctures the myths around the artist by exposing the production's artifice. But *Schalken the Painter* (1979) is in a different league. Working with his regular cameraman John Hooper, Megahey shot a *grand guignol* chiller in the style of 'Golden Age' Dutch painting. It was based on a tale by the Victorian writer Sheridan Le Fanu and concerns a picture by an artist apprenticed to the well-known Dutch master (and contemporary of Rembrandt) Gerrit Dou. Megahey explained:

> While the lighting and compositions are based on seventeenth-century Dutch art, it wasn't intended to be purely imitative of the paintings. Otherwise it becomes purely an academic exercise. In all my films visual imagery is used as a commentary, to make connections, so you don't have to have disembodied voices explaining things … We've done it so that you are, as it were, looking at paintings – we've tried to get a feeling of looking in. Which reminds us of the way people make icons of their possessions. (In Wyver 1979–80: 113)

As well as editing *Omnibus* during its best years, Megahey directed imaginative films about Landseer – *A Victorian Comedy* (1981) – and a minor Venetian painter, *Cariani and the Courtesans* (1987) and produced an exceptional film version of Bartók's *Duke Bluebeard's Castle* (1989). His trilogy of drama-documentaries *Artists and Models* (1986) is another singular achievement. This uses a single studio space in nineteenth-century Paris as a focus for studies of David, Ingres and Gericault. Most of the action and dialogue is taken directly from witnesses, and the paintings feature prominently, as does the historical context (achieved using silent footage from the French cinema). The assembled witnesses and testimonies frequently contradict each other, and perhaps especially so in the account of Gericault. The painter himself does not appear in this, and our guide is the biographer Charles Clément, who published the first study of the artist some forty years after his death. The drama about David is drawn from the intimate memoir of his life by his pupil Etienne Delecluze, and Ingres too is seen through the eyes of a pupil, Eugene-Emmanuel Amaury-Duval. The resulting mosaics of dramatisation, 'newsreel' and paintings create three of television's richest and most complex portraits of artists. Yet each study is also highly particular and partial. 'These are fragments really', Megahey said at the time. 'You just can't create a complete portrait of a man' (Wyver 1986).

Threaded through the history of British arts programming there are, in addition to the films by Russell and Megahey, a significant number of individual dramas that recreate artists' lives. Tony Palmer has made dramatised composer biographies of, among others, *Puccini* (1984), Handel – *God Rot Tunbridge Wells* (1984–85) – and Henry Purcell – *England, my England* (1995). The most successful of these is *Testimony* (1000), based on Solomon Volkov's edition of Shostakovich's highly contested memoirs. Colin Nears too made drama-documentaries of the lives of composers and writers, including *Carlo Gesualdo* (1983) and *Henrik Ibsen* (1979). The imagination of director David Wheatley brought forth characters from the tales of *The Brothers Grimm* (1979), and a film by Mai Zetterling of the life of *Vincent the Dutchman* (1972) was shown by *Omnibus*. Modigliani was another painter whose life was dramatised – *Requiem for Modigliani* (1970). In the courtroom drama *The Rothko Conspiracy* (1982) the disputed legacy of the abstract expressionist painter was examined along with the motivations of his art and events leading to his suicide. More recently, BBC Two screened a brilliantly distinctive film drama, co-written and directed by Chris Durlacher, of the life of the author of *1984* and *Animal Farm*. Not a single frame exists of archive film of the writer, so *George Orwell: A Life in Pictures* (2003) 'invented' footage of key events in his life, shot in the film styles of the 1930s and 1940s. Orwell's essays become authored documentary films; events described in diaries are 'captured' on home movies; and Movietone newsreel footage is manipulated to reveal Orwell in the trenches of the Spanish Civil War. In addition, artists' lives are the basis of three significant British feature films that were co-funded with television: Peter Greenaway's *The Draughtsman's Contract* (1982), *Caravaggio* (1986) directed by Derek Jarman and John Maybury's study of Francis Bacon, *Love is the Devil* (1998). All three directors trained as fine artists.

FRANTZ FANON: BLACK SKIN WHITE MASK

written and directed by Isaac Julien; co-written and produced by
Mark Nash
a Normal Films production for BBC and the Arts Council of England
52 minutes, 1996

Frantz Fanon: Black Skin White Mask is a complex drama-documentary about
the Martinique-born French author and theorist of anti-colonialism. Fanon's
Black Skin White Masks, written in 1951 when he was 27 and studying psy-
chiatry, is an influential exploration of the effects of colonialism on the human
psyche.

Director Isaac Julien had worked with the collective Sankofa, made innovative dramas – including *Looking for Langston* (1989) and the feature
Young Soul Rebels (1991) – and documentaries, among which was the *Arena/*
Arts Council co-production *The Darker Side of Black* about misogyny and homophobia in dance hall and hip-hop. After *Frantz Fanon: Black Skin White Mask*
he worked primarily producing sensual moving image installations within the
art world like *Long Road to Mazatlan* (2000). Certainly, a decade after the
production of *Frantz Fanon: Black Skin White Mask* there are no contexts in
British television where a documentary of this rigour and density would be
supported.

Julien draws together archive material outlining the historical context of
Fanon's life with readings from Fanon's work and interviews with Joby Fanon,
his brother, and Olivier Fanon, his son. Also contributing are the cultural critics Françoise Vergès, Homi Bhabha and, centrally, Stuart Hall. Hall speaks
with great clarity and precision about Fanon's core insights: the false and
depersonalised nature of the colonialised self, the implication of racism in
the field of vision, the sexualised nature of the
look, masculinity, homosexuality and the Oedipal
complex.

Colin Salmon as the doctor, theorist and activist
in *Frantz Fanon: Black Skin White Mask*

Illustrating and extending the arguments is
a succession of elegant, non-naturalistic scenes
with Colin Salmon playing Fanon. The drama is
played against projected slides and archive, with
layered tableaux expressing relationships between the figures in Fanon's life and giving form to
abstract ideas of the look and the gaze, desire and
subjection and identity.

Fanon's alignment with the National Liberation
Front (FLN) in the war for independence in Algeria leads to a deeper and ultimately fatal involvement with the anti-colonial struggle. The film presents this
journey with intelligence and passion, opening up Fanon's provocative ideas
but also providing a framework for critical engagement with them. 'He was
interested in independence, which is the seizure of liberty by the oppressed

people', Stuart Hall says, distinguishing this from decolonisation, where the colonial power is given away. 'He thought there was something liberating by that very act of armed seizure … and the self-respect that would arise from armed struggle of that kind.'

'My final prayer, oh my body', Fanon says at the close of this rich and profoundly relevant film, 'make of me a man who always questions.'

Alternative lives from the Arts Council

Just as the cinema offered one context for artists' lives to be imaginatively explored, so the funding context at the Arts Council similarly supported films in the drama form that would not have been funded and produced otherwise. There is first a distinct group of documentaries in the Arts Council collection that utilise a trace of the drama with extensive readings from an artist's words. Tristram Powell's *Landscape from a Dream* (1978) speaks only words from the writings of the painter Paul Nash, complementing these with his canvases and photographs together with beautifully filmed landscapes and sea scenes. *Stanley Spencer* (1979), directed by David Rowan, also restricts its script to Spencer's thoughts, some voiced by an actor but others drawn from recordings made with the artist. Again, the images are Spencer's paintings and the places associated with him, notably the village of Cookham. Rowan also incorporates some archive film and a handful of photos that are almost dramatisations, such as the silhouette of a figure meant to be Spencer's sister playing a viola in the nursery. Similarly making effective use of an artist's words is John Bulmer's *Keith Vaughan* (1984) which includes interviews of those who knew the painter alongside readings from his journals, including the moving final page scribbled on 4 November 1977 as he was dying from a deliberate overdose of drugs.

Europe after the Rain: Dada and Surrealism (1978), directed and written by Mick Gold, takes the step of having actors assume the roles of key figures like André Breton. In an exhaustive panorama of the two art movements in its title, the film has actors speak authored statements direct to camera. Gold's later *Schiele in Prison* (1980) also employs minimal elements of drama to consider the context of Secession Vienna and the question of whether what purports to be a prison diary written by the artist is in fact a fake. The sedate and slightly dull *News from Nowhere*, directed by Alister Hallam, was made in the same year as *Europe After the Rain: Dada and Surrealism*, and was the first full drama funded by the Arts Council. Timothy West plays William Morris travelling up the Thames with his friend Richard Grosvenor to his house at Kelmscott Manor.

THE THIRD FRONT
directed by Peter Wyeth, written by Wyeth and Don Macpherson,
produced by Margaret Williams
35 minutes, 1978

The Third Front is a drama about the theatre director Erwin Piscator, who worked primarily during the Weimar Republic in Germany. It is also a film about politics and art, and a political film which ends with a rallying call from Piscator: 'I should like to think that the result of this ... will be to help to unite the forces which share our desire to fight on the third, the cultural front for the breakthrough of a new epoch.'

The Third Front is a political film because it resolutely refuses the conventions of costume drama and, influenced by the theatre of Brecht (and Piscator himself), the films of Straub-Huillet and the radical theory of the moment, sets out to forge a new form of film. In this it is only partly successful, but the attempt alone ensures that it retains an interest that is more than historical.

An actor, Barrie Houghton, takes the role of Piscator, but he is dressed in modern clothes and filmed in contemporary settings. Terry McGinity, similarly attired, takes on a number of other roles, including (I think; the action is not always transparent) Piscator as well. Dramatic events, like the Revolution after World War One in Germany, are minimally suggested in austere shots of street cobbles, our actor running, the sounds of soldiers marching.

Dialectics and drama in *The Third Front*

Piscator speaks, reminiscing at one point for example about John Heartfield turning up late with a backdrop, but he faces off-camera, looking out of frame, refusing contact with either another character or the viewer. When a scene from one of Piscator's productions is staged, the camera keeps its distance, observing analytically and declining to enter among the figures.

The film is set in the London of the late 1970s, so as Piscator speaks about the power of film 'to show the link between events on the screen and the great forces of history' the camera pans around to show the recently completed National Theatre building on the South Bank. Indeed through the film, as Piscator develops his ideas of epic theatre and secures a base for his company, his character travels from a commercial theatre in the West End to the National Theatre.

Short, separate scenes, each introduced by a caption ('1928–31 Contradictions in the Times'), frustrate any sense of a developing narrative. The organising principle, although this is never made explicit, is Piscator's montage book 'Political Theatre'. The viewer must engage with the film's ideas, and is forced to construct meaning from clues, fragments, historical traces. At times, the film's refusal of conventional strategies seems simply obtuse, but it clearly communicates the energy, urgency and intelligence with which it was made.

As the Arts Council began to support filmmakers working with drama, a group of quiet, intelligent films emerged. *Käthe Kollwitz* and *Part of the Struggle* (1985), the latter about art and politics in the Weimar Republic, were made by Ron Orders working with Norbert Bunge and Arpad Bondy. Brenda Bruce movingly interprets extracts from the diary of Kollwitz who died near Dresden in April 1945, while in *Part of the Struggle* German actors portray George Grosz, Otto Dix, John Heartfield and others. Both films are complex engagements with the connections between politics and the arts, and are inflected by – and contributed towards – contemporary debates about socialist cultural practice. Their explicit leftist sympathies together with their austere aesthetic distinguish them strongly from any television dramas of artists' lives. But *Käthe Kollwitz* in particular is rewarding and challenging, and ends with a touching fragment of archive of the artist herself, shot in 1927. From the closing credits, she stares silently out of the frame. 'Without struggle', she has said earlier, 'there is no life.' Peter Wyeth's *Eugene Atget Photographer* (1982) is another minimalist drama, clearly beholden to the stark films of Robert Bresson and of Jean-Marie Straub and Danielle Huillet. But its deliberately affectless approach creates a surprisingly involving frame for presenting Atget's photographs of the buildings and public spaces of Old Paris. The most effective of these films, however, was made about the painter Mark Gertler by Phil Mulloy, who subsequently also directed for the Arts Council *Give Us This Day*, a drama of the life of Robert Tressell, author of the socialist classic *The Ragged-Trousered Philanthropist*.

Mark Gertler – Fragments of a Biography was co-written with actor Antony Sher, who plays the artist struggling with being Jewish in early twentieth-century England, with being a modernist and with being in love with Dora Carrington. Again, the drama is subdued and the characterisation pared back. But the film, which is shot in monochrome apart from Gertler's glowing paintings, remains exceptionally effective. Here is a drama that shows rather than tells, as in one brief shot where Carrington, whom Gertler has been pleading to sleep with him, buttons her coat and walks towards camera and out of frame. Gertler stares off into space, thinking perhaps of Ottoline Morrell's words in an earlier scene about Carrington's hopeless love for Lytton Strachey. What has passed between them remains unspoken, and unknown to the viewer. Yet built from tableaux like this, from pieces of exchanges, their relationship has a richness rare in television's artist lives. *Mark Gertler – Fragments of a Biography* was purchased and screened in 1981 in the BBC's *Omnibus* strand; the editor responsible was Leslie Megahey. But not all such experiments by the Arts Council with drama were as successful. David Rowan's *The Case of Marcel Duchamp* (1984) is an interminable 'investigation' of the artist's work, framed by scenes of two actors playing Sherlock Holmes and Dr Watson. The 'investigatory' conceit quickly feels specious and the film is further burdened by flat-footed scripting and realisation.

Extending the forms

The argument so far (in the breathless one-paragraph version): British television produced a rich, diverse range of programming with and about the arts from

1951 onwards. BBC2 after 1964 and Channel 4 after 1982 greatly extended the ambition and the distinctiveness of arts television, but during the later 1990s, with the rapid development of a multi-channel media world, the terrestrial broadcasters began to withdraw from the types of programmes, including the arts, felt to be marginal for mass audiences. Within the timeframe of this rise and fall of the arts on television, the Arts Council of Great Britain funded a complementary collection of documentaries and performance films, increasingly collaborating with broadcasters. Much of this work, for television and for the Arts Council, can be characterised as a mainstream elaborating three dominant programming forms, the essentials of which were in place by the late 1960s: the lecture, the encounter and the drama. These programme forms have been engagingly and productively explored by producers for four decades and more, but in the early twenty-first century their ritual repetition, coupled with the medium's expected populist address, too often closes down access to the arts and blunts the provocation, the delight, the challenge, the complexity and even the simple beauty of the arts.

As a viewer and someone who actively engages with the arts, as well as a programme maker, I find much of the arts output in the early twenty-first century frustrating and disappointing. In part this is because television's arts agenda is predictable and (predictably) reassuring. Truly contemporary original work, for example, whether in the visual arts or in dance or in new hybrid forms, is rare. There is little from abroad, apart from America: few programmes engage with the rest of Europe, with the arts of Asia and Africa and elsewhere. Work that is intellectually or formally challenging is only occasionally embraced. Complex ideas are resisted and work that takes time to weave its spell or unfold its strangeness is permitted neither time nor space to do so. The small screen no longer aspires to surprise and astonish.

What television mostly offers now, as suggested in Chapter 2, are the arts packaged and mediated by the forms and formats of entertainment today. *Ballet Hoo!*, like *The Singing Estate* (2006) and *The Choir* (2006), is engaging and uplifting reality television. Smart-looking contemporary journalism provides the framework for the items on *The Culture Show*. And an established presenter like Simon Schama employs fast-cut, heavily orchestrated dramatisations to add spice to a handful of conventional lectures about a familiar list of great artists. What is missing from all this – and which television is unquestionably able to offer effectively – is *experience* of the arts, culture without layers of mediation, ideas and images from which the viewer is encouraged to construct their own meanings, their own revelations. Opportunities are denied to those watching to be engaged and drawn in on its own terms to work which might be unfamiliar or even forbidding but which can be satisfyingly unveiled as involving and enriching.

Among the arts to which direct experience is denied by television is classic drama. In the decade since 1998, for example, the BBC has shown just three original Shakespeare productions: *The Merchant of Venice* (2001), taken from the National Theatre, Peter Brook's *The Tragedy of Hamlet* (2002) and live coverage (utilising the tropes of sports broadcasting) of *Richard II* (2003) from Shakespeare's Globe. In the same timeframe I can identify no production of any other drama written before 1900. Instead, as the centrepiece of the BBC's 2005 Shakespeare season, BBC One chose to screen adaptations of four of the plays' plot-lines for its *Shakespeare Re-told* modern-day dramas. The contemporary audience is not offered the opportunity to experience and engage with Shakespeare's language, his characters, concerns and ambiguities. Yet the arts are inherently, insistently ambiguous. Their meanings are messy and unstable and allusive. Television, however, driven moment-by-moment to retain the individual viewer's attention (and thus that of the mass), finds it all but impossible to reflect and protect these qualities, hence the concern – underpinned by an anti-elitist drive – to make the arts 'accessible', to homogenise them in formats familiar from other genres.

Perhaps television in today's world cannot cope with very much ambiguity. Perhaps complexity of ideas and experience is a step too far for how television understands its viewers. Perhaps the mass audiences to which all broadcasters (almost) all the time aspire have little interest in the resonances of the arts. Yet although they might not characterise their motives in this way, achieving the qualities of ambiguity, complexity, challenge and surprise has been fundamental for a succession of filmmakers (as well as certain commissioning executives), and a number of these have already been introduced. Ken Russell is unquestionably one, as are Leslie Megahey, Robert Vas, Nigel Finch, Mike Dibb, Isaac Julien and Jana Bokova. Their contributions are individual, particular and specific, and many of them work within other genres of filmmaking in addition to the arts. Although some like Russell and Megahey can perhaps best be understood in the context of the mainstream forms of arts programming, others simply stand outside these, sometimes self-consciously refusing them and offering up critiques. Collectively, they do not represent any kind of unified tradition, and they have worked across the broadcasters as well as outside them, sometimes supported by the Arts Council and by other funding, public, private and, on many occasions, from their own pocket.

As I was writing this book, I tried to identify attributes in the work of these filmmakers that were common to a number of them. Is it useful, for example, to consider many of them working with the form of the film 'essay' or to attempt to pinpoint the 'poetry' in their conjunctions of images, sounds and ideas? Yet their strategies, and those of many others, including some identified as artists, are so various that eventually I resisted grouping them in any way – or perhaps it was that the attempt to do so defeated me. As a consequence, the remainder of this chapter simply highlights in eight sections the oblique and occasionally oppositional works of significant individuals or groups seeking to do more than retread the dominant forms. Juxtaposed with these sections are further side-bars discussing individual films from the Arts Council collection. Here are some of the boldest engagements with the arts on film, including a number of those that have personally meant a great deal to me (and two of which I own up to having worked on). Complexity, challenge and surprise are common to them all, and even if some fall short of full achievement, each enhances our aesthetic understanding of the world in which we live.

STONES AND FLIES: RICHARD LONG IN THE SAHARA
produced and directed by Philip Haas
a Methodact Ltd production for the Arts Council of Great Britain in association with Channel 4, HPS Films Berlin and Centre Pompidou – La Sept – CNAP – WDR
38 minutes, 1988

Stones and Flies: Richard Long in the Sahara has the clarity and directness of its subject's art.

'A journey is a meandering line. To walk straight up and down many times makes a sculpture.' Richard Long's measured statements punctuate Philip Haas's film.

Stones and Flies: Richard Long in the Sahara is certainly a journey, as it follows Long out into the desert where he produces a number of impermanent sculptures. A tiny figure in an overwhelming landscape, he scuffs the sand to make a line. He drips water on to a rock: one line he calls 'Amazon', another 'Zambezi', a third 'Nile'. Rocks are collected into a circle before all of the stones within are removed.

'Sculptures are a stopping place along a journey. They are where the walk meets the place.'

The film, with its stripped-down aesthetic and single-minded concentration, has certain of the qualities that Long associates with sculpture. Anecdote and biography are rigorously excluded. We hear Long's ideas but these do not 'explain' his work. There is a formal beauty to the images. A precision also, to the framing and each edit. Camerawork and sound recording are acutely responsive to the landscape, but the world is abstract – there is no sense of any specific geography. Time passes, physical effort is expended, men and camels pass by, Long sleeps on the sand. The film has a deliberate rhythm, matching what it observes. To the (minimal) degree that a film makes possible, we enter the artist's world.

'I believe art even reduced to the simplest things can be the vehicle for new ideas.' *Stones and Flies: Richard Long in the Sahara* comprises only simple things, but it looks at Long's work (and listens to its environment) intently, intensively. From this, we can start to think about the land and our relationship to it, about time passing and time past, about solitude and community, about transience and permanence.

The film, inevitably, is a fiction. On this lonely Saharan journey he was accompanied by a crew of at least three, who have no presence here. But perhaps that is why the documentary opens with Long's shadow – any film of an artist working, creating, will only ever have the status of the shapes cast for the prisoners in Plato's cave.

When he makes a sculpture, Long may take a photograph of it, and then he breaks it down, returning the land to its original state. 'It is always my intention and hope to treat each place with respect.' The photograph remains, a trace, a sign of something special. The film, too, remains.

Artists and collaborations

As David Curtis documents in his book *A History of Artists' Film and Video in Britain*, artists in Britain were working with film outside the structures of the mainstream industry from the 1920s onwards. For a short period at the start of the 1970s the Arts Council's Art Film Committee invested in artists' films before (as is outlined in Chapter 3) responsibility for such funding was delegated to a sub-committee. David Hall produced a series of short 'interventions' for Scottish Television in 1969 and in the early years of Channel 4 artists were able to work directly for the medium, including initiatives organised by the producer Anna Ridley and, with the support of the Arts Council, for the second series of the anthology *Ghosts in the Machine* (1988). *One Minute Television* (1990–93) commissioned short artists' films, again with the Arts Council and these invariably inventive works were shown on *The Late Show*. Occasional more ambitious films include David Larcher's electronic extravaganzas *EETC* (1986) and *Granny's Is* (1989) produced for Channel 4, and Richard Billingham's *Fish Tank* (1998) and Tracey Emin's feature *Top Spot*.

Emin's film works with a comparatively conventional narrative language to explore relationships among six teenage girls in the artist's home town of Margate. But other artists have delighted in working entirely against the expectations of broadcasting, playing tricks with its technology and subverting its surfaces. Occasionally, the image- and innovation-hungry forms of commercials or title sequences drew directly from the ideas of visual artists, 'stealing', appropriating or creating *hommages* to their inventions. By the late 1990s, however, television's tolerance (and it was rarely more than this) of artists working directly with the medium was constrained by commercial demands. At the same time, artists increasingly found that galleries and museums, as well as clubs, outdoor screens and other less obvious venues, were far more congenial contexts for which to create works. For many, they were also more profitable, since a healthy market was stimulated for limited-edition film and video works and for the often complex installations within which the images are presented.

Among work funded by the Arts Council, *The World of Gilbert & George* (1981), directed by the duo and supported as a documentary (not an artists' film), intercuts intoned statements delivered direct to camera ('Beauty is my art') with images of London, of the artists' home and of the subjects in their pictures, including young men from the East End and the Union Jack. Comparably eccentric and (for many audiences) self-indulgent is *The Lacey Rituals* (1973) that starts with a clapperboard announcing 'Scene 1, take 1' and a scene of children preparing breakfast cereal. Made by the artist Bruce Lacey, his wife Jill and offspring Kevin, Tiffany, Saffron and Fred (they take turns to operate the camera, he explains) the film shows 'some of the rituals, obsessions and habits of the Lacey family'. (Hand-written credits on a single sheet at the end acknowledge that 'the sound recordist, lighting and technical adviser was Chris Robson'.) What they promise is exactly what you get, in an hour of home movies made with professional equipment, occasionally hinting that a parody of public information films is intended or perhaps a pastiche of an anthropology film, or even a Brechtian exposure of the constructed nature of documentary.

Other early artists' films from the Arts Council included David Hall's *Vertical* (1970) and Derek Boshier's *The Link* (1970), both intended to document the creation of an artwork (which is what secured the funding) but both engaging directly with the components of the filmmaking processes and, in David Curtis's phrase, 'documenting nothing but an idea'. *Vertical* consists of images of Hall's linear sculptures placed in landscapes and shot to create, and also destroy, illusions of 'squareness' and 'straightness'. Hall said at the time:

> In part, the film extends the ideas of my earlier sculpture but it exists as a statement in its own right. Something is created that could not be encountered within the conventions of object making. This film is not a documentary, although the material is of documented events, situations and structures. Participation exists conceptually, somewhere between the surface of the screen and the events themselves.[3]

Another early production, *Cast* (1971) made by artist Peter Dockley, features his human figures made of wax which across twelve minutes 'melt' away as time passes in stop-frame photography. Nicolas Monro's *Sailing Through* (1971) and William Pye's *Reflections* (1972) similarly show sculptures created by the artist-filmmaker, placed in lush landscapes of wind-blown grass in the former and seen close-up, fast-cut and revolving in the latter. Pye's film is fascinated by the sky, water and landscape viewed in the mirror-like surfaces of his forms.

Alongside the direct commission to an artist, there have been other forms of close collaboration between painters, sculptors and photographers with filmmakers to create something rather different. Almost all films, of course, and certainly those made with and about living artists, are – to a degree – collaborations with their subjects. Often the relationship involves a willingness to take part in some way, as well as the grant of rights, in exchange for a tacit understanding of sympathetic treatment. Occasionally subjects refuse to participate on camera, as Howard Barker did for *Refuse to Dance* (1986), a study of the recurring themes and preoccupations in his plays. Whether or not the artist is present in almost all cases the shaping force is the filmmaker's, however sensitive or responsive she or he may feel they are to an artist's work and ideas. But if the balance of influence can be made more equal, either informally or formally, the results can be compelling. Such creative collaborations were encouraged by the Arts Council funders (not least in the *Dance for the Camera* and *Sound on Film* series, both discussed in sidebars), and directors like James Scott and Philip

Haas demonstrated how working in this way can be revelatory about the artist and prompt formal invention. Haas is credited as producer on *The World of Gilbert & George* but his Arts Council collaborations with Boyd Webb, *Scenes & Songs from Boyd Webb* (1984) and especially *Stones and Flies: Richard Long in the Sahara*, made with the artist, are richer achievements.

James Scott's dazzling co-created film *Richard Hamilton* is considered in Chapter 3. Hamilton also appears in the extraordinary two-screen *The Great Ice-Cream Robbery* (1971), which Scott made with Claes Oldenberg, although he alone takes the directing credit. Scott's intention at the time was deliberately oppositional. He said in a 1972 interview:

> The whole [film] industry is in the hands of a few people with money who don't want the structure to change. One of the reasons I made *The Great Ice-Cream Robbery* for two screens and soundtracks was to fight this idea of a 'product'. It meant the film couldn't be treated in the normal exploitative way and only those people who really want to show it will take trouble with it. (In Hodgson 1973)

Although two-screen films were not uncommon at the London Film-makers' Co-operative, and Paul Morrissey and Andy Warhol had used the technique for *Chelsea Girls* (1966), there are few if any other documentaries about artists that project side by side separate image and sound tracks. Black spacing interrupts loosely-edited sequences which feature Oldenberg installing his retrospective at the Tate Gallery, preparations for an event combining a lecture and performance, policemen removing an unauthorised ice cream trolley, extracts from the artist's Super-8 film 'notebook', and a journey across London to find a pair of cooling towers that he had seen from the train. In the chaos of images and sounds, which can be seen as the documentary equivalent of the 'happenings' with which Oldenberg was involved during the 1960s in New York, the show is opened and an idea emerges for a sculpture transforming the chimneys into female knees. The police try to tow away the ice cream trolley, which has been illegally parked outside the Tate, and it topples over, spilling contents across the road. A number of Oldenberg's sculptures feature ice creams. Showings of the film have been exceptionally rare in the years since it was completed.

EXPANDING PICTURES
produced by Sophie Gardiner and Debra Hauer
a Euphoria Pictures production for BBC and the Arts Council of England
8 x c. 8 minutes, 1997

Expanding Pictures was intended to be a parallel 'collaborations' project, bringing television directors together to work with performance artists. Several of the eight completed shorts work with this model, including Deborah May's diverting, fast-cut montage of relationship dialogues, *You Don't Say*, with artists John Carson and Donna Rutherford. Ronald Fraser-Munro contributes a dull, shrill sci-fi fantasy, *LSDTV*, directed by Anne Parouty, and in *Spitting Mad* Margaret Williams makes an offbeat cooking show with Bobby Baker. For *How Do You Know It's Warren Beatty's Coat?*, the performance group Station House Opera worked with director Charles Garrad on a strange mime with three characters in an inhospitable world.

Rather more interesting is *The Link*, devised and performed by Glyn Davies Marshall and directed and edited by Judi Alston and Steve Richards. This has a conventional documentary imperative as Marshall wanted to discover how his grandfather died. He tells the story of his investigation into a mining accident as he exhausts himself by walking and crawling around with medical stretchers (made with his father) on his back, for he found out that his grandfather died from a heart attack after an intensive period of stretcher-bearing. 'I figured I would pick up the stretcher where my granddad left off.' He submits himself to more punishing physical exertion as he attempts to reproduce the monotony and toil of the 12-hour shift that his grandfather had just finished when he died. As 'a tribute to all miners' *The Link* has a moving poetic intensity.

The most notable aspect of the project, however, is that three of the key visual artists of the 1990s made works directly for television. Sam Taylor-Wood created the elegant *Misfit*, which has Kylie Minogue, filmed from behind, miming to the last-known recording of a castrato. For *2 into 1*, Gillian Wearing recorded a mother and her two 10-year-old twin sons, with one generation lip-synching the comments about themselves by the other. The twins appear to speak their mother's exasperated love for them, while she mouths their comments and criticism about herself. The effect is strangely disconcerting.

Perhaps the stand-out work from the series is Mark Wallinger's *Angel*, shot in a single continuous take. The artist takes the role of his sightless alter ego who he calls Blind Faith. Standing at the foot of an escalator in London's Angel tube station, he recites verses from St John's Gospel in the 1611 St James' Bible: 'In the beginning was the Word, and the Word was with God and the Word was God.' But he is speaking it backwards and the tape has been played in reverse, and people to either side can be seen walking in reverse. When he stops speaking he is carried backwards up the escalator in a kind of ascension as Handel's anthem 'Zadok the Priest' crashes in on the soundtrack. As the curator Imogen Cornwall-Jones has written,

> Appearances are inverted and Wallinger's contradictions reflect those which he perceives as inherent in Christianity, where God is man or bread is seen as flesh. The work's visual ambiguity is also echoed by the paradoxical nature of St John's Gospel recited by Wallinger and the spectator is asked to consider religious belief in a realm beyond the visible. (2002)

Expanding Pictures was made just as artists' video was beginning to be embraced by the art market, and while the BBC acquired limited broadcasting rights, exhibition rights were retained by the artist. *Angel*, for example, was issued in an edition of ten that, according to the *Daily Telegraph*, were sold for £3,000 each (a bargain given later prices) to among others Charles Saatchi, the Tate and the Arts Council Collection. After *Expanding Pictures* the focus for most visual artists working with film and video was the gallery rather than television: control of the work's circulation could be exercised more fully, especially if the video was embedded in an installation, and the returns were, potentially at least, significantly greater.

Each of the *Expanding Pictures* films includes one of a series of delightful title sequences, created by artists Paul Harrison and John Wood. Each fragment simply and elegantly challenges our sense of the television screen's space.

'Make it new': *State of the Art*

State of the Art (1987) is a series of six 50-minute documentaries made by writer Sandy Nairne, director Geoff Dunlop and myself for Channel 4 and WDR, Cologne, between 1985 and 1987. Transmission was accompanied by a book and a touring exhibition of a work by each of the artists in the series, and we put together an extensive series of screenings and discussions. The films developed from conversations begun after working with these collaborators on the Arts Council-funded film about new sculpture in Britain, *Just What Is It ?* We set out to consider the conventions and the inadequacies of dominant approaches to the visual arts on television, and to work towards new ways to present what the series sub-title details as 'ideas and images in the 1980s'. Each of the six programmes takes a theme which had and has as much importance in society in general as in the art world: for example Value, History and Identity. The work and ideas of four or five artists (and in the case of Value, dealers and critics) are explored within the framework of this theme, and those featured include Joseph Beuys, Cindy Sherman, Jean-Michel Basquiat and Antony Gormley. The concentration is exclusively on their work and associated understandings, not their biography or lifestyle.

'Make it new' was how Ezra Pound translated a directive from Confucius, and among the strategies we adopted in pursuit of this were the absence of a presenter or single narrator. Instead a quilt of quotations (from philosophers, critics, economists and social theorists) provides the intellectual framework, complementing the interview contributions of the artists. The quotations, together with minimal elements of conventional narration, imparting essential information, are read by four different voices in each film. Through the use of these quotations, and associated images – both of artworks and of sequences in the world – the films have a concentrated engagement with the ideas of postmodernism, with questions of sexuality and identity, and with a leftist politics. They aim to offer alternatives to the economy and the society given form in the contemporary urban world, in its media and its spectacles. *State of the Art* also has its artists and other interviewees speak direct to camera, not off to the side of frame as if to a surrogate for the viewer. Beuys and Eric Fischl, Basquiat and Barbara Kruger speak to the person watching, and the effect in many cases is vivid and direct. (A half-mirror mounted in front of the camera lens, realised by director Geoff Dunlop and director of photography Jeremy Stavenhagen, facilitated filming in this manner, allowing the interviewee to look straight towards the camera but in fact to see the questioner who was seated at a 90-degree angle off to one side.)

There is a rigorous avoidance of anecdote and an intense focus on artworks and ideas. These are intellectual films, documentaries that demand attention. If they want to attract and even seduce a viewer, they aim to do so by engaging the mind and the eye, but not by telling a story or introducing a quirky character. The films also demonstrate a precision in their filming of artwork that stands up to the passage of years and which has been influential on the styles with which Illuminations has worked ever since. Paintings and sculptures, for example, are filmed from originals not transparencies – we travelled extensively to shoot actual artworks, we persuaded owners to bring some out of stores and we hung or arranged them in spaces just for the camera. Canvases are shown full-frame, and then details of an image are selected; there is minimal movement across an artwork, and what there is is strongly motivated. The pace of the editing, especially of the artwork sequences, is more measured than is conventional in television, and seems strikingly so when compared with the faster-cut programming of the early twenty-first century.

Responses to the series were far from generally enthusiastic. For many, it came off the screen as inaccessible, alienating, humourless, relentless, confusing. Certainly there is not much humour, but its attempt to develop a new form for arts documentaries was bold and unquestionably appropriate for its moment. The critic Peter Fuller was among the more voluble critics of the series. He wrote in an article titled 'The great British art disaster',

> In so far as it is not just mindless cacophony [*State of the Art*] presents an alliance between two philistinisms: that of the old New Left, and that of the yuppie, or managerial, end of the (relatively) New Right. They are united in their 'progressive' contempt for duty, taste, skill and position … [Nairne] offers no vision, and affirms no value. He wishes only to assert the relativity of all aesthetics, and the validity of *any* idea, however venal, or contradictory, it may be. (1987: 17)

I cannot adopt any kind of distance towards the series, but while I recognise the charge of relativism, I feel firmly that the films resist precisely this. Their effect, earnest as it often is, is the opposite of asserting the equivalence of all positions and withdrawing from discrimination. Instead, they make explicit some of the assumptions behind value judgements, and offer a complex mesh of artworks and quotation to explore the politics of the visual arts, and more broadly of all systems of representation.

CORRECTION, PLEASE or HOW WE GOT INTO PICTURES
directed by Noël Burch
52 minutes, 1979

'Last night I was in the kingdom of shadows. If you only knew how strange it is to be there.' The first spoken words in Noël Burch's remarkable documentary are those of the well-known description of seeing a cinematograph show by Maxim Gorki, from 1896. On the screen, shadowy workers are leaving a factory, although not in the Lumière Bros.' version of this subject, but in a slightly later French short from c.1900. Gorki's testimony continues to the point where he acknowledges that the film show had taken place in a brothel.

The quotation introduces a celluloid study in which, as an opening title details, 'may be seen how the mechanics of certain very primitive films (made prior to 1906) shed light on the nature of both the language of Cinema and the audience attitudes associated with it.' The note that Gorki had been visiting a brothel when he first saw the cinema (which is often lost when the quote is used in film history books) also establishes the theme of the sexualised nature of watching figures on a screen.

Burch's distinctive method is to juxtapose selected film titles from the first years of the cinema, elements of didactic analysis and four elegantly-staged versions of a scene drawn (uncredited) from a Dorothy L. Sayers mystery story. In each of the four dramatisations, different elements of film language are utilised, beginning with a sequence of fixed wide shots without camera movement accompanied by a jaunty narration.

The scene involves a young man (named James Williamson, as a tribute to the early Hove-based filmmaker) delivering a letter to the alluring Countess Skladanovsky in her modernist home. When this is reprised, it includes expository titles, cuts on action and minimal camera movement. The third telling has editing working towards a more elaborate construction of space, and by the fourth there is sound and the smooth presentation of narrative according to the rules of what Burch has elsewhere called the Institutional Mode of Representation (IMR). IMR is the naturalised 'Hollywood' form of film language which developed only haltingly between 1895 and the arrival of sound, even if today we have all internalised this and accept it as the only 'correct' way of telling stories in film.

Noël Burch is a prominent academic and film historian and as such, is a rare figure interested in both writing about film and actively working with it. (Peter Wollen and Laura Mulvey, who are also represented in the Arts Council collection, are two others.) *Correction, Please or How We Got into Pictures* was made at a time when he was also working on the essays published in English in 1990 as *Life to those Shadows*. 'The point', he wrote in that book's introduction, 'was to show that the "language" of the cinema is in no way natural, *a fortiori* that it is not eternal, that it has a history and is a product of

History' (1990: 2). The films of the very first years of the cinema, precisely because of their difference, can help us recognise how constructed and conventional is the dominant film language of Hollywood and mainstream television today.

Paradoxically, given Burch's concern with locating film language in history, the extended extracts (and often whole films) included in *Correction, Please or How We Got into Pictures* are displaced from history, denied even a title or date until the closing credits. Fascinating one-reelers like *The Ingenious Soubrette* (1902) and *The Story the Biograph Told* (1905) are included (in sometimes disappointingly murky prints) without context, industrial background or authorship. Burch's interest here seems strictly formal.

Or perhaps not strictly formal, since he is engaged too by the seductive, fetishistic power of the film image. An inserted close-up of a young woman's ankle in *The Gay Shoe Clerk* (1902) has what one didactic inter-title calls a 'violent intimacy', and the vampish Countess hynotises Williamson with her alluring beauty and with her intense gaze directed out of the screen at the spectator. The words 'Keep looking!' are overlaid on the hypnotism in both instruction and admonition to us.

The formal, for Burch and for the film, is also political. Like *Correction, Please or How We Got into Pictures*, Burch's book *Life to those Shadows* was conceived in the late 1970s, as he writes, 'in the penumbra of a broad aspiration shared at the time by certain filmmaker theorists (the most prestigious of whom were Godard and Straub), an aspiration to *practices breaking with current standards*, pointers as it were to the political practices of the future Revolution' (1990: 2). The crude version of the associated argument runs that Hollywood's function is to 'misinform and anaesthetise the masses of the people'. New forms of film are necessary before the masses recognise – and follow – the true path towards social equality.

Thirty years ago, this did not seem as unlikely (or as naïve) an aspiration as it does in the early twenty-first century. Certainly a version of this analysis underpinned much theoretical writing in the 1970s as well as the production of many of the most interesting and challenging films from the time, among which, Noël Burch's *Correction, Please or How We Got into Pictures* undeniably earns its place.

The Brothers Quay: *Anamorphosis*

'If anamorphosis is the art of delaying access to deeper meaning', the narrator says, 'then we must learn to wait for revelation.' The comment could also apply to the films of the Brothers Quay, animators (and identical twins) who studied at the Royal College of Art and the creators of fantastical and bizarre filmic worlds. Their work since *Nocturna Artificilia* (1979), made for the BFI Production Board, has included pop promos, commercials, channel idents and feature films, and they collaborated with their regular producer Keith Griffiths on two documentaries with Arts Council support: *Punch and Judy* and *The Eternal Day of Michel de Ghelderode*. The latter focuses typically on a figure entirely marginal to the accepted mainstream of Western culture, the Belgian civil servant and playwright Michel de Ghelderode who between 1918 and 1937 developed an eccentric, surreal form of visual theatre. The documentary stages tableaux from these dramas, referencing Flemish painting, the traditions of carnival, the religious and historical memories of Flanders. Often the film is so oblique as to be obscure, especially as many of the scenes are staged in semi-darkness, yet there are also snatches of the Quays' entirely distinctive vision.

In 1991, again working with Griffiths and with the art historian Roger Cardinal (and Ernst Gombrich as consultant), they produced a film for the short-lived funding scheme Program for Art on Film, jointly supported by the Metropolitan Museum of Art and the J. Paul Getty Trust. This aimed to bring creative filmmakers together with prominent art historians to fashion new approaches to visual arts documentaries, an aim admirably achieved by *Anamorphosis*. The Quays' fastidious model animation brings to life ideas about this sixteenth-century artistic technique that, as an opening title explains, 'plays mischievously yet revealingly between the eye and what it sees'. A figure whose vision is directed by a picture frame fixed just before its face stares out at images that make visual sense only when seen from a specific viewpoint. The film employs a range of examples, including woodcuts by Erhard Schon from around 1535 and the skull in the foreground of Hans Holbein's 'The Ambassadors'. These artworks are spun and twisted, stretched and cropped, their concealed pictures mysteriously, magically appearing and vanishing. Animated figures embody the outline figures from historical engravings, inhabiting a sensuous, theatrical world

Animation and art history in the Quay Brothers' *Anamorphosis*

of threads and tassles, of mechanical turntables and light flickering on gilded frames. Most marvellously, the apparatus is reconstructed that is believed to have been used by the artist Emmanuel Maignan to create his 1642 anamorphic fresco of St Francis of Paola in the Rome monastery of SS Trinita dei Morti.

When the film looks at 'The Ambassadors' it directs the eye in a deliberate way that is distinct from the conventional manner of filming transparencies with a rostrum camera. Here, instead of the measured, even movement across the surface, the camera skitters and jumps, withdrawing into an imaginary environment for the picture, then caressing a line through its meticulously detailed, luxurious surface. When the skull is shown, the film explains that 'the visual trick of anamorphosis conceals, then discloses the truth which underlies appearances'. As this quote may suggest, *Anamorphosis* is, wonderfully, as concerned with seeing in general as it is with its ostensible subject. It is about how we look – or fail to look – at images, and about films, including films about the arts. For it is a quiet plea for slow looking, and for the understanding that can come from this. 'An image grasped too quickly', the script says, 'might not leave a lasting impression. To lead the eye slowly through incomprehension – and *then* to offer a resolution – that is insight.'

FRIDA KAHLO & TINA MODOTTI

script and direction Laura Mulvey & Peter Wollen
produced by Modelmark Ltd for the Arts Council of Great Britain
29 minutes, 1983

> 'Two choices for women. The personal: the traditional sphere of women, their suffering, their self-image. On the other hand: the political, the renunciation of home and family to produce images dedicated to social change. Frida Kahlo and Tina Modotti both provoke and defy such neat categorisation.'

The opening narration is read over a black screen with two exposed details, two women. After the title card, the portraits are revealed as the artists Frida Kahlo and Tina Modotti depicted in a 1929 mural by Diego Rivera for the Ministry of Education, Mexico City. Laura Mulvey and Peter Wollen's notably direct film parallels their lives and works, detailing the common elements in their lives (women, Mexico, art, revolution, as one of the film's numerous captions details them) but equally engaged by the differences between them.

In a succession of paired sequences – 'Roots', 'Biography', 'Inward/Outward', 'The Body', 'Injury/Beauty' – aspects are outlined of one woman and her work followed by comparable concerns related to the other. In the first of these, an unadorned presentation of Kahlo's paintings, as if in a slide-show, is accompanied by an outline of her life told in social terms, deliberately avoiding the story that she was crippled in a traffic accident. Here and elsewhere, the paintings are shown complete and without camera movement, just as Modotti's photographs are treated throughout the film. At the end of the sequence they are reprised, in reverse order, so as to give the viewer an opportunity to re-view them with the new awareness prompted by the narration. This is followed by a similar presentation of Modotti's work, stressing the political engagement demonstrated in her images which are characterised not as documentary but as emblematic.

The filmic dialectic pairs a discussion of Modotti's restless travelling throughout her life, illustrated by penny-plain maps with cities picked out from the continents of Europe and the United States, with a subjective Super-8 sequence of the 'Blue House' in Mexico City where Kahlo was born, lived for much of her life and died.

The most effective such conjunction is 'The Body' which shows first an extract from the 1920 movie *The Tiger's Coat* (credited simply to 'Hollywood', as if this suffices for capitalism's monolithic image industry). Modotti is the featured actress grieving at a bedside. Immediately following this is vivid home-movie colour footage of Kahlo and Rivera at the Blue House. The film contributes no discussion and refuses the viewer a narrative for either scene, but the counterpoint richly suggests questions about fiction and documentary, image and audience, drama and life.

The lives and the art of
Frida Kahlo & Tina Modotti

A suggestive analysis is offered of the images made by each woman. 'Frida Kahlo lived in pain and in crisis with her own body', the film puts forward. 'By painting her self-portrait she transcribed her injuries into emblems and allegory.' By contrast, Modotti 'was famous as a beauty, but she rebelled against the gaze of others to make her own images of the working women of Mexico'.

Biography and image are framed consistently by politics, and while the personal stories emerge, sentiment and pity, even admiration, are never on offer. A BBC film made more than twenty years later, distinguished in its own way, offers a revealing comparison, at least in relation to Kahlo. While Modotti is hardly better-known now than in the early 1980s, Kahlo's position in the popular imagination has been transformed, not least by the influential (1983) biography authored by Hayden Herrera (thanked in the credits on Mulvey and Wollen's film). By the mid-2000s, Kahlo's life of tragedy, as it is characterised, is almost as well known as Van Gogh's.

Mulvey and Wollen curated an exhibition of Kahlo and Modotti at around the same time at the Whitechapel Gallery, London and this accompanying film was their first shared attempt to use documentary alongside their fundamental contributions to film theory. (Wollen's book *Signs and Meaning in the Cinema* introduced ideas from Eisenstein and other theorists (the influential third edition was published in 1972) and Mulvey's much-anthologised 1975 essay 'Visual Pleasure and Narrative Cinema' is a foundational text of feminist criticism.)

For all that it is deeply informed by theory, *Frida Kahlo & Tina Modotti* has a directness, a formal clarity and an intellectual complexity that more than compensate for its avoidance of film's (too) easy pleasures. At its close, the opening narration is repeated through to '…Frida Kahlo and Tina Modotti both provoke and defy such neat categorisation'. Then it continues, moving beyond the dichotomy of the personal and the political, 'Frida's fascination with her own body and her national culture was deeply political. Tina's photography is strongly marked by her personal experience as a woman.'

There is a sense that the film, with its minimal but precisely-deployed means, has achieved a similar resolution, justifying its quiet but determined closure: 'The energy that each found to combat both personal calamity and political oppression survives in their art. We still feel it today.'

Memory and Outrage

In my 1999 obituary of Marc Karlin, I described him as the most significant unknown filmmaker working in Britain during the previous three decades. He was a central figure in the radical avant-garde of the 1970s and made a major contribution to the shaping of Channel 4. As a director he crafted innovative and passionate films for both Channel 4 and BBC2. Yet his rigour, his intellectualism and intolerance of anything he considered lazy or in bad faith conspired with the trends towards corporatism in television to render him and his work all but invisible.

In the mid-1960s he studied theatre direction in London but he was soon caught up in filmmaking and in the Paris events of May 1968. In part under the influence of the film essayist Chris Marker, he made *Dead Man's Wheel* (1969), a film about a train driver which combines a deep respect for one human being with an analysis of one political, social and cultural moment. Karlin was a political filmmaker: his socialist and libertarian beliefs frame every sequence he constructed. Yet his concern with the truths that an image can reveal ensured that his films avoid agit-prop and instead celebrate complexity, ambiguity and understanding. In the 1970s in London he was a member of two important filmmaking collectives, first Cinema Action and then the Berwick Street Collective. *Nightcleaners*, made by the Berwick Street Collective about the work and activism of the women who clean London's offices, is a defining film of this time, combining formalist experiment and political will with an unsentimental humanity.

Working as an individual director, he made *For Memory* (1986) for the BBC and the BFI Production Board, a challenging, rich, slow-paced and uncompromising engagement with history and the fragility of memory. Puzzled by a project which refused to conform to the expected etiquette of programmes, the BBC consigned its screening to an anonymous afternoon slot. Two series for Channel 4, one on the aftermath of the revolution in Nicaragua and one on utopias and the dreams of different socialisms, occupied much of the 1980s. Both series of films, like all his work, were only lightly disguised autobiography and both reflected an optimistic and unswerving belief in people's individual ability to resist the brutalising forces of contemporary society. Similarly shot through with the autobiographical is *The Outrage* (1995), a film that he wrote and directed for the *Tx.* strand that I edited. It was sparked by his feelings when confronted with a looming painting by Cy Twombly that appears to be chalk scribbles on a blackboard. The central character in *The Outrage*, M., a man who disappears after seeing this artwork, speaks of 'the anger, the feeling of being duped ... I suddenly felt violently seasick. The painting made me feel as if my life had no object, no intent.' M./Marc channels this anger into an intellectual and fantastical quest for the meaning of art in today's world, a quest that involves M. being transformed into a camel, a lion and a child, and a search for redemption through beauty that takes in iconoclasm during the English Civil War and Ricky Villa's winning goal for Spurs in the 1981 FA Cup Final against Manchester City.

The Outrage is a wonderful, sensuous film about Twombly's paintings (luminously filmed by Jonathan Collinson), but the viewer learns next-to-nothing about the artist. Rather it is a film about looking at art, and about art looking at us; about meaning and God and language and yearnings, 'yearnings for a time lost and a time to be regained'. Among the contributors, along with artist Michael Craig-Martin and curator Norman Rosenthal, is the philosopher Andrew Benjamin, who aptly suggests, 'It seems to me part of the job of art is to make people feel lost, to make people feel not at home, to make people feel not cosy.' At the close, M. is both lost and found, and, as the film's narration suggests, 'free to make his own traces'.

In the months before his sudden death, Karlin was working on a script about Milton, and he would delight in reading aloud passages of *Paradise Lost*; there seemed nothing incongruous about this radical, committed, modern man speaking the words of a seventeenth-century poet. The Milton script locates *Paradise Lost* amongst a group of eccentric intellectuals in a London of the near future. Karlin made a film test in which, because he could not afford an actor, he played the character of 'The Master'. He claimed to be uneasy with the role, a dominant recluse-like figure concerned above all to pass on the lessons of history and the revolutionary strengths of Milton's verse to later generations. But he had, of course, written it in his own image.

Dramatic screens

The history of performance on British television is far less researched and documented than that of the visual arts, and as a consequence of this, drama, dance and opera have received far less focus in this volume than films about painting and sculpture. A brief history of classic drama on-screen[4] begins with extracts from the classics shown in the very earliest years of broadcasting and then with a live relay from St Martin's Theatre on 16 November 1938 of J. B. Priestley's *When We Are Married*. The BBC's Annual Report for 1946–47 mentioned 'numerous transmissions direct from theatres, such as had become a feature of television programmes before the war' (BBC 1948: 28), and broadcasts of this kind continued into the 1960s when farces with Brian Rix were shown live from the Whitehall Theatre. Studio drama also started before World War Two, and Neil Taylor (1998) has noted that in 1937, for example, the BBC made 46 broadcasts of excerpts from stage plays and 56 of complete (and usually short) ones.

By 1950–51 the BBC was showing three live plays each week, many of them classics. The rhetoric of live transmission with four or five cameras from a studio space was constricting but could be employed with great flexibility and imagination. Classics including Jean-Paul Sartre's *In Camera* and Henry de Montherlant's *Malatesta* were featured in the first series of *The Wednesday Play* (1964–70) but increasingly they were confined to the Sunday night *Play of the Month* (1965–83) strand on BBC1. There were also singular events like the 15-part television series *An Age of Kings* (1960) drawn from Shakespeare's History plays (Sean Connery was in the cast) and its follow-up *Spread of the Eagle*

(1963), nine one-hour episodes taken from the same author's Roman plays. *The Wars of the Roses* (1964) was made with the Royal Shakespeare Company and 'entirely restaged at Stratford to suit television' (BBC 1965: 24). Fifteen years later, the BBC embarked on the complete works in the seven-year project *The BBC Television Shakespeare*. Shakespeare, as Taylor's research has revealed, is far and away the most performed theatre playwright on the BBC. From the early years to 1994, the BBC mounted 281 productions of the Bard's complete plays and significant excerpts. Shaw (99), Ibsen (57) and Priestley (45) were the most popular writers, whereas Brecht and Beckett, for example, come a long way down the list with just 26 and 18 productions respectively.

Significant one-offs continued to be produced in the 1980s, including Richard Eyre's production of Chekhov's *The Cherry Orchard* (1981), translated by Trevor Griffiths and starring Judi Dench, and distinguished studio productions under former RSC director David Jones for *Play of the Month* and also in *Theatre Night* (1985–91). By the 1990s, classic drama was increasingly rare even on BBC2, and the *Performance* strand, which in 1997 made only five productions, was discontinued the following year after Richard Eyre's *King Lear* with Ian Holm. In the 2000s it has been almost non-existent, although BBC Four tried a short-lived experiment in low-cost recordings from theatres; Chekhov's *Three Sisters* (2004), as adapted by Christopher Hampton, in an unwatchable television version, was as far back into theatrical history as this initiative ventured.

The focus of ITV drama in the early years was largely on original contemporary work, but there were occasional ambitious studio productions, including John Dexter's *Twelfth Night* (1970) with Alec Guinness and Ralph Richardson and *The Merchant of Venice* (1974), directed by Jonathan Miller, with Laurence Olivier and Joan Plowright. Trevor Nunn made three adaptations from his RSC productions: *Antony and Cleopatra* (1974), *The Comedy of Errors* (1978) and a claustrophobic *Macbeth* (1979) with Ian McKellen and Judi Dench. ITV also made a very smart and watchable updated *Othello* (2001), adapted by Andrew Davies with the Moor as the Metropolitan Police's first black head. Channel 4's commitment to theatrical events in the 1980s is outlined in Chapter 2, and the channel continued to fund a handful of major productions including Tim Supple's beautiful *Twelfth Night* (2003) with a predominantly Anglo-Indian cast, and Gregory Doran's *Macbeth* (2003) with Antony Sher and Harriet Walter. Doran took his acclaimed RSC production from the theatre and re-conceived it for the screen, shooting with a single camera across twelve days in London's Roundhouse.

Given the almost complete disappearance of classic drama from television, what opportunity is there for 'expanding the forms' of this art on the small screen? Three classic productions can perhaps give some sense of future paths for exploration. Roland Joffe directed John Ford's dark revenge tragedy *'Tis Pity She's a Whore* (1980), updating the action to Victorian times. Kenneth Cranham and Cheri Lunghi couple and kill their way through the violent tale, which Joffe filmed in and around a country mansion. Shooting on 16mm film gave him a far greater flexibility than could be achieved at the time with tape cameras in the studio, but this form of low-budget location-based classic adaptation has rarely been tried since. Two years earlier the brilliant director Alan Clarke had shown how it was possible to rethink the form of studio drama with a radical version of Georg Büchner's great tragedy of the French Revolution, *Danton's Death* (1978) with Ian Richardson and Norman Rodway. Clarke shot the production on long lenses, often achieving a tableau-like effect, with what producer David Jones admiringly described as 'a very cool, detached feel' (in Kelly 1998: 110). Penny Woolcock's film *Macbeth on the Estate* (1997), updated Shakespeare's tale to the present day, and set it on a council estate where people survive by dealing drugs, and Duncan is the local godfather. All three productions are revelatory and demonstrate how thrilling imaginative versions of theatre can be when translated intelligently to the screen.

The look of surprise: the films of John Akomfrah

To put London on the screen in a way that is totally original, as *Stan Tracey: The Godfather of British Jazz* (2003) does, is an achievement. Shot by cinematographer Dewald Aukema for director John Akomfrah, the film puts forward a sumptuous vision of the capital, a sepia-toned world of blues and browns, of extraordinary vistas and deep focus-pulls from close to far. Married with shimmering monochrome archive from the 1950s and 1960s, and with a dense sound mix, this creates a documentary that is quite out of the ordinary.

The subject is the life and music of pianist and composer Stan Tracey. His personal and professional life is followed from World War Two to today, through good times and hard times, with tributes and memories from, among others, Courtney Pine, Keith Tippett and Sonny Rollins. It is both a personal story and a tale of Britain through these years. The music is terrific and the journey through the years a moving one, but it is the visuals that truly distinguish the film. For what this vision of the city presents is a world where the past and present are seamlessly tied together, a world that is both familiar and yet strange, a world with reiterated motifs and sudden revelations. Val Wilmer says that Tracey's performances express a key component of jazz, 'the sound of surprise'. The film has the look of surprise running through it.

John Akomfrah was a key figure in the emergence of black British film in the 1980s. Working with the workshop group Black Audio Film Collective he made the astonishing *Handsworth Songs* (1986), a rethinking of documentary conventions and a complex exploration of race, memory and Britain's colonial past traced through the activities and culture of communities in Handsworth, Birmingham. *Seven Songs for Malcolm X* (1993) is a similarly unconventional but equally strong tribute to the African-American civil rights leader with testimonies and staged tableaux. He also directed the more conventional biographies *Dr Martin Luther King: Days of Hope* (1997) and *Omnibus: The Wonderful World of Louis Armstrong* (1999).

Working from the late 1990s with the company Smoking Dogs Films, Akomfrah made *Goldie: When Saturn Returnz* (1998), about the dance music superstar and *Riot* (1999) recalling the disturbances in Toxteth in July 1981, as well as the Stan Tracey film and even *Mariah Carey: Billion Dollar Babe* (2003). Even, or especially, when working with popular subjects, both Akomfrah and Smoking Dogs Films manage to give their documentaries an entirely distinctive visual and emotional identity, which within contemporary television is the more precious because it is so rare.

THE IMPERSONATION

prepared for screen and television by Noël Burch and
Christopher Mason
an Arbor International production for ZDF-Mainz and the Arts Council
of Great Britain
56 minutes, 1986

The Impersonation is truly a strange film. Few documentaries play quite so wholeheartedly and so successfully with ideas of truth and fiction, reality and invention. Its focus is an artist, Reginald Pepper, who seems to be real, at least to the extent that his images are sold in galleries and licenced to greetings cards, but who may well be a commercial fabrication. Around Pepper, the film spins skeins of storytelling and self-reflexivity. The film begins with a quote from Thomas Carlyle:

> Successful glimpses, here faithfully imparted, our more gifted readers
> must endeavour to combine for their own behalf.

It then purports, at least initially, to be drawn from rolls of unedited film and video found in a Salvation Army refuge with the body of Andrew K., who until recently was a tutor in film at the Swindon School of Art and Design. Ident cards and film leaders are included in an assembly of these 'rushes' along with readings from K.'s notes to his students. One of the groups is named after Jean-Luc Godard, and a student addressed in an instruction is called John Grierson. These students are working on a documentary about the disappearance of a local painter, Reginald Pepper, and we see some of Pepper's paintings done in a *faux-naif* folk-art style.

Into this game are dropped first interviews with seemingly 'real' people – a collector, Mrs Michael Carter, and gallery director Eric Lister – and then absurd and stylised visualisations of Pepper's paintings. These feature eccentric costumes and impossible camera angles, together with a Brechtian pull-back to show that all this is taking place in a film studio. Cut to two students in a kind of woodcut graphic with signs around their necks, one that says Gyorgy Lukacs, the other Ernst Bloch – more Brecht and more theory, for then they read quotes about artists from the Blue Rider, a group of painters in Munich, formed in 1911.

'Are you sure this is the most effective way of putting over your ideas?' K. asks his students. We might have been beginning to wonder the same thing.

'Aren't you afraid of boring your audience? I would beware of fashionable de-vices.' More interviews: Andras Kalman about the marginal status of folk art, and greetings card publisher Julian Royle on the history of cards. Then, oddly (although his contribution is very interesting) critic Guy Brett speaking about patchwork art from Chile: 'It's clearly the expression of people without power, powerlessness expressed. But at the same time it's an act of resistance.' Are we really meant to take Pepper's pictures of over-fed pigs as such?

Then *The Impersonation* gets really weird. Just after an art history lecture in German, which is concerned with Frans Hals and the notion of val-ue, a newspaper article is introduced, apparently genuine, headed 'The bogus life of a "primitive" artist'. According to this, the works of Reginald Pepper are in fact painted by a 'sophisticated' art-ist, Joanna Carrington. Off go a bunch of K.'s stu-dents to France, where Joanna supposedly lives. In an audio interview she continues the pretence of Pepper's separate existence and denies that she is actually he. Next, after finding the camera prowling around her property, she is chasing them away, saying forcefully that she did not want to be filmed or taped.

The strange world of artist Reginald Pepper from *The Impersonation*

Close to the end, a dialogue is recorded that, a title card assures us, is based on material supplied by the publisher Jonathan Cape. This consists of an exchange about a set of illustrations to the book 'Pepper and Jam' bet-ween Cape's Tom Maschler and Carrington. But Carrington's words are phrased as if Pepper has a separate existence. We learn of K.'s dismissal from Swindon, although by this stage the initial conceit has rather been abandoned. The final shot of the film is a tracking shot along railings which reveals first a yellow bin (like those kept by the roadside for icy days) on which is lettered 'Salt'. The shot continues to a second bin, on which is the word 'Pepper'; then Joanna Carrington is included in the credits as a contributor of 'Additional dialogue'. If the experience of watching the film is ultimately frustrating, it is nonetheless fascinating, and the refusal of any resolution either about the worth of 'primi-tive' art or as to what is true and what is not is integral to the film's lasting power. Go figure.

O Blue come forth

Blue (1993) is perhaps the boldest, purest film about painting to have been made for television. It is also of course about so much more: about Derek Jarman's response to the AIDS-related illness that he was suffering from, about loss, about sight, about love. There is no image, just an even, unchanging field of the colour. The soundtrack is composed of reminiscence, poetry, stories, raging and lamenting, spoken by Jarman himself, together with Nigel Terry, John Quentin and Tilda Swinton, plus a complex sound mix and score composed by Simon Fisher Turner. The text comes largely from Jarman's book *Chroma*, a meditation on colour, which he finished in 1993. The film is beautiful and haunting and desperately moving. What seems incredible now is that Channel 4 funded its production, with some support from the Arts Council of Great Britain, and showed it in prime time on a Sunday evening in September 1993, when it was simulcast with Radio 3. Jarman died five months later. Television is not like that any more.

Last notes from abroad

Since the notes about the 'pre-history' of the arts on film at the start of Chapter 1, the discussion has focused exclusively on films and television programming made in Britain. At the end of these thoughts about extending the forms, I want to recognise how these forms – especially of the encounter and the drama – have been engaged with, often in startling and radical ways, by filmmakers working in other parts of Europe, in North America and elsewhere. British television has tended to be narrowly parochial in the range of international programming that it has offered, and chances to see arts programming from France and Germany, from Canada and Japan, have been restricted to a handful of international festivals. A scattering of projects that suggest how to approach the arts for the screen in quite different ways might include the following:

– The films made for the Flemish-language service BRTN in the 1980s and 1990s by the director Stefaan Decostere. Often treating the television like a graphic canvas, Decostere collided original filming with treated archive and elaborate electronic effects to develop a personal screen language. His *Travelogue* (1991) is addressed to the ways in which we display the world to ourselves – television, museums, the city, the great exhibitions, the novel – to the ways in which these systems organise fragments to create a seemingly coherent whole, and to the structures of power, particularly of colonialism, which underpin these forms of display.

– Peter Watkins made *Edvard Munch* (1973) after visiting the museum which contains many of his paintings in Oslo. He has written that he was 'very moved by the artist's directness – with the people in his canvases looking straight at us'.[5] This is what many, many of the characters in his intense three-and-a-half-hour drama do, drawing us in to its tale of the artist, appealing to us and challenging us. Watkins filmed in Norway with an entirely amateur cast, reproducing the process that he had used on his BBC film *Culloden* (1964). The quiet, intense mood is totally distinct from the dominant tone of the drama about an artist made for British television. Watkins had written:

In the years that followed I made several further attempts to work at portraying the lives of other artists (including the Italian Futurist poet Marinetti, and the Russian pianist and composer Scriabin), but each of these projects collapsed in the early stages ... Part of the problem lies in the fact that in recent years TV productions have become very much afraid of working with 'ordinary people'. Which is why films like *Culloden* and *Edvard Munch* will never be made again. The direct involvement of the public in the creative process of TV – which has always been at the essence of my work – is seen as a threat, for it represents a change in the usual hierarchical relationship between producer and passive spectator. In a word – it represents a loss of control. Of course it is never stated in this way; TV executives usually resort to attacking the 'standard', the 'creative level' of the work instead.[6]

– The form of music documentaries has attracted a number of totally dedicated filmmakers who have developed personal styles to interpret and communicate their responses to compositions and performances. Christopher Nupen is one such, and Bruno Monsaingeon another. Monsaingeon is a filmmaker and violinist who has specialised in totally distinctive films about performers, including Glenn Gould, David Oistrakh and Yehudi Menuhin. His film *Richter – The Enigma* (1998) is an exemplary study made with a focus and precision that few arts documentaries attain. A third such filmmaker is the Dutch director Frank Scheffer who has made a cycle of films about the great composers of the twentieth century: *Conducting Mahler* (1996), together with films on Pierre Boulez's *Eclat* (1993), Schonberg's *Five Orchestral Pieces* (1994) and *Helikopter String Quartet* (1996) with Karlheinz Stockhausen.

– One other drama of an artist at work that can be brought in as a counterpoint to the tradition on British television is *The Chronicle of Anna Magdalena Bach* (1968), directed by Jean-Marie Straub and Daniele Huillet. Narrated by Bach's second wife, the film has only a minimal narrative and a focused concentration on performances of the composer's music. Made with a cool, detached style, it comprises a succession of scenes, many of which are shot in a single take. The historical detail is meticulous but there is little characterisation, although Anna Magdalena is presented as quietly devoted to her husband. 'The point of departure for our *The Chronicle of Anna Magdalena Bach*', Straub said of the film, 'was the idea of attempting a film in which music was utilised not as an accompaniment, nor as a commentary, but as aesthetic material.' (Roud 1972: 64)

– The television work of Jean-Luc Godard crept onto Channel 4 in the 1990s late at night, but his *Histoire(s) du Cinéma* (1989–98) remains far too little known. His entirely eccentric history of the cinema, co-produced with Canal Plus in France, is a personal meditation on film and its myths, and also very prominently on painting (see Shafto 2006), a personal notebook of visual notions and juxtapositions that we are privileged to be able to scroll through. It is a dense multi-layered montage and collage in electronic form of images and sounds and graphics. Nothing in British arts television comes close to matching its concern to re-invent the language of the medium.

CHAPTER 5
FUTURE VISION

On the night of 13 April 1994 BBC2 showed the first programme in a magazine series about computers produced by my company Illuminations. *The Net* (1994–98), as we called the show, was built on the documentary *MeTV: The Future of Television* (1993) that I had made the previous year. This, I have claimed without total confidence ever since, included British television's first use of the word 'Internet' in an interview with Mitch Kapor. Both *MeTV: The Future of Television* and *The Net* looked forward to a networked future, a world of screens of all kinds linked to information and movies, to shops and doctors and novel ways of communicating. In the credits of that first show we included a CompuServe address for feedback across a proprietary e-mail system. Having received just three or four letters after the transmission of previous programmes, I expected that the level of response might be comparable. In fact, when we returned from the pub three hours after the transmission of the show we opened the mailbox and found more than a hundred mails. Many of these pointed out, mostly politely, that we had managed to mis-transcribe the address (omitting the '@') but that nonetheless as viewers – and now users – of the series they had still managed to communicate with us – and that they had cogent, useful and thoughtful ideas to offer. Most people now have their own, but this was my 'a-ha' moment demonstrating just why the media of the future would be different.

Fast forward just over a decade. Any brief description of how the majority of people in Britain now engage with media, including broadcasting, will be inadequate. E-mail and the web, including both access to and the contribution of video, are integral to the lives of many. Digital television and radio services co-exist with online games of surpassing complexity and social networking facilitated both by the web and by mobile communication by voice, text and video. We watch what continues to be called television online, from DVDs and on mobile phones.

'Television is now part of a rich and exciting digital media landscape', the regulator Ofcom noted in a consultation document issued early in 2007:

> Time and money spent on other communications technologies have grown rapidly and significantly … In less than a year since it came to mainstream attention, YouTube developed into a $1.6bn company. And more than 2.5 million people now play *Second Life*, a media experience so innovative that it is prompting a reinterpretation of the idea of video games … For younger audiences, the mobile phone is now the most important communications medium – not television, and the internet represents an increasing proportion of their communications activity. (Ofcom 2007: 7)

Although many of these media forms have developed in parallel with broadcasting, in Britain at least the broadcasters – and most especially the BBC – have played a central role. 'The success of our new digital services', BBC director general Mark Thompson said in a 2005 speech, 'suggests that public demand for the core BBC content – news, music and the arts, drama and comedy, documentary, education – is as strong as it's ever been The difference is that audiences expect to be able to access and use all of these things whenever and wherever they want to' (2006: 10). With Thompson according such prominence to music and the arts in his characterisation of core BBC content (a prominence that they rarely appear to be given on the screen), what place do the forms, concerns and values of filmmaking and broadcasting about the arts, developed and debated with such passion and commitment over the previous fifty years and more, have in this 'now media' world? More generally, how can public service broadcasting, to which the arts have been so central, be re-imagined in ways appropriate for this present – and for the future?

> There is a long history of renewal and invention in delivering public service as technologies change … major museums were founded to reform and educate citizens in the 19th century; public service radio and television reached the whole of the UK in the 20th century; and now a new approach is needed for the digital media world of the 21st century. (Ofcom 2007:7)

The multifarious forms of this digital media world remain thrillingly and confusingly in flux, but at present user participation, together with personalisation and 'permeability' (the blurring of the distinction between producers and consumers), are three concerns seen to be central. Creation, annotation, comment and communication are all important activities. These radically extend the notions of interactivity with which many strands of leading-edge media have been working over the past two decades. This chapter locates arts media within these debates after considering how conventional linear forms are adapting and developing.

The continuing life of linear forms

One of the key benefits of digital technology is the availability of affordable video cameras of exceptional quality and powerful desktop editing systems. Individuals and groups can own or hire broadcast quality cameras for much lower costs than during the 1990s and before. The flexible software packages for editing Avid DV Express and Final Cut Pro run on domestic PCs and Macs and can be used for creating full-length documentaries, including those shot in Hi-Definition formats. Graphics and animation packages and programmes to assist music composition are accessible and comparatively easy to learn. In terms of the technology, making media of all kinds, including about the arts, has never been easier.

Arts documentary makers have exploited these possibilities – and especially those of new forms of distribution – to work outside of, and parallel to, the broadcasters who once provided them with their only production context. Jake Auerbach, who made distinguished films for the BBC including *Sickert's London* (1993; co-funded by the Arts Council) and a *Late Show* special *Kitaj, In the Picture* (1994) with the painter R. B. Kitaj, has worked outside the BBC since 2001 when he made *Frank Auerbach: To the Studio*. Both this and the independently produced film *Lucian Freud: Portraits* (2004) were purchased for screening by the BBC and released by Jake Auerbach Films on DVD, along with films about John Virtue and Rodin. Christopher Nupen has been making films with exceptional musicians as an independent producer since 1968. An earlier advance in the availability of technology, when lightweight, silent 16mm film cameras were introduced, prompted him to establish with colleagues Allegro Films, and three decades later he distributes his work on the Allegro DVD label. Illuminations, the company with which I work, began in 2001 to produce with its own resources a series of half-hour profiles of contemporary artists, *theEYE*, which we successfully distribute on DVD, licence to museums and galleries, and on occasions even sell to broadcasters or digital channels. At the end of 2007, the series featured 40 titles, including films with Anish Kapoor, Tracey Emin, Howard Hodgkin and Richard Deacon.

Recognising the changes in production and distribution, many cultural organisations have also begun to create and disseminate forms of arts-based media. With the exception of Arts Council-funded documentaries and a handful of explicitly educational projects, films made with performance companies and museums were until the late 1990s largely confined to broadcast programming. The reliance on the funding, production expertise and distribution systems of the broadcasters almost inevitably meant that once transmitted the film or recording would disappear into an obscure archive, from where access would be exceptionally limited and potential use restricted by constrained rights clearance. In the 1980s, encouraged by the success of Channel 4, ICA-TV was established by the London arts centre to make programmes from the activities of its gallery and performance spaces. It succeeded in producing films about Henry Moore and Helen Chadwick, together with a television version of Michael Nyman's chamber opera *The Man who Mistook his Wife for a Hat* (1987), but Channel 4 was interested only in commissioning occasional projects and the institution was unable to secure other forms of funding or distribution.

The creative and commercial potential for cultural institutions in the media landscape of the twenty-first century is far greater than before. Again, it is lower costs for technical production and new forms of distribution associated with developing forms of revenue that are prompting the explorations of many institutions. In the late 1970s, operas from Glyndebourne, including Stravinsky's *The Rake's Progress* with designs by David Hockney, were brought to the ITV network by the regional franchise holder Southern Television. Two decades later, Channel 4 financed the transmission of a number of Glyndebourne operas produced with NVC Productions. Early in the 2000s, it was the BBC that funded recordings, which were shown on BBC Two and distributed by BBC Enterprises' joint venture DVD label OpusArte. In 2005, however, Glyndebourne and OpusArte together resourced and produced without a broadcaster's direct involvement, recordings in Hi-Definition of two of that season's productions, *La Cenerentola* and *Giulio Cesare*. In a related development in the USA, New York's Metropolitan Opera (which pioneered radio broadcasts of opera in the 1930s) in early 2007 mounted live transmissions, again in Hi-Definition, of six productions which were transmitted to art-house cinemas in the United States, Canada, Britain, Scandinavia and Japan.

Museums and galleries also started to produce and distribute arts media. London's National Gallery made films for screening alongside exhibitions in the 1980s and 1990s, and in the mid-2000s began to release these on DVD. In 2006 the Tate announced a more ambitious approach with Tate Media, intending to work online, in broadcast production, with public events and magazine publishing. Its early programming included a short interview conducted by Tate Director Nicholas Serota with Howard Hodgkin and a handful of short films made for Channel 4 associated with the Turner Prize. The vision, however, was more ambitious. Working with the telecommunications giant BT, the press release announcing the launch of Tate Media predicted that the Tate's website would be transformed into 'a digital broadband arts channel over the next three years to allow people of all ages anywhere in the world to research, enjoy and participate in the visual arts'. The Tate also worked successfully with BT in 2005–6 on broadband presentations of contemporary works by Antony Gormley, Tracey Emin and Rachel Whiteread.

Broadcasters too began in the 2000s to complement their transmissions of arts programming with other forms of distribution. Although the focus of BBC Worldwide and the companies with which it worked for DVD distribution was firmly set on mass-market drama and entertainment titles, *Civilisation* was released on DVD in 2005, and *A Picture of Britain*, *How Art Made the World* and Simon Schama's *Power of Art* were similarly made available. The British Film Institute's DVD label negotiated the release of two early Ken Russell films, *Elgar* and *Song of Summer*, and the Classic Archive project, led by the French producer Ideale Audience and IMG Artists, released a wonderful range of classical music performances from the 1950s and 1960s recorded by the BBC and by broadcasters in France and Germany. In general, however, the BBC demonstrated little enthusiasm for truly opening up their arts archive, expecting distributors to guarantee an advance of £10,000 for each proposed title.

In 2006 LWT's *The South Bank Show*, working with iTunes, began to release free podcasts and vodcasts of interviews from the series, although rights difficulties meant that these did not feature film or music extracts. Damien Hirst, Steve Reich and J. G. Ballard were among the first offerings. Also in 2006 Channel 4 launched 4oD, a broadband video-on-demand service to Windows PCs. This featured current and past programmes from the channel (although the rights to many were unavailable); some presentations were free but a fee was payable for most. At the same time the BBC was developing and trialling its on-demand catch-up BBC iPlayer, which allows viewers to download BBC programmes for up to seven days after transmission. Archive programming will also be made available, although at the launch in July 2007 the offerings were limited.

All of these are significant pointers to a future where linear television, in the arts and in other genres, will be delivered to a host of platforms by a multitude of delivery systems. As with the other media outlined here, each of these entails new partnerships between funders, distributors, producers, cultural organisations, rights holders and artists (many of which may take more than one role). Yet a number of problems continued that had constrained arts programming production in the past. While production costs had fallen, in many cases the expectations of talent and rights holders had increased, and imaginative partnerships and/or revenue-sharing frameworks were often necessary to facilitate the use of artistes and copyrights. Business models for the worlds of streaming and downloading, as well as for other distribution systems, were at best unproven and frequently opaque. Nor, after the closing of production funding from the Arts Council in 1999, was any significant public cultural funding – apart from production monies from broadcasters – available in Britain for the creation of linear arts media. The digital new world in the mid-2000s could seem to an aspiring arts producer full of potential yet commercially tough as an environment within which to make programming.

MAKE ME THINK: BRUCE NAUMAN
written and directed by Heinz Peter Schwerfel
an Artcore Film production for the Arts Council of England in association with ARTE/WDR, Centre Georg Pompidou/DAP, Ministère de la Culture
50 minutes, 1997

'This film is not about what you see … It's about you, me, about our inner world as seen through the eyes of an artist whose problems reflect the topics of today's society: fear, contempt, hate, death … This film is about him, and you.' Heinz Peter Schwerfel's idiosyncratic essay on the work of Bruce Nauman is also very much about the filmmaker, and in the imaginative presentation of the artist's video works there is a frequent slippage between what is Nauman's art and what is Schwerfel's staging. Interviews, for example, appear on video screens in formats that directly echo Nauman's installations, and both works and Schwerfel's interventions are shot in a continuous abandoned industrial space.

Nauman usually resists appearing on-screen to explain his work, and here he pops up only right at the end as a photograph. Instead, artist Joseph Kosuth, dealer Leo Castelli and critic Robert Storr are among the witnesses who raise the themes and ideas that preoccupy the artist: space, scale, body, surveillance, language, material, emotion, politics A subjective camera prowls around the interviewees arrayed on screens in space, so that the viewer catches fragments and phrases and has to assemble meanings for themselves. The strong sense of observing and overhearing, and of being placed (trapped?) within an enclosed space, reinforces the effects of the art. 'Both the watcher and the watched', the narration says, 'are part of this film.'

Curator Robert Storr interviewed in *Make Me Think: Bruce Nauman*

The film, which was the last documentary to which the Arts Council contributed funding, unquestionably imparts a visceral sense of Nauman's art. Visually, and with its layered soundtrack, it cleverly juxtaposes images and ideas, and it offers an unsettling experience. I admire all this, but I worry about whether there should be a clearer boundary between the artist and the film. Should it be clearer who has contributed what? Or if the documentary is a true collaboration with Nauman, should that not be recognised in the credits? And is it important to have a boundary around the artworks? (Lawyers, the market and most artists usually think so.)

Also, I puzzle over the sequence towards the end when elements of the interviews are played together, with the voices speaking across and cancelling out each other, perhaps suggesting that what people have said is meaningless, just a babble of language that has little relevance to the integrity and the presence of the work itself.

'This film is not about what you see. It's not about images, but what is behind the images, who is behind the images, and who is standing in front of them, trying to understand what he sees. This film is about him, and you.'

Doing it digitally

In the summer of 2006 the BBC reorganised its commissioning and production structures to prepare it for a 'Creative Future' content strategy. Central to this vision was the notion of '360-degree commissioning', the designation for the idea that content creation going forwards should no longer be focused on one medium – television, say, or the Internet – with other services offering 'back-up', but that major projects had to be conceived as essentially cross-platform from their genesis. This was accompanied by reassurances that the BBC was not going to abandon traditional and sometimes stand-alone television programming, but it indicated how broadly and seriously the BBC had embraced the digital future.

Within arts programming at this date there was no standout project that fully demonstrated the 360-degree vision. However, interactive enhancements to a range of programmes suggested what the future might hold. On digital transmissions delivered through the Freeview box, 'red-button' interactivity extended (or, for some viewers, distracted from) prestige productions including the live transmission from Shakespeare's Globe of *Richard II* in September 2003. Throughout the evening the red-button access to iBBC services provided text information about the play and its plot plus commentary from Andrew Marr about contemporary political parallels, together with access to backstage cameras. BBC Proms concerts on BBC Four also regularly provided programme notes in this way. *The Big Read* (2003), a high-profile partnership between the BBC, the National Literacy Trust, the charity Booktrust and others to find the 'nation's best-loved book' (Tolkein's *The Lord of the Rings*, as it turned out) utilised similar red button enhancements alongside the broadcast programmes.

Painting the Weather (2004) was a more elaborate interactive project, centred on four BBC Four programmes about depictions of the climate in artworks from galleries around Britain. These were accompanied by an online exhibition of a hundred paintings from fifty galleries together with interactive television elements. Freeview homes could access through the red button a different picture each day for a fortnight. On digital cable, more than forty of the paintings were visible, and for viewers with a digital satellite receiver the full web exhibition could be explored. *The Beethoven Experience*, presented across the BBC on both radio (the composer's every note was played on Radio 3) and television in June 2005, also offered a supplementary interactive component. Included in the package for just a week were free downloads of the complete symphonies; these were downloaded 1.4 million times.

In 2007 Simon Schama's *Power of Art* took the ideas of working cross-platform further, with online city guides with galleries where featured artworks could be seen and interviews with artists (including Gavin Turk), museum directors (National Gallery director Charles Saumarez-Smith, ICA director Ekow Eshun) and critics detailing a choice – supposedly inspired by one of the artists profiled by Schama – of a selection of UK-based artworks. These interviews were accessible via the red button after each transmission and cut-down versions were posted online. The BBC and Arts Council England also commissioned ten contemporary artists to make new works 'that explored and documented the cultural power of a chosen UK city'. In Nottingham, Adele Prince made a 'meander map' using the web and GPS tracking technology which involved her setting off on a journey dictated by the people she encountered on the way. Richard Billingham, by contrast, explored the history of Brighton in ten films, some from the earliest days of the cinema and some that he shot, which could be accessed by mobile phone. Other elements of mobile content drawn from the series and the city guides could also be accessed.

These complements to the *Power of Art* were co-produced with Arts Council England, which after the closure of the Film, Video and Broadcasting department in 1999 and the withdrawal of production funding for documentaries and performance (see Chapter 3) found new ways to extend arts broadcasting. It worked with the BBC and others on projects predominantly for online, including the 2002 and 2003 *Shooting Live Artists* commissions. Six contemporary artists or groups were funded in each year by the BBC and the Arts Council to

Contemporary artist projects supported by Arts Council England, alongside the television series *Power of Art*

produce work that combined media technology with live art, with the finished pieces made available online. Arts Council England also worked with Channel 4 to develop *Operatunity*, co-commissioned short films with Channel 4 for *animate!* (1990–) and *Slot Art* (2001–3) and with the BBC established the 'Roots' project with jointly-funded co-ordinator posts in the eleven English regions to bring new audiences to culturally diverse arts. The Fivearts cities collaboration involved broadcast programmes on Five, together with tours, courses, talks and debates in a selected city each year. Liverpool was the focus in 2004 5, Newcastle/Gateshead in 2005 6 and Oxford in 2006–7, where the series *The Singing Estate* (2006) was filmed. In July 2006, *Big Dance*, organised by Arts Council England, the BBC and other agencies, mounted 700 events across the country. Arts Council England co-produced forty live dance events with BBC local radio and this prompted the largest simultaneous dance class in the UK. These live performances were co-ordinated with a BBC One programme, *Dancing in the Street*, broadcast live from Trafalgar Square.

More than fifty years after the first Art Film Tours took documentaries, including BBC films, to audiences in village halls across the country, these Arts Council 'beyond the broadcast' initiatives aim to prompt participation, particularly for people who may not have experienced the arts. As Chapter 3 documents, throughout those fifty years and more, the Arts Council sought a closer relationship with broadcasting for itself and the many organisations with which it works. The latest manifestation of this is the Arts Council/BBC 'Memorandum of Understanding 2006–8' intended 'to maximise our significant shared investment in the arts for greater public value and to work creatively together in developing new audiences for the arts.' (Arts Council England 2006b) The words are fine but, as has been the case throughout the relationship between the Council and the broadcasters, the achievements for the public funders feel comparatively modest. (The Arts Council also supported and encouraged a wide range of digital art creation, beginning in the mid-1990s with the Hub project, which was a showcase and online meeting point for digital art pioneers; like the Arts Council-funded artists' film and video made from 1972 onwards, such work is chronicled elsewhere and is beyond the modest scope of this volume.)

Public funding from other sources in the mid-2000s also helped cultural institutions begin to use the web for more than the provision of information and booking. The Royal National Theatre's *Stagework*[1] site is an exceptional example of an interactive educational resource, which was launched in 2004 alongside the Royal National Theatre's adaptation of Philip Pullman's *His Dark Materials*. The site, produced as a partnership between the Royal National Theatre, the production company Illumina Digital and the DCMS fund Culture Online, features video elements of productions from rehearsals through to final performances and encourages the user to look at aspects of production like lighting and costume design. There are learning resources for students and teachers together with an interactive guide to careers in the theatre.

Every Object Tells a Story[2] is another interesting online project with a strong cultural component. Developed by the V&A and a group of regional museums, produced with Channel 4 and Ultralab, and backed by Culture Online funding, the site is building an online archive of stories about objects that people value. Contributors compose brief stories in text (up to 250 words) or using audio and video; these are reviewed by a moderator before being posted to the site. Numerous museum professionals have made contributions about objects in their collections, alongside a wide range of other users. Culture Online also supported *soundjunction*,[3] an educational site developed by the music examining board, the Associated Board of the Royal Schools of Music. The site offers a range of resources for listening to, exploring, discovering and creating music, including software encouraging users to make and remix their own music.

Using *Stagework* as an exemplar, Ofcom in its document 'A new approach to public service content in the digital media age', wrote that it 'shows that some public institutions can create and deliver broadband content with the narrative structure and high production values normally associated with broadcasters' (2007: 21). At the same time Ofcom noted that successful online services working with the next generation of capabilities, those that commentators have linked under the title of Web 2.0, including social networking and user generated services, have focused on maximising commercial returns. 'Few have material public service value', Ofcom said. 'In particular, it is difficult to find examples of digital media content that address the most vulnerable areas of the PSB system' (ibid.). Also, while public service content may develop within the market, it will become increasingly difficult to locate as the amount of stuff online grows. Given this analysis, what is to be done?

So what's next?

Mark Thompson said in his autumn 2005 speech:

> We've learned that an important part of any big [broadcasting] idea is active participation by the public through personal choice, feedback, debate, creat-

ing content. Not all of this is new – fact sheets and audience research are as old as broadcasting – but digital technology has not only massively increased its scope, it's democratised it. It's handed the power to the people we used to call the audience. (2006: 12)

Through the 2000s Ofcom was much concerned with securing public service values in the changing media world. As detailed in their first public service broadcasting review, Ofcom believed that PSB should be defined in terms of its purposes and characteristics rather than by specific genres. Noting that audiences were 'drifting away' from specialist arts, religious and current affairs programming, Ofcom put forward a new definition of public service broadcasting, which included the idea that it should 'stimulate our interest in and knowledge of arts, science, history and other topics through content that is accessible and can encourage informal learning'. Essential characteristics of this 'new' PSB were that it should be 'high quality ... original ... innovative ... and challenging' (2005: 7).

To protect these purposes and characteristics as the media worlds change, continuing scrutiny and considered changes to broadcasting's regulatory frameworks are necessary responses but almost certainly not sufficient, especially if the values are to be translated into domains of digital media not conventionally identified as broadcasting. Nor are the broadcasters, grounded in one-to-many mass-market models of the *provision* of entertainment and information, necessarily the best contexts in which participatory projects with public service value, working in essence with many-to-many models, can best flourish. Hence Ofcom's idea of the Public Service Provider (PSP) which began to be shaped in consultations through 2006–7; the vision of the content facilitated and (part) funded by the PSP refines and extends Mark Thompson's sense.

At its heart, the content would be participative in nature. This enables a new approach to public service delivery – in which citizens are users rather than viewers of public service content, are able to personalise the content and experience, and where the distinction between producer and consumer of content is much less explicit. (Ofcom 2007: 6–7)

From the BBC Mark Thompson in his autumn 2005 speech offered a recent example of a large-scale cultural project which responded in part to the media spaces, even though this still relied on a centre disseminating programming and resources to a periphery, the audience, the members of which could respond and take part in numerous activities but were nonetheless not dominant to the creation and direction of the media. An autumn 2005 season of programming related to Shakespeare was built around four contemporary dramas for BBC One that used elements from the plots of *Much Ado About Nothing, Macbeth, The Taming of the Shrew* and *A Midsummer Night's Dream*. Online was 7NK, a Shakespeare Murder Mystery, in which the user took the role of a critic to solve various mysteries. Schools were encouraged to produce and submit a 60-second filmed interpretation of a play and a large-scale off-air drama event,

'One Night of Shakespeare', saw a hundred theatres across Britain feature 400 productions from more than 10,000 students.

The BBC's Shakespeare offerings also included a Flash-based interactive *Shakespeare's Stories*[4] accessed across broadband on a PC and through the red button on digital television. After an opening montage of 'teaser' interview elements, actor David Oyelowo promises 'a fascinating interactive journey that will take you right to the heart of Shakespeare's plays'. Scenes from a handful of

the plays are staged in a plain theatrical space and the concentration is focused on the playwright's language. At the end of each extract choices are put forward to allow the user to learn more about the plays, Shakespeare's history, the themes and language. So after a scene from *Macbeth*, the user has five seconds to choose bet-ween considering the idea of 'evil' in the modern world, hearing about a recent production of the play set in a fictitious Afri-can republic, digging deeper into the text, or explor-ing the historical context of the time under James I at the start of the seventeenth century when the play was first performed. The elements and path-ways, although still framed by the broadcasting,

The BBC website for the television and interactive experiences of *Shakespeare Re-told*

centre-to-periphery paradigm, make an imaginative use of video, graphics and audio and the experience is involving and enriching. 'What gives me the most confidence in the future of the arts on the BBC', Thompson noted, 'is the sheer intensity with which the public respond to events such as Beethoven and Shake-speare' (2006: 14).

Channel 4's broadband documentary site *four docs*[5] works with a participato-ry model that is closer to the user-generated content sites like YouTube. The site allows those who access it to watch four-minute documentaries from around the world and to contribute their own, which must comply with a checklist of legal and technical standards. These films are reviewed by a *four docs* editor

and rated by other users. Accompanying this are extensive materials about making documentaries plus rushes material and music that can be used under a variant of a Creative Commons licence.[6] Peter Dale, Head of the More4 digital channel, is quoted on the site explaining,

The rise of relatively cheap and easy to use digi-tal cameras and editing equipment means that the tools to make a documentary are more wide-spread than ever before. There's so much film-making talent out there but until now there's been no natural home for it – we wanted to find a way of harnessing all the energy and ideas.

Channel 4's *four docs* website offers new ways to distribute, watch and discuss documentaries

In early 2007 only a handful of the submitted short films engage with subjects from the arts. *Sargy Mann* (2006, directed by Peter Mann) suggests the world of a painter who continued to work although registered blind for over twenty years. As the note that accompanies the film says, 'many people believe that his paintings got better as his sight deteriorated'. Just before the film was shot, he went totally blind and the film presents one of the works done just after this occurred. 'When you are making a film about a blind painter it pays to see it from the subject's point of view', the *four docs* editor comments online. 'Here, prolonged sequences of black graphically underline the brilliant shock when the work of this extraordinary man is revealed. This is a serenely eloquent homage to all forms of optimism, particularly when the odds are totally tipped against you.'[7] Another film on the site, *Sight of Emotion* (2006, made by Gabriel Amarai and Nicolas Mandri-Perrott), looks at a group of photographers who encourage the blind to pick up a camera and take pictures. Two further films with the title *Art Savant* (2006, directed by Jan Bednarz) profile Gilles Trehin who has a rare type of autism resulting in an extraordinary ability to draw imagined detail.

Shakespeare Stories and *four docs* are two examples pointing towards the next generations of arts-related media, even if the arts have only a marginal presence in the latter. Also, only *four docs* has participation close to its creative centre, but new cultural forms for harnessing aspects of social networking and user contributions will undoubtedly soon emerge. Will they have a chance to grow and thrive in the marketplace? As already indicated, Ofcom is uncertain about this, and also about whether the users who might most enjoy and benefit from such services will ever be able to locate them. So once again, we return to their proposal for a Public Service Provider for digital media imbued with public service values. 'We continue to believe', Ofcom said in early 2007, 'that there is value in considering the creation of a new provider of PSC (public service content), with its centre of gravity in new media and with a remit specifically designed for new forms of content provision' (2007: 25).

Last words

Writing this final chapter has involved a recognition of my ambivalence towards my subjects. I have had a number of glancing but on occasions deep involvements with digital media since, in the early 1990s, I read a *New Yorker* article by Ken Auletta about the media executive Barry Diller. When Diller left Twentieth Century Fox in 1992 he looked around for something else to do and he eventually bought the television shopping network QVC ('Quality, Value, Convenience'). Not only was he engaged by the sense of putting a product on the screen and seeing people immediately calling in to purchase it (an image of phone lines lighting up as a barker made their pitch that I found as compelling as he did), but he recognised that this was the way into making money in the digital future. From this article came my documentary *MeTV: The Future of Television* which featured an interview with Diller, who since has built a £1 billion-plus group of companies with substantial online interests like Expedia.com, Ticketmaster, Ask.

com and Citysearch. I produced *The Net* for BBC2 and became involved in research-led work with online 3D worlds. I have lived with the arguments about the potential of digital media, and especially about many-to-many networks for a decade and more, but I have rarely felt overwhelmed or thrilled by the projects which I have visited, used, played, explored, entered or contributed to.

Too many online projects, whether games or community sites or aspiring to be art experiences, offer to me only a superficiality of experience, a thinness, a sense of surface that offers little in the way of emotional or intellectual engagement. I am not the target demographic, of course, for many digital experiences; I can see the attractions and pleasures of a collective online adventure like *World of Warcraft*, but it is not conceived for me. Hundreds of thousands of people clearly find the online *Second Life* community a rich and fascinating world. I respect this, and the satisfactions that many get from *World of Warcraft*, but they offer to me only minimal aesthetic or intellectual satisfaction. Perhaps it is nonsensical to compare them to a documentary by John Read or a dramatised biography by Ken Russell or, even, the experience of watching an episode of *Civilisation*. Yet I cannot shift my deep-seated sense that it is these – and many, many more such films – that have enriched my life, challenged me, provoked me and made me think in different ways about the world. Even as I write this, I recognise how absurd is the comparison, and I know that they have existed at different times, with different aspirations and for different audiences. *World of Warcraft* and *Second Life*, *Stagework* and *Every Object Tells a Story* are for now and tomorrow, whereas many of the films featured in this book are mostly fit for the archive and academia, and if they and we are lucky, for release on DVD or as downloads. Yet I am cautious about the embrace of the new and the loss of the qualities of the old that I fear may disappear. But even to try to detail these is to struggle to find appropriate words. 'Layers' is perhaps one such quality: layers within the shot and between shots, layers of meaning created by crafted juxtapositions and by the development through time of a directed narrative. 'Textures' is perhaps another: textures of an original artwork lovingly filmed, but also textures of thought alluded to by the poetic achievement of filmmaking.

Enough. One last example, a project with which I am involved at the time of writing that perhaps can combine some of the strengths of linear film with the potential of digital choice. Imagine that you are watching a programme about, say, the arts in Tudor England. You are interested in the subject but it is mostly the architecture of the late sixteenth century that fascinates you. Imagine then if the shape of the programme could be shifted by you, as you are watching it, to focus more on the architecture of Robert Smythson and less on, say, the poetry of Philip Sidney. This is the experience that our project *A Golden Age* aspires to offer. For the last two years, my company Illuminations has been a partner in the research project New Media for a New Millennium, or nm2.[8] With funding support from the European Commission's Framework 6 technology programme, nm2 is exploring new forms of what we call 'configurable' media for delivery across broadband. That is, that the user will be able actively to shape them as they are being watched.

nm2 wanted a project that would test the production tools that other partners have been developing for authoring media of this kind. The programme had
to help refine the way the tools work, and that would also demonstrate how
configurable media might be used in education and also in all kinds of entertainment and drama, and in news and factual programming. What we have chosen
to explore in *A Golden Age* is the culture of late sixteenth-century England: the
arts in the Elizabethan Renaissance. So we feature Tudor artworks and architecture as well as interviews with some of the key historians of the time. We have
actors to give a sense of the drama and poetry from the age of Shakespeare and
Marlowe, and also recordings of music extracts by John Dowland and Thomas
Tallis. *A Golden Age* organises these and other elements in extended narrative
arcs through which a user can simply and straightforwardly navigate. The choices are simple but the potential variants are boundless – and the experience, I
hope, has something of the quality of watching a good documentary yet with
the sense as you watch that you shape its direction and focus. Perhaps the final
version will suggest how the qualities I want to reserve from the fifty-year and
more tradition that this book has outlined can be combined with the possibilities
of digital participation and control and choice. Or perhaps *A Golden Age* will become just another tiny evolutionary path not taken by the digital developments
of the new century.

When John Read made *Henry Moore* for the BBC and *Artists Must Live*
with the Arts Council there was a single television channel in Britain and if you
wanted to see either again you had to go to a draughty village hall to a screening organised by the Arts Council's film tours. Now *Artists Must Live* is available online to students and researchers, one miniscule shard in a vast, dazzling,
provocative and above all accessible world of art and media. That's some kind
of progress.

NOTES

Chapter 1

1 Another survival is a sequence of the popular Cornish painter Samuel John ('Lamorna') Birch at work at Lamorna Cove filmed in 1924 by Claude Friese-Greene for his travelogue *The Open Road*.

2 Sacha Guitry made a film with a comparable intent during World War Two; his *MCDXX-IX–MCMXLII De Jeanne d'Arc à Philippe Pétain* (1943–44) presents images of and documents created by the great figures of French culture, arts and politics.

3 Thanks to the filmmaker and historian Robert McNab who first drew my attention to the films of Hans Curlis. McNab co-directs an important initiative to research and screen films of visual artists, The Artists on Film Trust, www.artistsonfilm.co.uk

4 Interviews with John Read conducted by the author in London, 30 December 1999.

5 Interview with the author, 30 December 1992.

6 The artists featured were Kenneth Armitage, Michael Ayrton, Reg Butler, Anthony Gross, Josef Herman and Victor Pasmore.

7 The out-takes of this interview were also released by the Arts Council in an extended form, as was done with two projects that did not involve Read: an extended, wonderfully eccentric encounter with Edward Burra (*Edward Burra: The Complete Interview*, 1982) and contributions to *Just What Is It ...?* (1984) by sculptors Tony Cragg, Anish Kapoor and others.

8 In the documentary film *K: Kenneth Clark 1903–83*, an Illuminations production for BBC Television produced in 1993.

9   Interviewed in BBC Television's tribute *Omnibus: Huw Wheldon, by his Friends*, broadcast 11 April 1986.

10   Interviewed in the documentary *K: Kenneth Clark 1903–83*, BBC Television, 1993.

11   Watching a *Full House* programme in December which included the French performance group Le Grand Magic Circus led by Jerome Savary prompted me to go to the Roundhouse to see them perform. For the edition of *Full House* on 17 March 1973 I secured tickets to be in the audience. With a friend, I travelled up to London from school, and we saw Melia introduce the Afro-rock group Osibisa, 'The British Soccer Dance' choreographed by Gillian Lynne, poems read by Brian Jones, Ivor Cutler and Glenda Jackson, and most remarkable the French composer Olivier Messiaen and his wife, pianist Yvonne Loriod, performing sections of 'Visions de l'Amen' on two pianos.

Chapter 2

1   Author's unpaginated typewritten notes of presentation, 'Television and the arts', ICA, London, 11–12 June 1983.

2   Speaking in the documentary *Arena at 30*, first broadcast on BBC Four on 3 September 2005.

3   From *Arena at 30*, first broadcast on BBC Four on 3 September 2005.

4   Speech at launch of *Signals*, 3 October 1988, at the offices of Channel 4, 60 Charlotte Street, London W1. Unpaginated, typewritten manuscript.

5   In 'Britain on the move', an unpaginated typescript submission by David Hinton to DBC Television in 2005.

6   UFCOM review of PSB 7.3 cultural identity, 7.3.2 Arts, consultation published 21 April 2004.

7   Discussed on the blog www.rereviewed.com/roguesemiotics/?p=556, accessed 3 January 2007.

Chapter 3

1   The Department of Information's 1942 documentary *CEMA* (discussed in Chapter 1) highlights a range of these activities.

2   *The Charter of Incorporation granted by his Majesty the King to the Arts Council of Great Britain, ninth day of August 1946*, p.3.

3   Interview with Rodney Wilson, 16 June 2006; subsequent quotations in this chapter are from this interview and from a follow-up on 8 December 2006. Interviews conducted by the author in the offices of Illuminations, in Islington, London N1.

4   The other two panels at this time were Drama and Music.

5   The *Painter and Poet* films were made for the BFI's Telekinema presentations on the South Bank and were, in the director's words, 'an attempt to interpret verse by means of illustrative drawings or paintings by contemporary artists'.

6   The BFI's Experimental Film Fund contributed £250, with the balance coming from private loans and investments.

7   Letter from Basil Wright to Philip James, 15 July 1955. Arts Council of Great Britain

papers, ACGB/56/78.

8   Humphrey Jennings, who with colleagues had written and directed *Spare Time* (1939) and *A Diary for Timothy* (1945), began work in late 1948 on a never-completed film about the London Symphony Orchestra. His last film, *Family Portrait* (1950) was commissioned by John Ryerson for the promotion of the Festival of Britain, but it is symptomatic of the funding context that the film he was planning when he died was financed not in Britain but by the European Economic Commission.

9   A viewer of the film today might respond with more muted enthusiasm, as it appears now as a largely conventional assembly of images of the sculptures filmed in landscapes.

10   Typescript memorandum by Tony Field. Arts Council of Great Britain papers, ACGB/54/124.

11   Minutes of the 91st Art Panel, 11 October 1967, 3(a).

12   Minutes of the first meeting of the Art Film Committee, 11 January 1968. Arts Council of Great Britain papers, ACGB/32/109.

13   Minutes of the Art Film Committee, 10 March 1969. Arts Council of Great Britain papers, ACGB/32/109.

14   E-mail to the author, 29 November 2005; James Scott maintains an informative website about his work at www.james-scott.com.

15   Wilson's paper was perceived by David Sylvester, a member of the Art Film Committee and director of recent films, as an attack on its practice to date; he wrote a peevish qualification, 'Some Notes on Rodney Wilson's paper ...', which sought to justify the committee's recent work.

16   Minutes of the Art Film Committee, 11 January 1968. Arts Council of Great Britain papers, ACGB/32/109.

17   Letter from Hugh Willatt, Secretary General, Arts Council of Great Brtain, to Richard Attenborough, 15 March 1971. Arts Council of Great Britain papers, ACGB/32/76.

18   Report of the Arts Council Film Committee of Enquiry, July 1973. Arts Council of Great Britain papers, ACGB/32/76, 14.

19   Ibid.

20   Letter from Keith Lucas, Director of the BFI to Hugh Willatt, Secretary-General, Arts Council of Great Britain. Arts Council of Great Britain papers, ACGB/32/76.

21   'Recommendations of the Film Enquiry Report with amendments suggested by the BFI and Art Film Committee', Council Paper 533. Arts Council of Great Britain papers, ACGB/32/76, 2.

22   Ibid.

23   David Curtis e-mail to the author, 12 March 2007: 'Part of this change from film tour to library was prompted by my belief that we should be making available BBC and other arts documentaries, not just Arts Council glories. And I was able to use the ex-film tour budget to buy them. I remember the BBC being totally unprepared for this interest and having to show me sep-mag prints.'

24   Cf. the discussion of the difficulties over 'Art and Austerity' (which became *Wot! No Art?*, about the arts in Britain in the period 1945-51) in the minutes of the thirty-second meeting of the Arts Film Committee, 22 October 1976.

25   Mark Kidel told the fortieth meeting of the Art Film Committee on 17 March 1978 that

'it was probably true that some people at the BBC saw Arts Council films as cheap fill-ins'. He also thought there was considerable jealousy on the part of BBC producer/directors at the freedom given to directors working on Arts Council productions.

26 This news was received with anger by the committee members. As minuted, Ian Christie 'considered it absurd that Council should remain wholly devoted to the traditional arts and not to an art form that was more visible to the general public'.

27 *Hansard* (House of Lords debate on the arts, March 6 1985), 5th series, Vol. CDLX, column 1326.

28 The idea of a separate Film Section, with a Film Panel, was first discussed at the Art Film Committee meeting in July 1975. Rodney Wilson attributes the setting up of FVB in part to the personal animus between Brian Young, Chair of the Art Film Committee, and Chairman of the Arts Council William Rees-Mogg; Young's response to one of the regular threats to the continuation of the film activities was to argue that instead they should become their own department.

29 Letter from Philip James to Basil Wright, 23 March 1955. Arts Council of Great Britain papers, ACBG/56/78.

30 Minutes of the eleventh meeting of the Art Film Committee, 2 October 1970.

31 By June 1992 gross sales totalled £18,360, against initial start-up costs of £24,000, according to the minutes of the Arts Films Production Committee, 5 June 1992.

32 Wilding Report, by Richard Wilding: 'Supporting the Arts: A Review of the Structure of Arts Funding', typescript presented to the Minister for the Arts, 1989, 20.

33 Off-the-record telephone conversation with anonymous Arts Council employee, conducted November 2006.

Chapter 4

1 Conversation with the author at the Dokuarts festival in Berlin, September 2006.

2 Information from Christopher Witcombe's website, 'Art history and technology: a brief history', at http://witcombe.sbc.edu/arth-technology/arth-technology5.html

3 *Vertical*, www.luxonline.org.uk/artists/david_hall/vertical.html, accessed 5 January 2007.

4 I am indebted to Neil Taylor's pioneering article 'A History of the Stage Play on BBC Television'.

5 Undated online statement, www.mnsi.net/~pwatkins/munch.htm; accessed 18 December 2006.

6 Ibid.

Chapter 5

1 www.stagework.org, accessed 6 December 2006.

2 www.everyobject.net, accessed 6 December 2006.

3 www.soundjunction.org, accessed 6 December 2006.

4 www.bbc.co.uk/drama/shakespeare/interactive.shtml, accessed 6 December 2006.

5 www.channel4.com/fourdocs/, accessed 6 December 2006.

6 Creative Commons licences offer alternatives to more restrictive forms of copyright,

allowing authors and artists to mark their creative work with the freedoms they want it to carry. Full details are at http://creativecommons.org, accessed 6 December 2006.

7   www.channel4.com/fourdocs/film/film-detail.jsp?id=23885#, accessed 6 December 2006.

8   www.ist-nm2.org, accessed 6 December 2006.

BIBLIOGRAPHY

Adams, Mary (1954) 'Foroward', in Mervyn Levy (1954) *Painter's Progress*. London: Phoenix House, 5–6.

Anderson, Lindsay (1954) 'Only Connect: some aspects of the work of Humphrey Jennings', *Sight and Sound*, April–June, 23, 4, 181–6.

Annan, Lord (Chairman) (1977) *Report of the Committee on the Future of Broadcasting* (Cmnd 6753). London: Home Office/HMSO.

Anon. (1969) 'How Like an Angel', *The Times*, 18 May, microfiche.

Appleyard, Bryan (1984) *The Culture Club: Crisis in the Arts*. London: Faber & Faber.

____ (1989) *The Pleasures of Peace: Art and Imagination in Post-War Britain*. London: Faber & Faber.

Arts Council England (1994–2006a) *Annual Report and Accounts*, 1 (1994–5) to 12 (2005–6).

—— (2004) *History of Arts Council England, information sheet*, June 2004, www.artscouncil.org.uk/regions/information_detail.php?rid=6&sid=1&id=52, accessed 2 December 2006.

____ (2006b) 'Arts Council England's response to "A public service for all: the BBC in the digital age"', 28 April 2006, www.bbccharterreview.org.uk/wp_responses/organisations/ArtsCouncilEngland.rtf, accessed 25 October 2006.

____ (2007) 'Arts Council England's response to OFCOM's discussion paper "A new approach to public service content in the digital media age"', www.ofcom.org.uk/consult/condocs/pspnewapproach/responses/arts.pdf, accessed 7 February 2007.

Arts Council of Great Britain (1945–94) *Annual Report and Accounts*, 1 (1945–6) to 49

(1993–4).

_____ (1951) *Sculpture and Drawings by Henry Moore*. London: Arts Council of Great Britain.

_____ (1953) *A Descriptive Catalogue of Art Films Presented by the Arts Council of Great Britain in co-operation with the British Film Institute*. London: Arts Council of Great Britain.

_____ (1977) *Documentaries on the Arts: Arts Council Film Library Catalogue*. London: Arts Council of Great Britain.

_____ (1985) *The Glory of the Garden: The Development of the Arts in England*. London: Arts Council of Great Britain.

_____ (1988) *Arts Council Film and Video Library: Documentaries on the Arts*. London: Arts Council of Great Britain.

_____ (1989) *The Arts and Broadcasting: Bringing the Best to the Most*. London: Arts Council of Great Britain.

_____ (1991a) *Films on Art from the Collection of the Arts Council of Great Britain*. London: Arts Council of Great Britain.

_____ (1991b) *National Arts (& Media) Strategy: Film, Video and Broadcasting – A Discussion Document*. London: Arts Council of Great Britain.

_____ (1993) *A Creative Future: The way forward for the arts, crafts and media in England*. London: HMSO.

Auty, Chris (1983) 'Greenaway's Games', *Stills*, May–June, 62–5.

BBC (1948) *BBC Annual Report and Accounts 1946–47*. London: HMSO.

_____ (1962) *Programmes: The Arts* (unpaginated promotional material).

_____ (1965) *BBC Annual Report and Accounts 1964-65*. London: HMSO.

_____ (1995) *People and Programmes: BBC Radio and Television for an age of choice*. London: British Broadcasting Corporation.

Bakewell, Joan and Garnham, Nicholas (1970) *The New Priesthood: British TV Today*. London: Allen Lane.

Banham, Mary and Hillier, Bevis (1976) *A Tonic to the Nation: the Festival of Britain 1951*. London: Thames and Hudson.

Barnett, Steven and Curry, Andrew (1994) *The Battle for the BBC*. London: Aurum Press.

Baxter, John (1973) *An Appalling Talent: Ken Russell*. London: Michael Joseph.

Berger, John (1972) *Ways of Seeing*. London: BBC/Penguin Books.

Berthoud, Roger (1987) *The Life of Henry Moore*. London: Faber & Faber.

Bianchini, Franco (1987) 'RIP GLC: Cultural Policies in London', *New Formations*, 1, Spring, 103–17.

Billen, Andrew (1999) 'Art critique', *New Statesman*, 14 June, microfiche.

Black, Peter (1961) 'Television review', *Daily Mail*, 16 December, microfiche.

_____ (1967) 'Television review', *Daily Mail*, 8 July, microfiche.

Bragg, Melvyn (1978) 'Art for the people?', Observer, 8 January, microfiche.

_____ (1982) 'Open Space for Arts', in Brian Wenham (1982) *The Third Age of Broadcasting*. London: Faber & Faber, 28–47.

_____ (1988) 'Something to brag about', *Sunday Times Magazine*, 10 January, 41–6.

Briggs, Asa (1979) *The History of Broadcasting in the United Kingdom, Volume IV: Sound & Vision*. Oxford: Oxford University Press.

____ (1995) *The History of Broadcasting in the United Kingdom, Volume V: Competition 1955–1974*. Oxford: Oxford University Press.

Brooke, Michael (2006) 'Ken Russell and the *South Bank Show*', *screenonline*, www. screenonline.org.uk/tv/id/1026310/index.html, accessed 12 October 2006.

Brown, Maggie (1997) 'Lost art of TV', *Guardian G2*, 7 May, 13.

____ (2003) 'Too little, too cheap, too dumb?', *Guardian*, 19 May; available at http://arts.guardian.co.uk/features/story/0,,959110,00.html, accessed 3 January 2007.

Bugler, Jeremy (1990) 'Art and good form', *The Listener*, 11 October, 14–15.

Burch, Noël (1990) *Life to those Shadows*. London: British Film Institute.

Burnett, Claire (1990) 'Pie in the sky promises for arts TV', *Broadcast*, 5 October, microfiche.

Carpenter, Humphrey (1996) *The Envy of the World: Fifty Years of the BBC Third Programme and Radio 3 1946–1996*. London: Weidenfeld and Nicolson.

Carter, Meg (1989) 'Arts go pop', *Televisual*, January 1989, 37–8.

Channel Four Group (1979) 'Open letter to the Home Secretary', *The Guardian*, 10 October, microfiche.

Clark, Kenneth (1969) *Civilisation: A Personal View*. London: BBC/John Murray.

____ (1977) *The Other Half: A Self Portrait*. London: John Murray.

Clarke, Steve (1998) 'Into the Arena', *Broadcast*, 18 December, 19.

Clifford, Andrew (1991) 'Professors of the Closed University', *Guardian*, 10 July, 38.

Collings, Matthew (1999) 'Everyone's a critic …', *Observer Review*, 7 July, 14.

Considine, Pippa (1998) 'Shock of the new?', *Broadcast*, 27 February, 18–19.

Cooper & Lybrand (1989) *Arts Council Television: A Feasibility Study*, unpaginated internal report. Arts Council Great Britain papers, ACGB/54/4.

Cornwall-Jones, Imogen (2002) 'Angel', www.tate.org.uk/servlet/ViewWork?workid=26106&searchid=24397&tabview=text, accessed 4 November 2006.

Crisell, Andrew (1997) *An Introductory History of British Broadcasting*. London: Routledge.

Curtis, David (2007) *A History of Artists' Film and Video in Britain*. London: British Film Institute.

Davay, Paul (1949) 'Compelled to see', in UNESCO, *Films on Art*, 18.

Davies, Bernard (1972) 'Television review', *Television Mail*, 22 December, microfiche.

____ (1981) 'One man's television', *Broadcast*, 1 June, 12–13.

de Koster, Richard (1998) 'On connoisseurship', www.highlands.com/art/, accessed 4 February 2007.

Dickinson, Margaret (ed.) (1999) *Rogue Reels: Oppositional Film in Britain, 1945–90*. London: British Film Institute.

Donovan, Paul (1999) 'Lost Horizons', *Sunday Times Culture*, 12 September, 6.

Dorment, Richard (1999) 'Art betrayed by the BBC', *Daily Telegraph*, 1 December, microfiche.

Dugdale, John (1988) 'Culture clash', *The Listener*, 28 July, 33.

____ (1990) 'Broadcast and be damned', *The Listener*, 26 July, 26–7.

Dunkley, Christopher (1999) 'High culture knocked from its pedestal by pop', *Financial Times*, 25 August, 14.

Dyer, Geoff (1985) 'Time out', *The Listener*, 9 May, microfiche.

____ (1987) *Ways of Telling: The Work of John Berger*. London: Pluto Press.

Ellis, John (ed.) (1977) *1951–1976 Catalogue British Film Institute Productions*. London: British Film Institute.

Ferris, Paul (1990) *Sir Huge: The Life of Huw Wheldon*. London: Michael Joseph.

Fiddick, Peter (1973) 'Television review', *The Guardian*, 8 October 1973, microfiche.

Finch, Nigel (1984) 'Margins of Error', in Chris Garratt (ed.) *Broadcast Television and the Visual Arts*. London: Television South West, 33–8.

Fisher, Mark (1992) 'Pulling at the arts strings', *Media Guardian*, January 27, 23.

Forgan, Liz (1992) 'Pulling at the arts strings', *Media Guardian*, January 27, 23.

Fuller, Peter (1980) *Seeing Berger: a Revaluation of Ways of Seeing*. London: Writers & Readers.

____ (1987) 'The great British art disaster', *New Society*, 23 January, 14–17.

Gable, Robin (1989) *Resources of Hope: Culture, Democracy, Socialism*. London: Verso.

Gill, John (1990) 'Fate of the arts', *Television Week*, 15–21 February, 16–17.

Gomez, Joseph (1976) *Ken Russell: The Adaptor as Creator*. London: Frederick Muller.

Graham-Dixon, Andrew (1991) 'Hatching a scheme', *The Independent*, 16 July, microfiche.

Gray, Muriel (1991), 'The bad smell of success', *The Independent*, 17 June, microfiche.

Hall, David (2005) *Vertical*, www.luxonline.org.uk/artists/david_hall/vertical.html, accessed 5 January 2007.

Hall, Peter (1993) *Peter Hall's Diaries: The Story of a Dramatic Battle*, ed. John Goodwin. London: Hamish Hamilton.

Hambley, John (2004) Letter submission to DCMS BBC Digital Services Review, 8 June, available at http://www.culture.gov.uk/Independent_review/Artsworld.pdf, accessed 7 November 2006.

Harris, Jonathan (2001) *The New Art History: A Critical Introduction*. London: Routledge.

Hayman, Patrick (1957) 'Art films by John Read', *Sight and Sound*, Spring, 26, 4, 217–8.

Hayward, Philip (1988) 'Introduction: Echoes and Reflections: The Representation of Representations', in Philip Hayward (ed.) (1988) *Picture This: Media Representations of Visual Arts & Artists*. London: John Libbey, 1–26.

____ (ed.) (1988) *Picture This: Media Representations of Visual Arts & Artists*. London: John Libbey.

Hebert, Hugh (1995) 'Culture mulch', *Guardian*, 1 November, 12.

Hellen, Nicholas (1995) 'Royal Opera stung by fly-on-the-wall film', *Sunday Times*, 17 December, 3.

Hewison, Robert (1977) *Under Siege: Literary Life in London 1939–45*. London: Weidenfeld and Nicolson.

____ (1981) *In Anger: Culture in the Cold War 1960–75*. London: Weidenfeld and Nicolson.

____ (1986) *Too Much: Art and Society in the Sixties 1945–60*. London: Methuen.

____ (1990) *Future Tense: A New Art for the Nineties*. London: Methuen.

____ (1995) *Culture and Consensus: England, Art and Politics Since 1940*. London: Methuen.

Hodgson, Clive (1973) 'From artists to cleaners: an interview with James Scott', *Film*, 2, 4, July; available at www.james-scott.com, accessed 14 January 2007.

Hogenkamp, Bert (2000) *Film, Television and the Left in Britain 1950–1970*. London: Lawrence & Wishart.

Hoggart, Richard (2002) 'Dumb and dumber', *Guardian G2*, 14 March, 3.

Holmstrom, John (1964) 'Memento Monitor', *New Statesman*, 5 June, microfiche.

Holroyd, Michael (2002) 'Our friends the dead', *Guardian*, 1 June, microfiche.

Hood, Stuart (1968) 'Loud loving', *The Spectator*, 8 November, microfiche.

Hunt, Lord (Chairman) (1982) *Report of the inquiry into cable expansion and broadcasting policy*. London: HMSO.

Hutchins, Patricia (1954) 'The Drawings of Leonardo da Vinci', *Sight and Sound*, April–June, 23, 4, 200.

Hutchison, Robert (1982) *The Politics of the Arts Council*. London: Sinclair Browne.

Independent Film-makers' Association (1980) 'Channel Four and Innovation – The Foundation', February, unpaginated booklet.

Institute of Documentary Film (2006) 'Time is the greatest expense: interview with Jana Bokova', web.docuinter.net/en/doc_texts.php?id=27&PHPSESSID=0cd43270ab6aafc58c3055fca7ee3f7c, accessed 118 December 2006.

Isaacs, Jeremy (1989) *Storm Over 4: A Personal Account*. London: Weidenfeld and Nicolson.

____ (2001) 'Battle stations', *Independent on Sunday*, 26 November, microfiche.

Jackson, Michael (1992) 'Introduction', in Mills & Allen, *Commissions and Collaborations*. London: Mills & Allen/BBC/*Radio Times*.

Januszczak, Waldemar (1989) 'Up yours, Melvyn', *Guardian*, 25–6 March, 19.

Jeffries, Stuart (2002) 'Back in the frame', *Guardian G2*, 30 September, 16–17.

Jennings, Mary-Lou (ed.) (1982) *Humphrey Jennings: Film-maker, Painter, Poet*. London: British Film Institute in association with Riverside Studios.

Jones, Jonathan (2002) 'Come back, Rolf Harris, all is forgiven', *Guardian Review*, 6 April, 4.

Jordan, Stephanie and Allen, Dave (1993) *Parallel Lines: Media Representations of Dance*. London: John Libbey/Arts Council of Great Britain.

Keating, Roly (2006) 'Summer Exhibition', *RA*, Summer, 49.

Kelly, Richard (ed.) (1998). *Alan Clarke*. London: Faber & Faber.

Keynes, J. M. (1945) 'The Arts Council: Its Policy and Hopes', *The Listener*, 12 July, 31.

Kinnersley, Simon (2007) 'Taking the microphone', *State of Art*, January-February, 8–9.

Kinnes, Sally (2000) 'Dressed up or dumbed down?, *Sunday Times Culture*, 12 March, 33.

Kustow, Michael (1982) 'The arts on Channel Four', typescript memorandum to Jeremy Isaacs, 7 January.

____ (1984) 'The arts on Channel Four', loose leaf press brochure distributed in January.

____ (1987) *One in Four*. London: Chatto & Windus.

Lambert, Stephen (1982) *Channel Four: Television with a Difference?* London: British Film Institute.

Lanchester, John (2002) 'The TV channel that thinks it's a radio station', *Guardian G2*, 24 April, 2–3.

Lawson, Mark (1995) 'And so farewell "Late Show"', *The Independent*, 4 April, microfiche.

___ (1999) 'Not a pretty picture', *The Independent*, 29 November, microfiche.

Leapman, Michael (1993) '"Elitist" BBC admits it must go downmarket', *The Independent*, 14 July, 1.

Lennon, Peter (1983) 'Portrait maker', *The Listener*, 15–21 January, microfiche.

Levinson, Nick (1984) 'History of Mystery', in Chris Garratt (ed.) *Broadcast Television and the Visual Arts*. London: Television South West, 39–48.

Levy, Mervyn (1954) *Painter's Progress*. London: Phoenix House.

Lewis, Peter (1962) 'Can Art be box-office and remain Art?', *Contrast*, Spring.

Lovell, Alan (ed.) (1976) *BFI Production Board*. London: British Film Institute.

McCann, Graham (2002) 'Come the cultural revolution', *Financial Times*, 27 February, 16.

Marks, Laurence (1992) 'The men on the BBC omnibus', *Observer*, 23 August, 63.

Marshall, John (1989) 'The politics and style of an art dealer', *Television Week*, 16–22 March, 13.

Matheson, Hilda (1933) *Broadcasting*. London: Thornton Butterworth.

Myerscough, John (1988) *The Economic Importance of the Arts in Britain*. Policy Studies Institute.

Nairne, Sandy, with Dunlop, Geoff and Wyver, John (1987) *State of the Art: Ideas and Images in the 1980s*. London: Chatto and Windus.

Nelson, Robert S. (2000) 'The slide lecture, or the work of art history in the age of mechanical reproduction', *Critical Enquiry*, 26, 414–34.

Norman, Matthew (1992) 'The great late show', *The Mail on Sunday*, 22 March, 37.

Nupen, Christopher (1979) 'Inside Outside', *Edinburgh International Television Festival 1979 – Official Programme*. London: Edinburgh International Television Festival, 43.

Ofcom (2005) 'Ofcom review of public service television broadcasting: Phase 3 – competition for quality', 8 February 2005, www.ofcom.org.uk/consult/condocs/psb3/, accessed 20 December 2006.

____ (2007) 'A new approach to public service content in the digital media age', 24 January 2007, www.ofcom.org.uk/consult/condocs/pspnewapproach/, accessed 28 January 2007.

Ogilvie, Sir Frederick (1946) 'Future of the BBC: Monopoly and its Dangers', *The Times*, 26 June, microfiche.

Peacock, Alan (1986) *Report of the committee on financing the BBC* (Cmnd 9824). London: HMSO.

Penman, Robert (1993) 'Ballet and contemporary dance on British television' in Jordan and Allen (eds) *Parallel Lines: Media Representations of Dance*. London: John Libbey/Arts Council of Great Britain, 101–26.

Phillips, Stephen (1991) 'Strategy document about arts broadcasting', written for the Arts Council Film, Video and Broadcasting Panel.

Pilkington, Lord (Chairman) (1962) *Report of the Committee on Broadcasting* (Cmnd 1753). London: HMSO.

Potter, Jeremy (1989) *Independent Television in Britain, Volume III: Politics and Control 1968–80*. London: MacMillan.

____ (1990) *Independent Television in Britain, Volume IV: Companies and Programmes 1968–80*. London: MacMillan.

Preston, Trevor (2007) 'The Medium Size Cage', *State of Art 2007*, Jan–Feb, 6.

Read, Benedict and Thistlewood, David (1993) *Herbert Read: A British Vision of World Art*. Leeds: Leeds City Art Galleries/The Henry Moore Foundation/Lund Humphries.

Read, Herbert (1965) *The Origins of Form in Art*. London: Thames and Hudson.

Read, John (1948) 'Is There a Documentary Art?', *Sight and Sound*, 17, 65, 157–9.

Reed, Stanley (1977) 'Appendix One', in John Ellis (ed.) (1977) *1951–1976 Catalogue British Film Institute Productions*. London: British Film Institute, 130–31.

____ (1955) 'Television film and the artist', unpublished typescript dated June 1955.

Reith, John (1925) 'Memorandum of information on the scope and conduct of the Broadcasting Service', BBC Written Archives, Caversham, 3.

Ridgman, Jeremy (ed.) (1998) *Boxed Sets: Television Representations of Theatre*. Luton: John Libbey Media/Arts Council of England.

Roberts, Helene (ed.) (1995) *Art History Through the Camera's Lens*. Australia; United Kingdom: Gordon and Breach.

Roberts, John (1988) 'Postmodernism, Television and the Visual Arts – A Critical Consideration of *State of the Art*', in Philip Hayward (ed.) (1988) *Picture This: Media Representations of Visual Arts & Artists*. London: John Libbey, 47–62.

Roud, Richard (1972) *Straub*. New York: The Viking Press, Inc.

Scannell, Paddy and Cardiff, David (1991) *A Social History of British Broadcasting, Volume One 1922–1939: Serving the Nation*. Oxford: Basil Blackwell.

Sendall, Bernard (1982) *Independent Television in Britain, Volume I: Origin and Foundation 1946–62*. London: Macmillan.

____ (1983) *Independent Television in Britain, Volume II: Expansion and Change 1958–68*. London: Macmillan.

Shafto, Sally (2006) 'On Painting and History in Godard's *Histoire(s) du cinéma*', www.sensesofcinema.com/contents/06/40/histoires-du-cinema.html, accessed 10 January 2007.

Shils, Edward (1955) 'The British Intellectuals', *Encounter*, 4, 4, April, 6.

Sinclair, Andrew (1995) *Arts and Cultures: The History of the 50 Years of the Arts Council of Great Britain*. London: Sinclair-Stevenson.

Stoneman, Rod and Thompson, Hilary (1981) *The New Social Function of Cinema: Catalogue: British Film Institute Productions '79/80*. London: British Film Institute.

Stubbs Walker, J. (1951) 'Television review', *Daily Mail*, 1 May, microfiche.

Swallow, Norman (1966) *Factual Television*. London: Focal Press.

Sykes, Frederick (1923) *The Broadcasting Committee Report*. London: HMSO.

Taylor, Neil (1998) 'A History of the Stage Play on BBC Television', in Jeremy Ridgman (ed.) (1998) *Boxed Sets: Television Representations of Theatre*. Luton: John Libbey Media/Arts Council of England, 23–38.

Thistlewood, David (1993) 'Herbert Read's Paradigm: A British Version of Modernism', in Benedict Read and David Thistlewood (eds) (1993) *Herbert Read: A British Vision of World Art*. Leeds: Leeds City Art Galleries/The Henry Moore Foundation/Lund Humphries, 76–94.

Thompson, Mark (2006) 'Culture and the new broadcasting', speech at St Hilda's College, 21 October 2005, reprinted in *Oxford Today*, Hilary Issue 2006, 10–12.

Thorpe, Vanessa (2002) 'The culture vultures are gathering', *Observer Review*, 3 February, 7.

_____ (2007) 'Overview: culture and sport', *The Blair Years* supplement, *Observer*, 8 April, 47.

Tobin, Betsy (1989) 'Art attack', *Broadcast*, 6 October, 18–19.

Tusa, John (2007) 'Blair's lips may say "culture" … but his heart is not in art', *Observer*, 11 March, available at http://arts.guardian.co.uk/art/news/story/0,,2031074,00.html, accessed 23 March 2007.

Tynan, Kathleen (1987) *The Life of Kenneth Tynan*. London: Weidenfeld.

UNESCO (1949) *Films on Art: A Specialised Study, An International Catalogue*. Paris: UNESCO.

Ure-Smith, Jane (1990) 'Down to a fine art', *Television Week*, 19–25 September, 33.

Walker, Janey (1999) 'Has TV deserted the arts?', *Guardian G2*, 26 June, 7.

Walker, John A. (1993a) *Art and Artists on Screen*. Manchester: Manchester University Press.

_____ (1993b) *Arts TV: A History of Arts Television in Britain*. London: John Libbey/Arts Council of Great Britain.

Wall, Anthony (2005) 'The producer speaks!', www.bbc.co.uk/music/bobdylan/tvradio/no-directionhome/interview/, accessed 14 December 2006.

Watkin, David (1974) *The Life and Work of C. R. Cockerell*. London: A. Zwemmer.

Wenham, Brian (ed.) (1982) 'Into the Interior', in Brian Wenham (ed.) (1982) *The Third Age of Broadcasting*. London: Faber & Faber, 15–27.

_____ *The Third Age of Broadcasting*. London: Faber & Faber.

_____ (1984) 'There is no ratings war', *The Listener*, 13 September, 2–4, 6.

Wheldon, Huw (1962) 'Foreward', in Huw Wheldon (ed.) (1962) *Monitor: An Anthology*. London: Macdonald, 9–14.

_____ (ed.) (1962) *Monitor: An Anthology*. London: Macdonald.

White, Lesley (1991) 'The Jackson Drive', *Vogue*, September, microfiche.

Whitehead, Phillip (1984) 'The price of ratings', *The Listener*, 6 September, 6–8.

Williams, Nigel (1997) 'Raise your brow', *Independent on Sunday*, 10 August, 16.

_____ (2000), 'You just can't get the quality anymore', *Guardian Saturday Review*, 19 August, 3.

Williamson, Judith (1986) 'The problems of being popular', *New Socialist*, September, 14–15.

Willis, John (2000) 'Arts: going down the tube?', *Guardian G2*, 27 March, 7.

Wilson, Angus (1964) *Tempo: The Impact of Television on the Arts*. London: Studio Vista.

Wilson, H. Hubert (1961) *Pressure Group: The Campaign for Commercial Television in England*. London: Secker & Warburg.

Witcombe, Christopher (2001) 'Art history and technology: a brief history', http://witcombe.sbc.edu/arth-technology/arth-technology5.html, accessed 20 January 2007.

Worsley, T. C. (1970) *The Ephemeral Art*. London: Alan Ross.

Wright, Patrick (1985) *On Living in an Old Country*. London: Verso.

Wyver, John (1978) 'Television: selections', *Time Out*, 15–21 December, 24.

_____ (1979/80) 'Ghosts of Christmas Past', *Time Out*, 21 December–3 January, 113.

_____ (1980) 'Is There Life after *Civilisation*?', *Time Out*, 19–25 September, 18–19.

_____ (1986) 'Artists and models', *Radio Times*, 7–13 March, microfiche.

_____ (1998) 'Safety catch' *Broadcast*, 27 February, 19.

_____ (1999a) 'Obituary: Marc Karlin', *The Independent*, 28 January, microfiche.

_____ (1999b) 'Victory for the middlebrow', *Guardian G2*, 14 June, 7.

Yentob, Alan (1999) 'Has TV deserted the arts?', *Guardian G2*, 26 June, 7.

Two web sites in particular have been invaluable during the writing of *Vision On*. The British Film Institute's Film and TV Database at www.bfi.org.uk/filmtvinfo/ftvdb/ is a wonderful source for credits and dates, as is what the BBC continues in 2007 to call an 'experimental prototype' of the BBC Programme Catalogue at http://open.bbc.co.uk/catalogue/infax/.

INDEX